VMware vSphere® 5
Building a Virtual Datacenter

VMware Press is the official publisher of VMware books and training materials, which provide guidance on the critical topics facing today's technology professionals and students. Enterprises, as well as small- and medium-sized organizations, adopt virtualization as a more agile way of scaling IT to meet business needs. VMware Press provides proven, technically accurate information that will help them meet their goals for customizing, building, and maintaining their virtual environment.

With books, certification and study guides, video training, and learning tools produced by world-class architects and IT experts, VMware Press helps IT professionals master a diverse range of topics on virtualization and cloud computing and is the official source of reference materials for preparing for the VMware Certified Professional Examination.

VMware Press is also pleased to have localization partners that can publish its products into more than forty-two languages, including, but not limited to, Chinese (Simplified), Chinese (Traditional), French, German, Greek, Hindi, Japanese, Korean, Polish, Russian, and Spanish.

For more information about VMware Press please visit **http://www.vmware.com/go/ vmwarepress**.

VMware vSphere® 5
Building a Virtual Datacenter

Business IT

Eric Maillé and René-François Mennecier

vmware® PRESS

Upper Saddle River, NJ • Boston • Indianapolis • San Francisco
New York • Toronto • Montreal • London • Munich • Paris • Madrid
Capetown • Sydney • Tokyo • Singapore • Mexico City

VMware vSphere® 5 Building a Virtual Datacenter

ISBN-13: 978-0-321-83221-4

ISBN-10: 0-321-83221-3

The Library of Congress Cataloging-in-Publication data is on file.

Text printed in the United States on recycled paper at RR Donnelly in Crawfordsville, Indiana.

First Printing: August 2012

Warning and Disclaimer

Corporate and Government Sales

VMware Press offers excellent discounts on this book when ordered in quantity for bulk purchases or special sales, which may include electronic versions and/or custom covers and content particular to your business, training goals, marketing focus, and branding interests.

For more information, please contact:

U.S. Corporate and Government Sales
(800) 382-3419
corpsales@pearsontechgroup.com.

For sales outside the United States, please contact:
International Sales
international@pearsoned.com.

VMWARE PRESS PROGRAM MANAGER
Erik Ullanderson

ASSOCIATE PUBLISHER
David Dusthimer

ACQUISITIONS EDITOR
Joan Murray

SENIOR DEVELOPMENT EDITOR
Christopher Cleveland

MANAGING EDITOR
Sandra Schroeder

PROJECT EDITOR
Mandie Frank

TECHNICAL EDITOR
Thomas Keegan

COPY EDITORS
Richard Carey
Keith Cline

PROOFREADER
Sarah Kearns

BOOK DESIGNER
Gary Adair

COMPOSITOR
TnT Design, Inc.

EDITORIAL ASSISTANT
Vanessa Evans

COVER DESIGNER
Chuti Prasertsith

I want to thank René-François for his collaboration, which was rich in emotions, and my father for his support throughout the drafting process. I dedicate this work to my wife, Céline, and my two children, Agathe and Aloys, who gave me (for the second time) the strength to make this new project a reality. And just as I did at the end of the first book, I swear I'll never write another one!

Eric Maillé

Thank you, Eric, for having allowed me into this wonderful, stormy, and rich adventure. Thanks to Nam, Mamie, and Nathalie, to whom I've paid too little attention recently. I dedicate this book to my father, who will finally be able to understand his son's wonderful, fascinating profession.

To conclude, I want to pay homage to Eric Duval, my mentor. He succeeded in transmitting his passion and know-how. Thank you.

René-François Mennecier

Contents

8   Managing a Virtualization Project   257

About the Authors

Eric Maillé is Pre-Sales Consultant at EMC (after successful experiences at IBM, NEC Computers, and HP). Eric works on virtualization infrastructure and cloud computing projects upstream. He helps corporate enterprises make the best technological decisions based on their business requirements. Eric draws from his expertise to explain the transformations that VMware vSphere® 5 implies and the challenges that need to be addressed to ensure the proper architecture is selected and that its components are optimized. Eric has been honored with VMware vExpert 2011 and 2012 award, and he is an author of a previous book on VMware vSphere® 4: *Mise en place d'une infrastructure virtuelle* (in French and Spanish). He is certified a VCP (VMware Certified Professional), Cloud Architect (EMC), and co-founder of a site dedicated to virtualization technologies (www.virt-now. com).

René-François Mennecier works as a Cloud Architect Senior Consultant at EMC. René-François first specialized in disaster recovery plans and service continuity. Then, his experience at Dell allowed him to gain expertise in virtualization, including rationalization, consolidation, and datacenter-relocation challenges. At EMC, he is now in charge of strategic transformation and private cloud IT projects for enterprise accounts. He is a certified VCP VMware and EMC Cloud Architect and was awarded the title vExpert 2012.

About the Technical Reviewer

Tom Keegan has tech edited numerous technology books on Microsoft and VMware technologies, and has enjoyed tech editing for 14 years. He is also co-author of *VMware vSphere® for Dummies*. He has designed several VMware infrastructures, and began working with VMware ESX at the product's inception. A VCP3, VCP4, VCAP-DCD, and VCP5, he continues to advance his expertise by taking advantage of the many remarkable features the vSphere family offers. Tom currently is a Technical Director at Fresenius Medical Care, and lives with his family in Massachusetts.

Acknowledgments

We first want to thank those who assisted us in the making of this book and enabled us to deepen our knowledge in very specialized fields. Your help was invaluable. Special thanks to the following people:

Denis Jannot, Lothaire Lesaffre, Cody Hosterman, Philippe Audurieau, Rolland Zanzucchi, Jérôme Fontanel, Hervé Gilloury, Jean-Baptiste Grandvallet, Hervé Oliny, Emmanuel Bernard, Philippe Rolland, Mickaël Tissandier, Emmanuel Simon, Nicolas Viale, Jean-Louis Caire, Jean Strehaiano, Gwenola Trystram, Philippe Chéron, and Bernard Salvan.

Many thanks to Sylvain Siou, Technical Director at VMware France, for his contribution and sound advice, and to Richard Viard for his extremely specialized expertise in all topics related to VMware. Many thanks also to our virtualization ecosystem network: Eric Sloof, Iwan Rahabok, Ilann Valet, Olivier Parcollet, Julien Mousqueton, Jérémie Brison, Raphaël Schitz, Vladan Seget, and Damien Peschet. We also want to thank technical reviewer, Thomas Keegan, and copy editors Richard Carey and Keith Cline, for helping us deliver the book to the English-speaking VMware community.

Special thanks to Chad Sakac, who found time in his overloaded schedule to write the Foreword for this book.

We Want to Hear from You!

As the reader of this book, *you* are our most important critic and commentator. We value your opinion and want to know what we're doing right, what we could do better, what areas you'd like to see us publish in, and any other words of wisdom you're willing to pass our way.

As an associate publisher for Pearson, I welcome your comments. You can email or write me directly to let me know what you did or didn't like about this book—as well as what we can do to make our books better.

Please note that I cannot help you with technical problems related to the topic of this book. We do have a User Services group, however, where I will forward specific technical questions related to the book.

When you write, please be sure to include this book's title and author as well as your name, email address, and phone number. I will carefully review your comments and share them with the author and editors who worked on the book.

Email: VMwarePress@vmware.com

Mail: David Dusthimer
         Associate Publisher
         Pearson
         800 East 96th Street
         Indianapolis, IN 46240 USA

Reader Services

Visit our website at www.informit.com/title/9780321832214 and register this book for convenient access to any updates, downloads, or errata that might be available for this book.

Foreword

The management of *datacenters* epitomizes the issues and challenges that today's IT departments must face when confronted with a difficult dilemma: providing more services within budgets that shrink each year. As critical business ecosystems, datacenters are growing ever more complex, with their components ever more intricately interlinked. Despite this complexity, corporate computing must remain flexible and must answer the business needs that generate income for the company.

At the same time, the quantity of data generated is constantly increasing. According to estimates, the quantity of information generated 10 years from now will be *44 times* what it is today, and to manage such a data flow, we will need *10 times* as many servers.

Legal constraints add to these challenges by imposing business-continuity and data-protection plans that increase the workload of IT teams. Adding further constraints, many datacenters are affected by a lack of space, causing serious problems to arise when lines of business demand new machines to meet new needs. Energy is another topic of concern because datacenters can reach their electricity limit if not managed properly. Some companies find they cannot increase their datacenter's electrical capacity and must find alternative solutions.

We must also think about *us*: *the users*. We have a multitude of means of communication at our disposal (tablets, PCs, smartphones), and we want and expect immediate access to information (social networks, text messages, the Internet). It is hard to understand why, within our companies, we have to wait several days for access (which is sometimes denied) to some services when it is so simple and quick (and most of the time free) to get access outside the corporate environment.

For services intended for the general public, such as Facebook, it is important to recognize how easy it is for the user to open an account and start using the services with standard technology—no different from the technology used by traditional enterprises. What makes the difference in everyday use is the *way* these technologies are used—the way processes are established and the degree to which automation methods are employed. Only by understanding this coherent whole, orchestrated and automated, can we form the foundation of a truly new way to process data. In this context, we also have to understand that the usual methods currently in place within IT departments must evolve and that transforming the information system is necessary.

Server virtualization holds the key to this transformation and is often discussed as the fundamental solution for facing the challenges at hand. It allows the setup of an efficient technical platform to support business needs and offer services to users within the company while reducing cost and power use. This technology, combined with network and storage virtualization, provides a new generation of datacenters. When automation and self-service are added, it is the basis for *IT as a service*, or *the cloud*.

The VMware vSphere 5 server-virtualization solution is an essential component in advancing this transformation. It provides an agile, flexible, scalable environment that allows a migration to cloud-computing services. Indeed, cloud computing is tomorrow's greatest IT opportunity. With cloud computing, end users can access a range of fully virtualized datacenter-based services without the need to go through the traditional, cumbersome provisioning processes.

To get there, we must master server-virtualization technology and its components. And it is absolutely necessary to understand that this set of components ultimately determines the technical platform's stability, elasticity, and scalability. Such technological complexity can raise issues of choice that are not always easy to resolve. That is why it is crucial to understand how the components interact and how to use VMware vSphere 5 in an optimal fashion within the datacenter.

In this book, Eric Maillé and René-François Mennecier expertly explain the operational mechanics of using VMware vSphere 5 without ever losing sight of the best practices for its optimal use within the production constraints of a datacenter. This book is thorough and lively, providing many examples and recommendations based on their professional experience.

I highly recommend this book to anyone looking for a practical guide to this complex but fascinating topic.

Chad Sakac

Chad Sakac is Senior Vice President and Global Manager of Systems Engineering at EMC and vExpert, vSpecialist, founder and author of virtual Geek (http://virtualgeek.typepad.com).

Preface

We have been passionate about virtualization for many years and have been paying attention to everything going on in the field. Once again, we found ourselves impressed by the newest version of VMware and the possibilities it offers. With vSphere 5, VMware demonstrates anew its ability to innovate and offer solutions that push the limits in terms of availability, performance, and flexibility of use. Yet this rapidly evolving field, with its many functionalities, can be confusing. For this reason, it seemed important to us to synthesize, in book form, the information essential for properly comprehending this technology, showing how to use it in an efficient manner within the datacenter.

We wanted to offer a general book that would touch on the themes we deem most important. Our goal was to provide a global view of vSphere 5, with a maximum of information and advice drawn from the experience we have acquired in our daily work with the companies that require our interventions.

Choices needed to be made, however. We decided not to develop our explanations in a highly technical fashion; we aimed, instead, to make the text accessible to most readers, not to only a few experts.

The first chapters are devoted to understanding VMware vSphere 5's functionalities. In the subsequent chapters, we explain the links between this technology and the datacenter's various elements—servers, storage, network—as well as the possibilities in terms of backups and service continuity (local and distant), including a chapter that covers vSphere 5 installation and how to manage its operation.

In the last chapter, we examine the practical case study of a migration to a virtualized environment within a large company's datacenter, with objectives clearly defined by the corporation's management. We detail the steps to be followed in the different stages, the target architecture to be set up, the method used to carry out this project, and the benefits obtained. This practical chapter highlights the challenging areas and zones at risk in this type of project and outlines a method that allows for a successful, smooth migration.

This book is intended primarily for those in charge of infrastructure projects within information systems: system/network/storage administrators, project managers, consultants, architects, sales specialists, evangelists, and so on. It will also be of interest to students and future engineers, who will need a solid understanding of virtualization as they prepare for their careers in IT.

Disclaimer

Even though we belong to the EMC group, we strove to remain objective and agnostic about the technologies discussed. This book is intended as a true representation of what our experience has taught us. Our goal was to provide the information we deemed essential to enable readers to make their own choices—with full knowledge of the facts and based on their needs—without taking sides ourselves for a particular technology. The opinions expressed are our own; neither the EMC group nor any of this book's technology stakeholders are responsible for the opinions expressed herein.

Eric Maillé and René-François Mennecier

Chapter 1

From Server Virtualization to Cloud Computing

In the past few years, corporate information systems have greatly changed, due both to changing technologies and rapidly increasing demand for services and resources. The need for computer resources has never been greater. Using new means of communication such as smartphones, social networks, and instant messaging, users want immediate access to information from anywhere and at any time. Moreover, company executives require a high level of services to support their corporate and business needs in the context of budgetary restrictions.

Virtualization: The Heart of IT Transformation

IT managers face strong pressure to transform and modernize their information system. To meet these growing needs while controlling costs, server virtualization is a must. It has become the cornerstone of modern computing, paving the way to *cloud computing*. We have entered a new computing era where the technology once used for testing and development is now being deployed for critical applications.

In 2012, VMware vSphere 5 is the server-virtualization solution most often deployed in corporate environments. It has become the standard in production environments. Alternative solutions do exist, such as those offered by Microsoft, Citrix, and Oracle, but none to date offers as much integration and compatibility with the various datacenter components as VMware vSphere 5 when it comes to both hardware and software.

To benefit from the many advantages VMware offers, IT teams must understand the interactions between this technology and the datacenter's various components. These teams must evolve toward cross-disciplinary competencies and adopt the methodology required to take advantage of the technology's potential and to accelerate its integration within the datacenter. System administrators, along with network, storage, and security teams, are the folks primarily affected by virtualized environments. Involve them early on so that they can support the project rather than hinder it. They must have the ability to train themselves and the motivation required to change their traditional methods. Such a change must be supported using training, information found online, and webinars. It can be useful to call upon service providers to share their knowledge during some project phases.

This is an opportunity to rethink the work processes and procedures in place. A *proof of concept (POC)* can be planned to determine the solution's functional aspects, although this phase now seems pointless given how successfully the technology has already proven itself in all sectors of activities and types of businesses.

The management team must also be sensitized. Management must be aware of the changes pertaining to the organization and work processes as well as the investment required for the project to succeed.

With this support, everyone—at every level of the organization—should be aware of the issues and in-depth changes involved and of the benefits the company will reap.

Server Virtualization

Server virtualization is an *abstraction layer* that masks the physical resources of hardware equipment to provide a system with resources that differ from what they actually are. By its very nature, hardware has limited resources. Server virtualization removes these constraints, opening up a world of possibilities. As a concept, server virtualization is nothing new; IBM invented it for its large mainframe systems at the end of the 1960s. For the longest time, it seemed the technique could not be adapted to x86 environments; VMware, however, succeeded in 1998.

VMware's technology virtualizes an entire x86 server into a logical entity called a *virtual machine (VM)*. As shown in Figure 1.1, the low-level virtualization layer—called the *hypervisor*—can run several operating systems on a single physical machine.

The hypervisor makes an operating system independent from the hardware on which it has been installed, which opens up many possibilities for the consolidation of various server-based services on a single machine.

Server Virtualization Adoption Factors

The following sections examine the factors you should consider when adopting server virtualization in your IT environment.

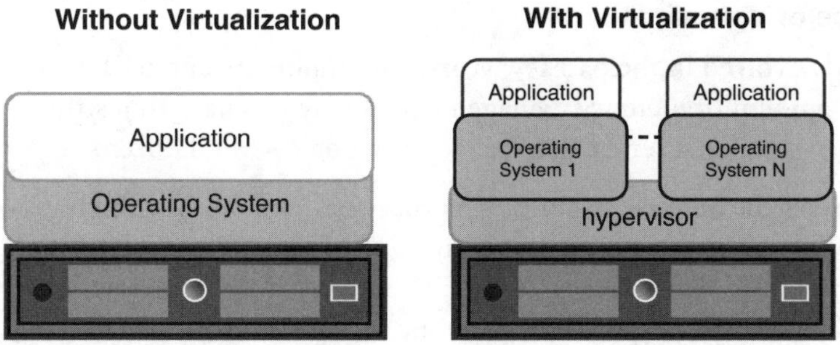

Without Virtualization   **With Virtualization**

Figure 1.1 Without virtualization, only one operating system can run on a physical machine, whereas virtualization allows the simultaneous use of several operating systems on a machine.

Waste of Resources

In a physical environment, an estimated 80% of a datacenter's servers have an average use rate less than 10%. Yet datacenters are reaching their limits in terms of floor space, energy, and cooling. This waste stems from the fact that companies have invested heavily in x86 servers to run a single application. This has led to a proliferation of physical servers and, given their actual use, to astronomical operation costs. According to estimates, administrators spend approximately 70% of their time on support or maintenance operations that bring no added value to the company.

> **NOTE**
> Overhead costs, such as management, administration, and power-consumption costs, become astronomical when compared to the cost of acquiring servers and can represent up to four times the initial cost of a server.

The high cost of maintaining the operational conditions of the server infrastructure wastes corporate funds and creates an operational inefficiency, hindering both innovation and the ability to manage new projects.

Opposing this waste, executives are putting pressure on IT managers, asking that they guarantee a certain level of service while managing an increasing volume of requests using IT budgets that remain the same—or are even reduced—each year. Virtualization is a way to meet these requirements while reducing costs and bringing the company's IT system up to date.

Technology in the Service of Virtualization

Server technology has greatly evolved in the past few years, with multicore and 64-bit processors and a significant amount of memory management. Today it is hard to justify installing a single operating system on a server that can accommodate several dozen.

Virtualization technology makes the best use of multicore processors, and reaching high levels of consolidation is now possible. Servers are currently *10 to 12 times* as powerful—in terms of performance—than they were just four years ago. This power increase rivals UNIX servers such as AIX, SUN, and HP-UX. Beyond a few specific configurations, strategic applications such as SAP or Oracle work quite well in a virtualized x86 environment.

Many functional capabilities have been integrated into the hardware to support native virtualization:

- The processors have built-in virtualization capabilities with Intel VT (Virtualization Technology) or AMD V (Virtualization).

- Storage-bay manufacturers interface directly with VMware technology to offload the server from certain storage-related tasks (called VAAI: vStorage APIs for Array Integration).

- Some network switches such as Cisco's Nexus 1000V and, more recently, IBM DVS5000V can simplify network management in this environment.

As you can see with these few examples, hardware and software companies have begun to develop their products to have a complete integration with and to exploit the full potential of virtualization technology.

Specifications for a Virtualized Environment

After considering the adoption factors for virtualizing your environment, you should familiarize yourself with the basic specifications for that environment.

Changing the Datacenter Model

Replacing physical servers with virtual entities encapsulated into files changes the datacenter's current model. Before virtualization, a distributed model using many small-scale physical servers was used. With virtualization, the model becomes centralized, consolidated around a single site. Storage becomes the cornerstone, and to host virtual machines, it must offer high performance and provide solutions to secure data. Networks take on a vital role because once cloud computing becomes the chosen model, companies are completely dependent on network and Internet connectivity. Therefore, the network's bandwidth must be adequate.

This evolution is forcing businesses to redefine their current infrastructures.

Virtual Machines

In a virtual environment, the administrator manages *virtual machines* (VMs). A VM encompasses the entire content of a physical server: its operating system (called a guest OS), applications, and data.

With regard to infrastructure, a VM is in every way identical to a physical server; application porting is not necessary. Administrators can fine-tune the size of VMs very precisely. This configuration granularity allows them to provide VMs with the resources they need.

VMs are completely *isolated* from one another (operating system, registry, applications, and data). If one VM is infected by a virus or if its operating system crashes, the other VMs are in no danger. To this day, this barrier between VMs has never been broken.

All the VM's components are contained in files. This is called *encapsulation*. Encapsulation simplifies backups, copies, disaster recovery plan processes, and migration to new environments, leading to great flexibility of use.

Furthermore, VMs are completely independent from the hardware on which they operate. In a traditional physical environment, the operating system is closely linked to the hardware on which it is installed. (The environment is monolithic and requires each server to have a master image with specific drivers to install.) In a virtualized environment, however, a virtualization layer always provides the VM with the same virtual hardware (graphics card, SCSI card, and so on), so identical VMs can be created no matter what hardware lies beneath. This makes it easier to proceed with large-scale deployment by reducing the creation of numerous masters dedicated to each type of hardware.

> **NOTE**
>
> Many companies host critical applications on aging servers, the renewal of which has been endlessly postponed because of how complex migration would be. With virtualization, these servers can simply be converted to virtual servers—without the need to reinstall operating systems or applications.

Mobility

Mobility is one of the major characteristics of virtualized environments. VMs can be moved from one physical server to another in a completely transparent fashion. This reduces service interruptions and simplifies day-to-day management for administrators when performing planned maintenance or migration to new platforms. Distributing the load to servers that are not as busy is also easy.

Instant Provisioning

Virtualization revolutionizes traditional server-management methods and server operation. With instant provisioning, a new server can easily be put into service in a few minutes, whereas it takes several weeks in a traditional physical environment. This completely changes the time frame, allowing companies to adapt very quickly to business-related change and evolution—for example, mergers and acquisitions or implementation of new services or new projects. Specific needs can be met quickly. This also improves service for users.

Grouping Resources into Clusters

ESXi host servers can be grouped into a single entity called a *cluster*, which allows the environment to be managed as a whole rather than as separate units. Because material resources are shared within a cluster, advanced functionalities of high availability can be obtained. In times of high activity, the load can also be shared automatically by all servers within the cluster. This simplifies the work of administrators and guarantees service levels for applications.

Quality of Service

To guarantee that each VM has access to the resources it needs, *quality of service (QoS)* can be implemented. QoS is parameterized on several levels—VM, ESXi host server, or at the cluster level.

Benefits of Virtualization

Server virtualization offers undeniable direct benefits, the main ones being as follows:

- **Cost reduction:** Cost reduction is a major concern for businesses. Virtualization is one way to reduce CAPEX (capital expenditures) and OPEX (operational expenditures). Fewer servers within datacenters means lower investments, lower maintenance costs, less floor-space use, and reduced power consumption and cooling costs. Reducing the cost of power use and cooling is fundamental because this can represent up to three times the cost of infrastructure hardware. Also, electricity rates tend to increase each year, making it crucial to limit or even reduce how much power is used.

  As shown in Figure 1.2, server virtualization is one way to reduce power usage in datacenters.

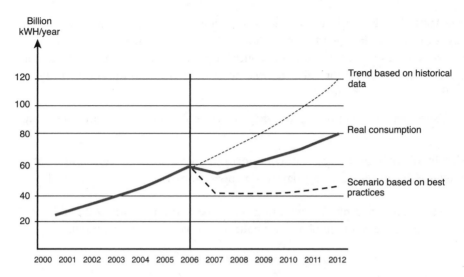

Figure 1.2 Reduction of power usage in datacenters through server virtualization.

Graph excerpted from Jonathan G. Koomey's research (Stanford University), August 2011

The growth curve of electricity consumption by datacenters between 2000 and 2010 started slowing down in 2006–2007. Between 2000 and 2005, consumption doubled (30–60 billion kWh/year), but between 2005 and 2010, it grew only 56% instead of doubling. Three factors contributed to this slowdown: the economic crisis slowed investment; electricity usage within datacenters was increasingly well managed; and virtualization was massively adopted, drastically reducing the number of servers.

- **Improvement of service-level agreements (SLAs):** The advanced functionalities of vSphere 5 make it very easy to implement high-availability solutions while freeing up administrators from time-consuming clustering solutions. Furthermore, implementing activity recovery plans and backup operations is much easier, which solves issues related to excessively narrow backup windows and the associated time constraints.

- **Flexibility:** Virtualization easily accommodates your growing needs, whether these are business needs, corporate needs related to mergers and acquisitions, or user needs. Flexibility improves reactivity and innovation because the dedicated infrastructure required for any project can be set up simply without a significant financial investment.

- **Operational efficiency:** The inherent functionalities of virtualization greatly simplify programmed maintenance operations, migration phases, and software updates—all operations that can be extremely resource demanding in a physical environment.

- **Automation:** This frees up administrators for other tasks and allows users to make use of resources independently, without requiring assistance from IT teams. Automation reduces repetitive tasks that contribute no added value and is key to cost reduction. A direct correlation exists between cost reduction and the automation level of the information system.

- **Users:** Users benefit the most because they consume IT as a service without having to go through IT teams.

- **Standardization:** The ability to apply uniform standards leads to legal conformity and enables efficient processes for day-to-day operations.

Yet it would be a mistake to think implementing such an environment will solve all issues at once. Various phases are required before virtualization reveals its full potential.

Phases of Virtualization

Let's take a look at the three phases of virtualization, illustrated in Figure 1.3, that result in the benefits that lead to successful cloud-computing services.

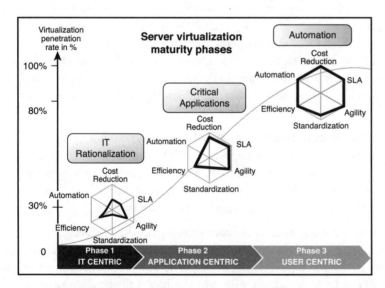

Figure 1.3 The first phase revolves around the infrastructure services directly controlled by IT services. Phase 2 focuses on business critical applications, while Phase 3 is concerned with services offered to users.

Phase 1: IT Rationalization

Replacing energy-hogging old servers with new-generation servers *rationalizes* the infrastructure. It reduces the power usage and floor-space use of datacenters, some of which have reached the end of their useful life. Furthermore, with vSphere *distributed power management (DPM)*, servers can be stopped or rebooted at will to optimize power use based on a cluster's resource needs.

Benefits

Virtualization has often been introduced in noncritical testing and development environments. This allows developers to work with a multitude of operating systems and application versions as needed. Administrators can test the production environment without calling upon network or storage teams. IT managers take advantage of this phase to virtualize servers directly under their control (such as infrastructure servers); domain controllers, printing servers, and web servers are easily virtualized. During this phase, the penetration ratio of infrastructure virtualization reaches 0% to 30%.

This phase allows teams to become familiar with the new environment. Thanks to *instant provisioning*, these teams can better react to new needs because new servers can be ready in minutes instead of requiring several weeks in a physical environment. This also improves service for users.

Using *snapshots* also makes it easy to update applications because it becomes possible to quickly backtrack if the applications fail.

Challenges

Generally, cost savings expected from this technology do not materialize during the rationalization phase. Indeed, new servers, storage bays, and VMware licenses must be purchased, and teams must be trained. This is an *investment phase*. After this introductory phase, some managers conclude that the technology does not lead to cost reductions, which is not surprising. Real savings will occur during the next phases, when the technology is mastered to perfection and automation is in place. Costs are then reduced—spectacularly so.

During the rationalization phase, consolidation is low (5 to 10 VMs per server), so performance problems are rare. Most problems revolve around storage space. Given how easy it is to provision VMs, a phenomenon known as *VM sprawl* is observed and should be curbed before it makes the environment unmanageable. To retain control, strict VM management rules must be applied. The following are examples:

- A VM inactive for a defined period (a few weeks) is automatically decommissioned (deleted).

- A VM that remains dormant (started but with no activity) over several days must be identified so that the cause of its inactivity is understood. If the VM has been forgotten, it should be stopped and eventually deleted.

- Production VMs must be identified and kept separate from other VMs. For example, folders can be created to classify VMs.

Phase 2: Critical Applications

In the second phase, service levels of critical applications are increased and operational efficiency is significantly improved. Virtualization can now be deployed on a large scale within the information system. The focus shifts. The first phase was about infrastructure; it is now about applications. Examples of critical applications include Microsoft Exchange, Lotus Notes, SAP, Oracle, Microsoft SQL, SharePoint, Citrix, and VDI.

Benefits

Today, aside from a few specific application loads, there is no contraindication to running the most critical applications in a VMware environment. Under vSphere 5, thanks to performance improvements within VMs, 95% of application loads can be put in VMs without a glitch.

As shown in Figure 1.4, the progression observed between January 2010 and April 2011 proves that these applications perform well in a virtualized environment. Note the high adoption rate of Microsoft SharePoint (67%) under VMware.

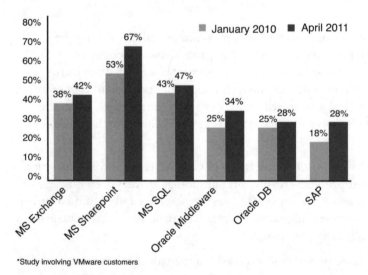

*Study involving VMware customers

Figure 1.4 Most traditional critical applications are executed by clients using VMware.

Rapid application provisioning with cloning

One reason why IT administrators virtualize Oracle or SAP is because it's the easiest way to clone applications. In a physical server world, the cloning application process can be a cause of inefficiencies. IT administrators must configure each application tier, including the hardware, OS, and application, which is time consuming and can result in potential configuration errors. Virtualization simplifies the cloning process for the creation of an optimized golden image for rapid provisioning. Furthermore, an application can also be packaged as a vApp, which includes multiple pre-configured virtual machines containing the different application tiers (for example, web, app, and database). This package can be provisioned on demand onto the production (as well as test and pre-production) infrastructure quickly.

Simplify High Availability implementation

In physical environment, High Availability can be painful. Each application needs a specific method of availability, which requires expensive licenses, dedicated standby infrastructure, and highly skilled staff to configure and manage each solution (Oracle RAC and Data Guard, Microsoft clustering, Data Base Mirroring [SQL Server], Database Availability Group [DAG] Exchange Server...). The alternative to this expensive approach is a standardized approach using vSphere technology, without the complexity of other technologies. Some companies have taken advantage of this move toward the virtual to replace their time-consuming clustering solutions with integrated high-availability solutions such as vSphere HA, vSphere FT or App-Aware HA, which is an API that allows users to plug in one of two currently available third-party App-Aware products from Symantec or Neverfail. Furthermore, thanks to the use of vMotion and Storage vMotion, anticipating service interruptions for planned maintenance operations is no longer necessary. Service levels are thus improved.

Guarantee Resource Reservations

During this phase, the penetration ratio of virtualization reaches 30% to 80%.

Challenges

Because it relates to critical applications, this phase is very sensitive. According to a July 2011 *International Data Corporation (IDC)* study, many businesses find their deployment is slowed for the reasons listed in Figure 1.5.

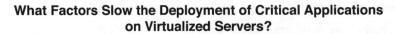

What Factors Slow the Deployment of Critical Applications on Virtualized Servers?

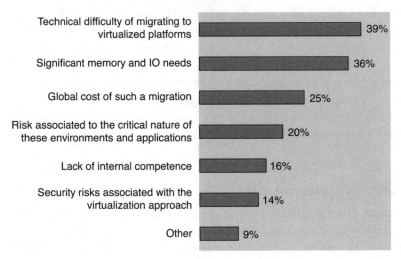

Figure 1.5 Factors that can affect application deployment.

This phase usually requires an approach that can effectively overcome technical hurdles. The issues relate to performance, backups, and *disaster recovery plans (DRPs)*. In this phase, the challenge is to implement adequate target architecture to support the application load. Existing methods must be revised because they are usually not well suited for virtualized environments.

Some companies can face strong internal resistance to this change. For this reason, it is crucial to get all IT teams involved in the project early on and support them throughout this transformation.

Storage architecture is essential because it hosts VMs. Because data volume can be very significant, it becomes important to optimize data management. Data-compression, thin-provisioning, and backup de-duplication technologies are well adapted to these environments. The environment's dynamic nature must also be taken into account and requires a revision of existing architectures.

It is essential for administrators to acquire cross-competency skills and obtain training in the new environment. Their roles and tasks must evolve until they have a global vision and a good understanding of the interactions between the various components of the technology and the datacenter.

Phase 3: Automation

In the third phase, *automation* leads to *cost reduction*. By freeing up their time, automation allows administrators to devote more energy to the update and improvement of their information systems. The 70% maintenance to 30% innovation ratio is now reversed. Automation holds the key to managing growth and meeting the new demands voiced every year. Bringing business needs and computer resources closer, without recourse to IT teams, favors innovation and provides the possibility of getting new projects started without the hindrance of financial issues. Indeed, many projects are abandoned due to a lack of IT budget.

This phase also includes the industrialization of processes and the optimization of resources to reach very high levels of consolidation. This serves to justify the investments made in previous phases.

> **NOTE**
>
> An administrator can usually manage 50 physical servers in a physical environment, up to 200–300 VMs in a virtual environment, and up to several thousand VMs when automation is implemented.

Because infrastructure problems and application service levels were solved in the first two phases, and given the implementation of process and provisioning automation, it is possible in this phase to focus on user needs. Using service catalogs, the user is independent and consumes IT resources without relying on extensive IT advice or effort. This is called *IT as a service*.

Challenges

During this third phase, IT teams face challenges of a different nature. Problems used to be related to technical or infrastructure issues—for example, maintaining operational conditions and updating platforms and migrations of all kinds (applications, hardware, operating systems, and so on). Virtualization solutions reduce these problems, but companies must now face organizational and governance issues. Server virtualization has an impact on all hardware and software elements of the datacenter, and governance rules must be put into place to establish who has decision-making power.

Automation is very convenient, but a VM is by no means free. Adopting strict rules and defining a VM management policy is absolutely indispensable. If chargeback is set up, it is necessary to define the criteria it will be based on (for example, per consumption or per VM).

All aspects of *VM lifecycle management* are of concern when determining which VMs can be removed and which must be preserved and archived (for legal conformity).

Toward Cloud Computing

The third and final phase of virtualization is also the one in which we introduce what is commonly called *cloud computing*. Cloud computing is a broad subject, one that could fill a book of its own, so we do not go into extensive detail here.

Definitions abound; here is an interesting one from NIST (National Institute of Standards and Technology):

> Cloud computing is a model for enabling ubiquitous, convenient, on-demand network access to a shared pool of configurable computing resources (e.g., networks, servers, storage, applications, and services) that can be rapidly provisioned and released with minimal management effort or service provider interaction.

In essence, it is a new way to consume computing resources, the objective being to reduce the complexity of IT infrastructures by offering completely automated computing services.

In this model, the information system moves from a cost center to a profit center in which available resources can be re-invoiced via subscription or fee-based services. Users consume computing resources through a gateway offering a catalog of services. What makes this new model viable, both technically and financially, is the appearance of virtualization technologies that allow physical components to be disregarded.

The model's major advantages are its speed of activation and the agility offered, allowing very quick reaction to meet the company's business needs. Using available services, projects can be created almost instantaneously, which changes day-to-day work methods.

One of the model's main issues involves understanding where data is located and who has ownership. This is an issue for the cloud service provider, who must be able to explain where the data is and whether the regulations in effect conform to the legislation of the country or society buying this type of service. Both the data flow and its ownership must be well documented and validated by all parties, in a clearly understandable manner.

When the cloud is created within a corporation, it is called a *private cloud*. When the service is offered by an external supplier (a *service provider*), it is called a *public cloud*. In cases where activity spikes occur and the private cloud does not suffice, additional resources from the public cloud can also be allocated for a defined period of time. This is called a *hybrid cloud*.

A public cloud is a service offered by external providers (service providers) to final users. The provider and client concur on minimum required performance or delivery times, called a *service-level agreement (SLA)*. The client no longer needs to manage an internal IT infrastructure and can focus on its core business, making this model perfectly suited for *small and medium businesses (SMBs)*, for which IT is usually not the core. Service levels (usually 24/7 with DRP, backup, and so on) and safety levels offer much better performance than what most SMBs are currently experiencing, mainly because of issues related to internal skills and financial means. Operation costs are clearly lower than with internal solutions, and *users always have access to the most recent software version*. Furthermore, computing resources become flexible; they adapt to activity fluctuations and their seasonal character.

Several models exist, including the following:

- **Software as a service (SaaS):** Users have no control over the underlying infrastructure. They make direct use of applications found in the cloud. Examples: Mozy, Zimbra, Gmail, Google Apps, Microsoft Office 365, Cisco WebEx.

- **Platform as a service (PaaS):** Users deploy applications they have created or acquired using programming languages or tools supported by the service provider. They do not control the underlying infrastructure. Examples: SpringSource, Microsoft Azure.

- **Infrastructure as a service (IaaS):** Users themselves provision resources such as processor, memory, network, and storage. They keep control of the operating system and applications. Examples: EMC, VMware, Cisco, Amazon Web Services, IBM, HP, CSC, Verizon.

Virtualization Ecosystem

The following sections provide a quick overview of the virtualization ecosystem and various solutions.

Server Virtualization

A distinction must be made between bare-metal virtualization products and those on a host server, called *host based*. Host-based virtualization applications on a server can be used for testing but never for production. If host-based versions are put into production, the side effects can be catastrophic, yet these solutions are interesting for test environments.

The best-known products of this type are as follows:

- Microsoft Virtual Server 2005, Virtual PC

- VMware Server

- VMware Workstation, VMware Player, VMware ACE, VMware Fusion (for Mac)

Bare-metal applications are those in which the virtualization layer is installed directly over the hardware. Installation is done in the same manner as a traditional operating system—by booting from a CD-ROM. These are the only solutions optimized and usable in a production environment. They are installed over the hardware, just like an operating system.

The following are the main bare-metal virtualization solutions:

- VMware vSphere
- Microsoft Hyper-V
- Citrix XenServer
- Oracle VM
- Red Hat KVM

Although Citrix XenServer, Oracle VM, and Red Hat KVM perform well, the market is geared for a battle between Microsoft and VMware. VMware leads the virtualization market and is technologically ahead of Microsoft.

VMware is now well established in large companies where its domination is quasi-complete. It has attained great maturity in production environments and is well integrated with the various datacenter elements at the software and hardware levels, which are great advantages.

Microsoft offers Hyper-V, a solution that is well adapted to today's SMBs but does not yet offer all of VMware's advanced functionalities for large corporations.

Desktop Virtualization

Workstation virtualization allows each user to remotely log on to a virtual machine located in the datacenter. Remote access can be attained through many hardware solutions—traditional PC, laptop, low-speed terminal, or even a smartphone—without the need to configure anything on the client workstation.

The following are the best-known current solutions:

- VMware View
- VMware WSX (New VMware project: Windows desktops via HTML5 technologies)
- Citrix XenDesktop
- NEC Virtual PC Center
- Quest vWorkspace

- Systancia AppliDis Fusion
- Neocoretech NDV

For laptops and desktops, client-hypervisor type solutions can be installed directly on top of the existing hardware. These enable several isolated VMs to run on a single PC. With such a solution, the user could use several distinct and completely isolated environments (for example, one image for professional use and one for private use) that are managed through a centralized management console.

Existing solutions are as follows:

- Citrix XenClient
- Virtual Computer NxTop (now part of Citrix)

Performance and Capacity Planning

When critical applications are used in a virtual environment, it is important to have tools both for monitoring performance and for capacity planning.

The main software tools that focus on virtual environments include the following:

- VMware vCenter Operations Management Suite
- Quest vFoglight (acquired by Dell)
- Orsyp Sysload
- vKernel (acquired by Quest Software so now part of Dell)
- Veeam One
- Xangati

P2V Conversion Tools

Migration projects require the use of tools to convert physical machines to virtual ones. This migration is called *physical to virtual* (*P2V*).

The following are the best-known tools for P2V:

- VMware vCenter Converter
- Vizioncore vConverter
- HP Server Migration Pack
- Plate Spin Migrate (Novell)

Backup

Traditional backup solutions are available for virtual environments. A number of manufacturers offer solutions that have been very well adapted to such environments. Here are the most popular:

- EMC Avamar

- Symantec NetBackup

- Veeam Backup

- IBM Tivoli Storage Manager TSM

- VMware Data Recovery

- Quest vRanger Pro

- CommVault

- Acronis vmProtect

These backup solutions do not generally require agents; they interface with the APIs supplied by VMware to provide seamless integration. Certain solutions allow file-level restoration in the virtual machine and provide de-duplication.

Packaged Cloud Offerings

A few years ago, blade server management was innovated by the regrouping of several servers in the same rack to simplify their integration within the datacenter (fewer cables, reduction of floor space use, reduction of power usage, and so on). Packaged cloud offerings adopt a similar philosophy, but for the *entire* datacenter, in a solution packaged at the hardware and software levels. The whole is ready to use and integrates provisioning and orchestrating tools. The goal is to reduce the lead time before a virtualized environment is available on an industrialized platform. All major IT players now offer products based on this model.

In the private cloud

- Vblock (EMC/VMware/Cisco alliance)

- FlexPod (NetApp/VMware/Cisco alliance)

- IBM CloudBurst

- Oracle Exadata/Exalogic

- Dell vStart

- HP CloudSystem

In the public cloud

- Google

- Amazon

- Microsoft

- Salesforce.com

Cloud Data Storage

With this new type of service, any content can be automatically stored within the cloud, so its data can be accessible from anywhere, from any type of terminal (for example, PC, smartphone, tablet). These solutions are widely popular. As soon as a change is made, data is automatically synchronized between the different terminals (which also secures the data). This makes it easier to work collaboratively when several users need to modify the same documents.

> **NOTE**
>
> We wrote this book using Dropbox services, which was a simple way for us to share our files.

The following are the best-known solutions of this type:

- Dropbox

- Oxygen

- VMware Project Octopus

- Apple iCloud

- Ovh hubiC

- EMC Syncplicity

The Future Looks Bright

As you can see, there is a tremendous ecosystem for the virtual environment of today's datacenter. These solutions support the radical transformation of computing, using fewer resources and providing greater efficiency. However, virtualization alone does not solve all the issues IT staffs face, and in fact, virtualization can create some issues if not managed properly. Therefore, when planning a virtualization strategy, it is important to build a VM lifecycle and properly manage the allocations to reduce sprawl. By working from the beginning with all facets of IT, including storage, network, and security groups, your virtualization project will be successful.

Today's challenges are different from those of the previous decade because the needs are different. Instant news and social networks generate a phenomenal amount of data to manage. It is therefore necessary to lay the bricks to move toward cloud computing services and build the next generation data center in phase with the new challenges.

Chapter 2

The Evolution of vSphere 5 and Its Architectural Components

Before we delve into the software components and architecture of VMware's new vSphere 5 offering, let's take a look at how the company itself, as well as its virtualization portfolio, has evolved since its founding.

VMware Overview

VMware was founded in 1998 by the following people:

Diane Greene, President and General Manager (1998–2008)

Dr. Mendel Rosenblum, Chief Scientist (1998–2008)

Scott Devine, Principal Engineer (since 1998)

Dr. Edward Wang, Principal Engineer (1998–2009)

Edouard Bugnion, Chief Architect (1998–2004)

VMware was acquired by EMC in 2004 for $625 million. At the time of the acquisition, sales figures were about $100 million, and the company had 370 employees. In 2011, sales were nearly $3.7 billion, and by 2012, the company employed more than 9000 people.

Pat Gelsinger is the CEO of VMware as of September, 2012 (formerly it was Paul Maritz, since July 2008).

VMware Portfolio

VMware's product portfolio has greatly expanded over the past few years. In its early years, the company concentrated mainly on the hypervisor offering, but it is now highly focused on cloud-computing services, administrative tools, collaborative tools, and applications. This book focuses on vSphere 5's datacenter virtualization platform, and components that are fundamental for managing the datacenter are covered in detail; others are mentioned for information purposes only. Figure 2.1 provides an overview of what VMware offers today.

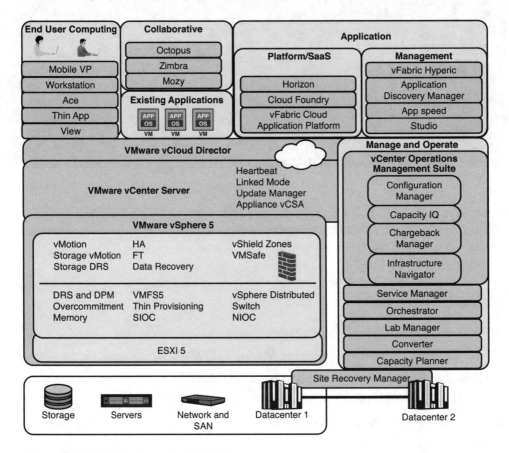

Figure 2.1 The VMware product portfolio.

VMware's strategy is clearly oriented toward cloud-computing offerings. The cloud offering comprises the elements shown in Figure 2.2.

VMware Evolution

The first version of VMware ESX was released in 2001; vSphere 5 is its fifth generation. The evolution and the technological leaps that accompanied each new version are worth reviewing here. Figure 2.3 provides an evolutionary timeline.

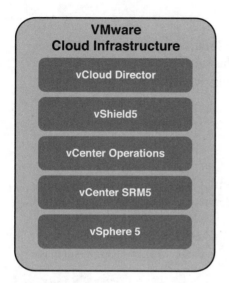

Figure 2.2 VMware's cloud infrastructure elements.

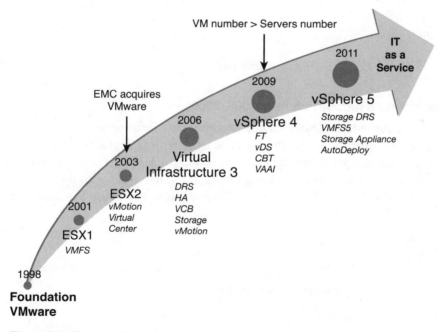

Figure 2.3 The evolutionary product development leading to vSphere 5.

First Generation (1998–2003)

ESX1 is the first hypervisor for x86 platforms to offer local storage. Centralization does not yet exist, and servers are managed one by one. This version is adapted for low-charge machines. The hypervisor is mainly used for testing and developmental environments. There is no direct competition.

Available version: VMware ESX1.x

Second Generation (2003–2006)

vMotion is the first technology enabling the movement of live virtual machines. Administration is centralized using Virtual Center, and several physical servers can be managed. Virtualization is no longer limited to testing; it is now used for production as well. VMware has more than 20,000 customers worldwide and completely dominates this market. Competition is weak, although interesting open-source solutions exist, such as KVM and Xen. EMC acquires VMware in 2004.

Technological leaps:

- vMotion

- Virtual Center

Available versions: VMware ESX 2.x, Virtual Center 1.x

Third Generation: Virtual Infrastructure 3 (2006–2009)

Hypervisors are no longer independent from one another. They form a pool of resources clustered under a unified entity to provide high service levels with high availability and load distribution. Backups are performed by Framework VCB. VMware is an imperative asset in most large corporations worldwide. Competition is put into place with the acquisition of Xen by Citrix (in 2007) for $500 million. Microsoft launches Hyper-V to catch up in this field.

Technological leaps:

- VMware HA (High Availability)

- VMware DRS (Distributed Resource Scheduling)

- VCB (VMware Consolidated Backup)

- Storage vMotion (since version 3.5)

Available versions: Virtual Infrastructure 3: VMware ESX 3.x, Virtual Center 2.x

Fourth Generation: vSphere 4 (2009–2011)

vSphere 4 extends storage and network functionalities and provides even more function-alities for availability and security. Even though VMware dominates this market, competition increases from Citrix Xen Server and, in particular, from Microsoft with the launch of Hyper-V R2. The year 2009 is significant—more VMs are in production than physical servers.

Technological leaps:

- VMware FT (Fault Tolerance)
- vNetwork Distributed Switch
- Various APIs
- Changed Block Tracking
- Data Recovery

Available versions: vSphere 4: VMware ESX4/ESXi4, vCenter Server 4

Fifth Generation: vSphere 5 (2011–...)

Today vSphere 5 positions itself as the datacenter's virtualization platform optimized for cloud computing. Several improvements at the storage level and a solid relationship with the most important software editors and hardware manufacturers make VMware the solution that best meets the most important requirements to deploy critical applications. The licensing strategy is modified. It is based both on processors and on the memory configured in the VMs. The service console is abandoned for a lighter version of ESXi. Many new products complete the offering, such as vCenter Operations Management Suite, SRM 5, vShield 5, and vCloud Director 1.5.

Technological leaps:

- Storage DRS
- New storage APIs
- VMFS-5 (Virtual Machine File System 5)
- vStorage Appliance
- vSphere Replication for SRM 5

Available versions: vSphere 5: VMware ESXi 5, vCenter Server 5

Table 2.1 shows a comparison of the last three versions.

Table 2.1 Feature Comparison: VMware V13, vSphere 4, and vSphere 5

Functionalities	VMware VI3	vSphere 4	vSphere 5
Host server			
ESX version	ESX 32 bits	ESX4 64 bits	ESXi5 64 bits
Maximum host memory	256 GB	1 TB	2 TB
Administration			
Centralized management	Virtual Center	vCenter Server 4	vCenter Server 5
vCenter linked mode		Yes	Yes
Host Profiles		Yes	Yes
DPM (Distributed Power Management)		Yes	Yes
vApps		Yes	Yes
Update Manager		Yes	Yes
Host Update		Yes	Yes
vCenter Appliance			Yes
Auto Deploy			Yes
Image Builder			Yes
Advanced functionalities			
vMotion	Yes	Yes, with EVC	Yes, with EVC
Storage vMotion	Yes (Snapshot)	Yes (DBT)	Yes (Mirror)
DRS (Distributed Resource Scheduler)	Yes	Yes	Yes
Storage DRS			Yes
Availability			
HA	Yes (AAM agent)	Yes (AAM agent)	Yes (FDM agent)
FT		Yes	Yes
Storage			
VMFS	VMFS3	VMFS3	VMFS3 and VMFS-5
Maximum LUN size	2 TB	2 TB	64 TB
Thin provisioning		Yes	Yes
Storage I/O Control (SIOC)		Starting with vSphere 4.1	Yes (SAN and NAS)
vSphere Storage Appliance		No	Yes
Storage API		Starting with vSphere 4.1	Yes, VAAI2 and NAS VAAI
Backup			
Backup API	VCB	Yes, VADP	Yes, VADP
Changed Block Tracking		Starting with vSphere 4.1	Yes
Backup software		Yes, Data Recovery	Yes, Data Recovery

Functionalities	VMware VI3	vSphere 4	vSphere 5
Network			
vNetwork Distributed Switch		Yes	Yes
VMDirectPath		Yes	Yes
Network I/O Control (NIOC)		Starting with vSphere 4.1	Yes
NIC Teaming	Yes	Yes	Yes
Security			
vShield Zones		Yes	Yes
VMsafe		Yes	Yes

vSphere 5 Licenses

The following sections provide some important licensing information you should be familiar with before you adopt the vSphere 5 solution.

vSphere 5 Versions

The following vSphere editions oriented toward *small and medium business (SMB)* are available:

- vSphere Essentials
- vSphere Essentials Plus

vSphere Essentials and vSphere Essentials Plus are designed for small-scale deployments. With these editions, up to three host servers can be managed using two physical processors each and up to a maximum 192 GB vRAM entitlement per host server. A vCenter Server Foundation license is integrated.

The free hypervisor can use only vSphere's basic hypervisor functionality. It can be transparently upgraded to the more advanced versions of vSphere. Unlike the paid versions, the vSphere hypervisor cannot be managed by vCenter Server. It is exclusively managed with the vSphere Client through a direct connection to the host.

NOTE

Certain studies show that only 10% of SMBs have deployed virtualized servers. To simplify the deployment of VMware in SMBs, VMware offers VMware Go, a free web-based service that guides users through the installation and configuration of VMware vSphere. This service allows users to virtualize their servers in a few clicks and is a simple way to approach virtualization.

Three editions are intended for medium and large accounts:

- vSphere Standard
- vSphere Enterprise
- vSphere Enterprise Plus

Table 2.2 compares the features of these three versions.

Table 2.2 Feature Comparison: Standard, Enterprise, and Enterprise Plus Editions

Functionalities	Standard	Enterprise	Enterprise Plus
ESXi5.x	✓	✓	✓
vCenter agent	✓	✓	✓
Virtual SMP (vCPU)	8	8	32
vRAM pooled / CPU	32 GB	64 GB	96 GB
Update Manager	✓	✓	✓
VMFS-5	✓	✓	✓
Image Profiles	✓	✓	✓
vStorage API for Data Protection	✓	✓	✓
Thin provisioning	✓	✓	✓
vSphere HA	✓	✓	✓
Data Recovery	✓	✓	✓
vMotion	✓	✓	✓
Hot Add	X	✓	✓
vSphere FT	X	✓	✓
vShield Zones	X	✓	✓
Storage vMotion	X	✓	✓
DRS	X	✓	✓
DPM	X	✓	✓
vStorage API for Multipathing	X	✓	✓
vStorage API for Array Integration	X	✓	✓
Virtual Serial Port Connector	X	✓	✓
Distributed vSwitch	X	X	✓
Host Profiles	X	X	✓
Storage I/O Control	X	X	✓
Network I/O Control	X	X	✓
Profile-Driven Storage	X	X	✓
Storage DRS	X	X	✓
Auto Deploy	X	X	✓
View Accelerator	X	X	✓

✓ = Included   X = Not included

NOTE

The Advanced version available with vSphere 4 is no longer offered. It is replaced by the Enterprise version. Customers who use the Advanced version are automatically upgraded to vSphere 5 Enterprise, as long as their maintenance agreement is up-to-date.

Licensing Model

As shown in Figure 2.4, VMware vSphere 5 is licensed on a per-processor basis with a vRAM entitlement. Each VMware vSphere 5-processor license comes with a certain amount of vRAM capacity, or memory configured to virtual machines (called *pooled vRAM*). This amount of memory represents the total *configured* memory in the VMs (that are powered on) within a vCenter.

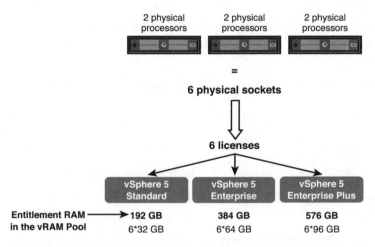

Figure 2.4 Example of a vSphere 5 licensing model.

To further explain the model shown in Figure 2.4, here is an example: One standard vSphere license entitles 32 GB of vRAM per CPU socket within a pool. If there are three dual-processor (two sockets) physical servers, six vSphere Standard licenses are required. These six licenses entitle a total quantity of configured VM (and powered on) memory of 6 * 32 GB = 192 GB in the vRAM pool. If each VM has 2 GB of configured memory, for example, this translates into an entitlement to 96 VMs functioning within the pool. Extending the vRAM capacity is easy: Just add more Standard vSphere licenses to the memory pool.

> **NOTE**
>
> vRAM calculation is based on average annual use. The theoretical cap (192 GB in this example) can be exceeded over defined periods. If the average is below the cap, this has no bearing. (Alerts are populated in vCenter, but performance is not hindered, and functionality is not blocked.) If the average exceeds the cap, the company must sort out the situation to take advantage of all vSphere capabilities.

> **NOTE**
>
> If one configured VM memory exceeds the maximum vRAM value (96 GB for Enterprise Plus), a single license is required. For example, one VM with 256 GB of configured memory requires the purchase of only one license.

There is no longer any limitation on the number of cores per CPU as there was in vSphere 4 (limit of 6 or 12 cores per CPU, depending on the license). The host server's RAM is also no longer limited.

vSphere 5 and vCenter Server licenses are sold separately. License keys are made up of 25 alphanumeric characters.

vCenter Server 5.0 Licenses

vCenter Server requires one license per server instance. Three licenses are available:

- **VMware vCenter Server for Essentials:** License integrated with vSphere Essentials and Essentials Plus.
- **VMware vCenter Server Foundation:** For small-scale deployments, up to three ESX host servers (dual processor).
- **VMware vCenter Server Standard:** For large-scale deployments with an unlimited number of ESX host servers.

vCenter Server licenses include the following:

- vCenter linked mode (only with vCenter Server Standard)
- vCenter Orchestrator (only with vCenter Server Standard)
- vCenter Server
- vSphere Client

- VMware vSphere Web Client

- VMware vSphere Update Manager

- VMware ESXi Dump Collector

- VMware Auto Deploy

- VMware vSphere Authentication Proxy

- vCenter Host Agent Pre-Upgrade Checker

Figure 2.5 shows the vSphere 5.0 installation screen with the different products and tools available.

Figure 2.5 Installation page for vSphere 5.

What's New in vSphere 5?

vSphere 5 brings many new features (more than 200 announced), a great number of which relate to storage—the critical component of virtual architectures. Here are the key points to remember about this new version:

- The ESX4/ESXi 4 hypervisor has been replaced by the lighter 144-MB ESXi5 version that has no service console. This lighter version requires fewer updates and is less vulnerable.

- VMs can now use new virtual hardware (version 8) that offers high levels of performance, supporting up to 32 vCPUs and 1 TB of RAM, as well as I/O that can support very high application loads.

- The file system has been upgraded from VMFS-3 to VMFS-5, which removes some limits in terms of volume sizes.

- A new storage appliance, called *vSphere Storage Appliance (VSA)*, helps small deployments benefit from advanced features (such as vSphere HA, vSphere DRS, vSphere DPM, vSphere FT, and vMotion) without the need to invest in shared storage bays.

- vSphere *High Availability (HA)* has been completely rewritten. The agent from the purchase of Legato *Automated Availability Manager (AAM)* is replaced by a *Fault Domain Manager (FDM)* agent.

- The Storage vMotion mechanism has been redeveloped. The technique was previously based on block-change tracking. This presented some difficulties when significant I/O loads carried a malfunction risk during the convergence phase. Under vSphere 5, Storage vMotion uses a new mechanism with a host-level split driver, which simplifies convergence.

- vSphere Storage DRS is a new feature (DRS equivalent for storage) allowing the balance of datastore load according to available space and I/O load. A new concept is introduced: the *datastore cluster*.

- vSphere Profile-Driven Storage makes it possible to create rules to qualify storage performance. Using this, a VM can be associated with the storage service option it should use without worrying about its exact location.

- The new *vCenter Server Appliance (vCSA)* in Linux SUSE simplifies deployment in small-scale environments.

- ESXi Image Builder is a PowerShell CLI command set that creates an ESXi image preconfigured with the latest drivers and updates (a type of master or gold image commonly used by administrators). The image created in this manner can be exploited and preconfigured following a defined policy.

- Auto Deploy simplifies large-scale rollouts and enables the ESXi image to be loaded in memory rather than physically installed on the server's hard drive; this is called *stateless ESXi*. To provision a server, Auto Deploy is based on a *preboot execution environment (PXE)* architecture in relation to host profiles.

- Using the Host Profiles functionality, an industrial deployment of ESXi servers can be performed by predefining installation and configuration parameters. In this way, it is possible to implement a configuration policy to guarantee the ESXi servers' infrastructure and comply with the defined policy. You can use Host Profiles to configure the network, the storage, vSwitches, license keys, and so on.

> **NOTE**
>
> Auto Deploy can be associated with Image Builder and Host Profiles to automate the deployment of a customized image onto a large number of servers.

- vSphere 5 introduces a new *command-line interface (CLI)* that simplifies things for administrators who once had to juggle multiple command-line tools. VMware provides a single tool that offers unified commands using the same syntax rules.

- Storage I/O Control is *Network File System (NFS)* supported.

- ESXi VM swap space can be moved to local *solid-state drive (SSD)* disks or shared storage space. In cases where a memory swap is necessary, performance degradation is reduced.

Existing Features

Here is a summary of vSphere 5's current features. Some features are essential; these are explored in depth in the chapters that follow.

- The environment's dynamic nature simplifies maintenance operations and migration phases using the following:

  - **vMotion** makes it possible to move VMs between physical servers within a cluster. This migration occurs only after a manual intervention by the administrator. *Enhanced vMotion Compatibility (EVC)* ensures the compatibility between processors from different generations of vMotion.

  - **Distributed Resource Scheduler (DRS)** automates vMotion to distribute the VMs' workload among ESXi servers.

  - **Distributed Power Management (DPM)** is coupled with DRS to run VMs on fewer physical servers to reduce the datacenter's power usage.

  - Storage vMotion is a manual intervention by the administrator that allows the hot migration of virtual disks from a datastore's VMs to another datastore in the same storage bay or between two different storage bays—without service interruption. **Storage DRS** automates its operation to distribute the datastores' workload.

High availability and high service levels are ensured by the following:

- **vSphere HA (High Availability)** ensures that when an ESXi host server fails, all VMs connected to that host are immediately and automatically restarted on the other ESXi servers within the cluster.

- **vSphere FT (Fault Tolerance)** provides very high availability. When an ESXi host server fails, FT-protected VMs experience no service interruption or data loss. They continue running on other servers within the cluster. As opposed to vSphere HA, in which VMs are restarted, vSphere FT is fully transparent, both for the application and users.

- **vCenter Data Recovery** is vSphere 5's infrastructure backup solution, which is fully integrated into vCenter Server. It is based on the vStorage API for Data Protection that allows the hot backup of running VMs.

Quality of service (QoS) is provided by the following:

- **Storage I/O Control (SIOC)**, existing since vSphere 4.1, provides QoS at the datastore level by distributing the I/O load when contentions occur.

NOTE

Storage DRS and SIOC should not be confused. When contentions occur at the datastore level, SIOC guarantees a certain bandwidth and latency for critical VMs, whereas Storage DRS distributes the load of datastores by migrating the VMs from one datastore to another.

- **Network I/O Control (NIOC)** is equivalent to SIOC for networks. It provides QoS related to network traffic between VMs. Other forms of QoS to share VM resources are obtained through shares, reservations, and resource pools.

Security is ensured through the following:

- **vShield Zones** is a VM-protection virtual firewall that takes the form of an appliance also used to analyze all network traffic. The vShield Zones firewall is located at the level of vSwitches, using rules that block or allow certain ports or protocols or network traffic.

- **VMware VMsafe** is an API dedicated to the protection of VMs. Software editors using VMsafe have the option of protecting their VMs without installing agents within those VMs.

Effective storage management is achieved through the following:

- With **thin provisioning**, the disk space allocated to a VM does not need to be physically reserved. The space is attributed dynamically as the quantity of data in the VM increases. This contributes to the optimization of storage space.

- **Volume Grow** allows the dynamic extension of an existing VMFS without shutting down the VMs.

- The **Hot Add feature** allows the hot addition of components such as CPUs and memory to VMs.

NOTE

This functionality must be activated in the VM's advanced parameters. (To enable the parameter's activation, the VM must be shut down.) Most Windows 2008 Server and some Windows 2003 guest operating systems are supported.

- Using **Hot Extend**, you can dynamically extend virtual disks without shutting down the VM.

Network management is achieved through the following:

- **vSphere Standard Switch (vSS)** provides a virtual switch for each ESXi host.

- **vSphere Distributed Switch (vDS)** is a virtual switch that can be shared among several ESXi servers. A network-related security policy can be implemented and applied to all datacenter servers. vDS allows a VM to keep its network attributes by moving from one server to another, facilitating administration.

Other features include the following:

- **Virtual Serial Port Concentrator** allows the establishment of communication between a VM and serial IP devices. It is possible to connect the VM's serial port through the network using Telnet or *Secure Shell (SSH)*.

- **View Accelerator** allows the de-duplication of some memory pages from a VM image on each ESXi server. This serves to accelerate the startup of a large number of identical VMs, which is very useful in Virtual Desktop Infrastructure (VDI) environments because it solves boot storm issues (intense activity arising from the simultaneous boot of a large number of VMs).

Software Sold Separately

The software products described in the following sections can be obtained separately.

vCenter Site Recovery Manager 5

vCenter *Site Recovery Manager 5 (SRM 5)* is a business-recovery solution that guarantees a simple protection against incidents that can occur on a production site. SRM ensures the central management of *Disaster Recovery Plans (DRPs)* and automates the resumption of production on an emergency site. Through SRM 5, administrators can perform rollover tests without impacting production. They can also use it for planned migration operations. This version's new features are as follows:

- Replication integrated at the host level (asynchronous mode only)
- Integrated failback (nonexistent in the previous version)
- Enabling of planned migration

vCenter Converter

A *physical-to-virtual (P2V)* tool allows the conversion of a physical machine into a virtual machine. VMware offers its VMware Converter as a conversion tool. This tool is well suited to convert a small number of machines. For larger-scale migrations, other tools on the market are better suited because they can industrialize the process and offer much richer functionality.

> **NOTE**
>
> Under vSphere 5, VMware Converter is not provided as a plug-in in vCenter, so it must be installed in standalone mode.

vCenter Operations Management Suite

VMware continues to invest in research and development to enhance this powerful new tool, which is already considered one of the building blocks for any cloud-computing project. The value proposition of this suite is to bring visibility to the environment, full automation that frees administrators from manual tasks, and proactive management of incidents. The tool also ensures compliance by using an approach based on configuration policies, and it helps administrators provision the virtualized infrastructure. The solution provides the following:

- Capacity and configuration management for cloud-computing environments or extended production environments

- Performance management feature and root cause analysis functionality

- Overall visibility of the environment to correlate configuration changes and performance anomalies

- Chargeback feature for the IT services

- Reporting feature spanning the past months

- Topology mapping of the infrastructure and of the applications dependencies

This tool supports administrators in their daily tasks and provides factual input to help achieve the best virtualized infrastructure dimensioning. Figure 2.6 shows the vCenter Operations interface.

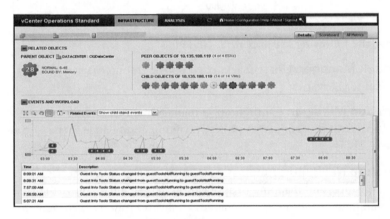

Figure 2.6 vCenter Operations interface.

NOTE

Service providers are the main stakeholders interested in this tool because it enables them to exploit the infrastructure in an optimal fashion. This in turn allows them to attain very high levels of consolidation and thus generate more cost savings.

Four editions of vCenter Operations are available: Standard, Advanced, Enterprise, and Enterprise Plus. The Enterprise Plus version extends the analysis to the physical environment as outlined in Table 2.3.

Table 2.3 vCenter Operations Versions

vCenter Operations Management Suite				
	Standard	**Advanced**	**Enterprise**	**Enterprise Plus**
Scope	Small environment	Large environment	Virtual and cloud infrastructure	Cloud and heterogeneous environments
vCenter Operations Manager	✓ performance only	✓	✓	✓
vCenter Infrastructure Navigator			✓	✓
vCenter Chargeback Manager			✓	✓
vCenter Configuration Manager			✓ vSphere hosts only	✓

Depending on the version, the following features are included:

- **vCenter Chargeback Manager:** Chargeback based on the resources used per VM. Data comes from vCenter Server.

- **vCenter Configuration Manager:** Configuration management according to defined criteria and based on the company's policy, verifying compliance at the server and software levels.

- **vCenter Infrastructure Navigator:** Automatic discovery of application services, visualization of relationships, and mapping of application dependencies on virtualized computer, storage, and network resources. It enables application-aware management of infrastructure and operations, helping the administrator to better understand the impact of change.

NOTE

vCenter Capacity IQ is a capacity management tool for determining what use is made of the virtual environment. This tool is now fully integrated into vCenter Operations Management suite, so it cannot be sold separately anymore.

- **vCloud Director:** A provisioning and application-deployment solution for a fully virtualized datacenter. It manages all virtualized components, from machines to virtual networks, using high security levels just like a physical datacenter. This solution means IT resources are consumed as a service.

- **vApp:** Encapsulates a group of VMs to manage this group as a single virtual unit, simplifying deployments and day-to-day management.

Other software can be used to complement vCenter Operations, including the following:

- **vCenter Lab Manager:** Provides automatic VM provisioning in a testing/development environment, with snapshot/rollback features.
- **vCenter Service Manager:** Based on 100% web architecture, allows administrators to manage the company's processes—managing incidents and issues, change, configurations, service levels, and availability, based on compliance with *Information Technology Infrastructure Library (ITIL)* concepts.
- **vCenter Orchestrator:** Automates certain tasks to create workflows.
- **vCenter Capacity Planner:** Provides provisional capacity to determine the physical resources that will be necessary in the future.

vSphere 5 Technical Architecture

Technically, vSphere 5 is a suite of components that operates as a virtual infrastructure. vSphere 5 provides many new features, but its architecture, illustrated in Figure 2.7, is primarily the same as vSphere 4's.

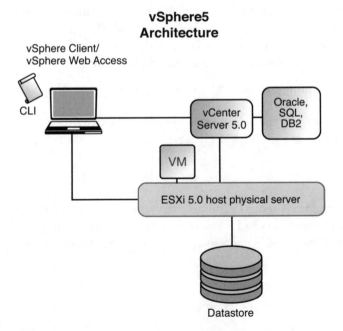

Figure 2.7 vSphere 5's basic architecture.

The basic components of the architecture are as follows:

- **vCenter Server:** Provides centralized management for all ESXi servers within the infrastructure, backed by a database server: Oracle, Microsoft SQL, IBM DB2, and Microsoft SQL Server 2008 Express are supported.

- **ESXi 5.0 host server:** The infrastructure's core.

  ESXi 5.0 is the *hypervisor*, which is a virtualization layer that can run several operating systems on a single physical machine. The ESXi server is directly linked to vCenter Server, whose actions are received by the vSphere Client.

- **Datastore:** Infrastructure storage space.

  The datastore is a virtual representation of the datacenter's physical storage resources. It simplifies the complex nature of the market's various storage types and solutions by proposing a standard model for the storage of VMs.

- **vSphere Client:** User interface to the infrastructure.

  vSphere Client is an indispensable component because it is the interface required to create, administer, and supervise VMs and ESXi hosts. vSphere Client can connect directly to an ESXi server or to a vCenter Server.

- **vSphere Web Access:** Web interface.

  This web interface was developed in Adobe Flex to perform basic administration and configuration actions on virtual and ESXi machines. It allows the virtual environment to be administered from a simple browser without the need to install vSphere Client on Windows-based and Linux-based platforms.

- **Virtual machine (VM):** Representing a server with its OS, applications, and data.

In the following sections, we drill down into the architectural details of the two major components of vSphere 5: vCenter Server 5 and ESXi5 Hypervisor.

vCenter Server 5

vCenter Server is the virtual infrastructure's central administrative tool. It supervises and administers all activities from ESXi host servers and VMs. vCenter Server 5 can manage up to 1000 host servers and 10,000 VMs per vCenter Server install. Figure 2.8 shows the vCenter Server Administration console.

Figure 2.9 illustrates vCenter Server 5's architecture.

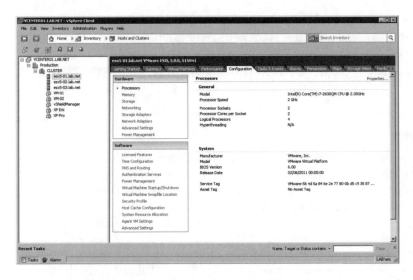

Figure 2.8 vCenter Server 5 Administration console.

Architecture vCenter Server5

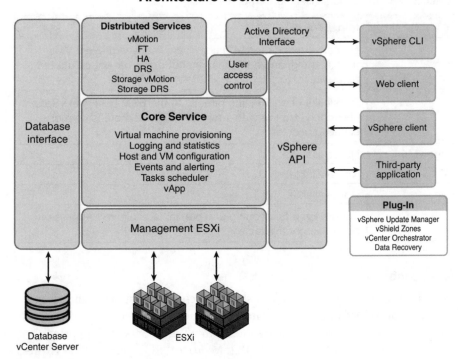

Figure 2.9 vCenter Server 5 architecture diagram.

The components of vCenter Server 5 are the user access controls, basic services, distributed services, plug-ins, and interfaces. vCenter Server can be installed on a VM or on a physical server, but only in a 64-bit Microsoft Windows environment. For small-scale environments, a vCenter Appliance called vCSA and based on Linux SUSE is also available.

RECOMMENDATION

Because vCenter Server is an essential element of VMware architecture, this server requires high service levels. For this reason, to benefit from VMware's HA features, VMware recommends installing it on a VM rather than on a physical server. Deactivating DRS and giving HA a high priority is recommended for a vCenter Server VM.

---

vCenter Server is the virtual infrastructure's central administrative tool. VMs can function without vCenter Server, but some features cannot run without it. Table 2.4 details the impact an interruption of vCenter Server would have on various components.

Table 2.4 vCenter Server Interruption: Affected Components

Components	Impact of vCenter Server Interruption
Virtual machines	No consequence for 14 days. Then, licenses prevent VMs from starting, and a VM that is shut down cannot be started up again.
ESXi server	Possibility of connecting directly to the ESXi host with vSphere client only. No live web interface because there is no more service console.
vMotion/Storage vMotion	Not available.
vSphere DRS	Not available.
vCenter plug-in	Not available.
vSphere HA	Agents keep functioning and can initiate failover. Admission control is not available.

vCenter Server Database

This is the virtual infrastructure's database. The state of each VM, host, user, and so on resides in the vCenter Server's database. The database is installed and configured when vCenter Server is installed. It can be local or remote from vCenter Server. Supported databases are Oracle, Microsoft SQL, and IBM DB2. Microsoft SQL Server 2008 Express can also be used for small-scale deployments of up to 5 ESX and 50 VMs.

vCenter Linked Mode

vCenter linked mode enables you to connect to any instance of vCenter Server in the infrastructure to visualize and manage all the objects forming the group. This simplifies management for the administrator, who, although not needing to connect to every instance of vCenter Server, can have a global view of the infrastructure within a single client management console. It also allows the administrator to define roles only once and apply them to all vCenter instances within the group.

This mode uses Microsoft's *Active Directory Application Mode (ADAM)*—automatically installed with vCenter Server and based on *Lightweight Directory Access Protocol (LDAP)*—to store and synchronize data between various vCenter Server instances. This mode can be configured when installing vCenter Server or integrated post-installation. The following data is replicated among the different instances:

- Login information (IP address and ports)

- Certificates

- License information

- User roles (Each user can view and act on the instances in which it has rights.)

vCenter Server instances within a linked mode group can be located on different domains if a trusted relationship exists between the domains.

> **NOTE**
>
> A vCenter linked mode group is not a vCenter Server HA solution. It facilitates the administration of the infrastructure's various vCenter instances from a single console. To secure HA, use vCenter Server Heartbeat.

vCenter Server Heartbeat

vCenter Server Heartbeat is a feature that provides HA for vCenter Server. It also provides failover management when vCenter Server and other services are interrupted. Failover is triggered when the primary server does not respond. In such a case, the passive server immediately takes on the role of active server. Primary and secondary servers can be made up of two physical servers, two VMs, or one physical server and one VM.

The service interruption can be caused by a physical server outage, a network-related problem, the SQL database, or the application itself.

vCenter Server Heartbeat protects the following services:

- vCenter Server
- ADAM
- vCenter Management Web Server
- Update Manager
- Guided Consolidation Service
- Orchestrator

vSphere Update Manager

vSphere Update Manager (VUM) allows the centralized and automated management of updates and patches for the various versions of VMware vSphere.

Update Manager can be used to do the following:

- Upgrade ESXi hosts (VMkernel)
- Install and update third-party software (for example, Nexus 1000v, PowerPath/VE)
- Upgrade the VM virtual hardware and VMware Tools
- Upgrade to the next version of VMFS

VUM performs the following tasks:

- It collects the latest patches by directly connecting to VMware's website looking for ESX-related patches.
- Information gathered by Update Manager is used to define baselines. There are two types of baselines: *upgrade baseline* defines the version level required from a host server, VM, or virtual appliance; *patch baseline* defines the required update level that must be applied.
- vSphere Update Manager analyzes the state of ESX host servers and VMs and compares these to the administrator-defined baselines. When the analysis is done, noncompliant machines are tagged for patch updates.

Applying Patches to Virtual Machines

To reduce the risk of outage on a VM while a patch is applied, Update Manager can take a snapshot of the VM's state prior to the application of VMware Tools or virtual hardware updates. Snapshots are stored for a period defined by the administrator.

Applying Patches to ESX Host Servers

vSphere Update Manager also allows the disruption-free application of patches on ESX host servers using VMware DRS. It puts hosts in maintenance mode and performs a hot migration of VMs to other hosts before applying patches. After the patches are applied, the host comes out of maintenance, and VMs can go back into production mode on the ESX server. VUM then applies the patches to the cluster's next host.

> **NOTE**
>
> With vSphere Update Manager 5, maintaining VM application patches and OS patches is no longer allowed. To perform these operations, you must use software-delivery tools such as Microsoft's *System Center Configuration Manager (SCCM)* or *Windows Server Update Services (WSUS)* or IBM's Landesk or Tivoli.

vCenter APIs

VMware provides APIs for vCenter Server. Software editors and integrators can develop their own solutions and offer additional value-added products and functionality that complement those provided by VMware.

Plug-In vCenter Server

Plug-ins consist of a client and a server. When the server plug-in is installed, it registers to vCenter Server and becomes available for download on the client side through the vSphere Client. VMware offers some plug-ins as options, including Update Manager, Site Recovery Manager, Data Recovery, and Auto Deploy.

vCenter Server Appliance

vCenter Server Appliance (vCSA) is a prepackaged 64-bit version of SUSE Linux Enterprise Server 11. It includes an embedded database (DB2 Express) that can manage up to 5 ESXi servers and up to 50 VMs. Connecting to an external Oracle or IBM DB2 database is possible.

With this appliance, the *total cost of ownership (TCO)* is reduced because the purchase of a Windows license is not required. Deployment is simplified because importing the *Open Virtualization Format (OVF)* file to the vSphere 5 platform is all that is necessary. Updates are also made easier thanks to Update Manager. At the administrator level, there is no difference when connecting to the vSphere Client.

Appliance configuration is done through a web interface, and authentication is done through the Active Directory or *Network Information Service (NIS)*.

All classic VM functionality is supported (for example, HA, Snapshot, or vStorage API for Backup).

The vCSA VM is configured as follows:

- 2 vCPUs
- 8 GB) vRAM
- 1 vNIC
- 2 vDisks:
  - **vDisk1:** 5.3 GB thin
  - **vDisk2:** 25 GB thick

In this first version, vCSA has the following limitations:

- There is no support for third-party software plug-ins and no support of SQL Server databases. Linked mode and IPv6 are not supported.
- vCenter Server Appliance is sold separately from the vSphere and vCenter license.

ESXi 5 Hypervisor

ESXi 5 is a hypervisor that forms the core of vSphere 5's infrastructure. It is the virtualization layer that allows several operating systems to run on a single physical machine. This 144-MB version is called "light" because it contains no service console. Some manufacturers integrate ESXi directly into the server's internal memory, USB key, or SD card.

Advantages of this version include the following:

- ESXi 5 provides light 144-MB architecture versus 2 GB for previous versions with a service console.
- Security is reinforced and requires fewer maintenance operations such as OS patches and updates.
- ESXi can be loaded into memory without a boot disk (thanks to Auto Deploy).

ESXi 5 Components

Figure 2.10 provides a diagram of the ESXi 5 component architecture.

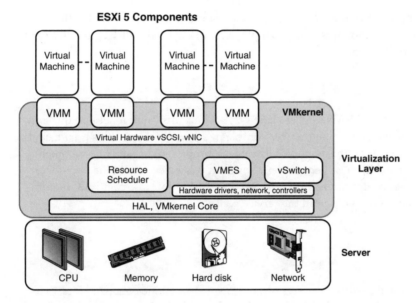

Figure 2.10 ESXi 5 components.

ESXi 5.0 contains these main components:

- Virtualization layer
- VMs

Virtualization Layer

The virtualization layer has two components: *Virtual Machine Monitor (VMM)* and VMkernel.

The virtualization layer hides the various hardware components from the VMs by always offering the same virtual hardware (vNIC, vSCSI) to a given VM. The layer allows VMs to operate simultaneously and is responsible for the host server's resource sharing.

Each VM possesses its own instance of VMM. VMM executes all virtual CPU instructions. It ensures communication between the VM's memory and the host system's memory. VMM intercepts I/O requests coming from VMs and submits them to VMkernel. VMM also controls the guaranteed minimum allocations (for example, memory, disk) upon startup and their isolation.

VMkernel is virtualization's core and drive. It is a system entirely developed by VMware (in 64 bits for ESXi 5). VMkernel controls and manages the server's material resources. It dynamically allocates CPU time, memory, and disk and network access to VMs by sequencing them using the Resource Manager. It also contains device drivers for the physical server's various components—for example, network card and disk controller card, VMFS file system, and vSwitches.

> **NOTE**
>
> Many people assume ESX and VMkernel are based on a Linux distribution because they can use Linux command prompts (from the service console in earlier versions). This is false, and VMware has been very clear on this point: VMkernel is a proprietary product development. The service console available on earlier versions, however, was indeed a modified version of Red Hat Enterprise that could, among other things, boot ESX. Note also that ESXi is sufficient unto itself to boot; it does not need the service console.

> **NOTE**
>
> The service console available with older versions of ESX was an online command interface that could grant access to VMkernel to modify and configure the ESX host server's parameters and could be used to power ESX. For security and stability reasons, the service console was removed from the virtual platform in favor of a lighter version of ESXi.

Virtual Machines

A *virtual machine (VM)* consists of a guest *operating system (OS)* with virtual hardware.

Figure 2.11 Guest OS with virtual hardware.

The host (or ESXi host) is the main physical server on which ESXi is installed. The guest OS is the operating system installed on the VM. Virtual hardware is composed of virtual components such as *virtual networking card (vNIC)*, vSCSI, and vCPU.

Hardware version 8, introduced in vSphere 5, supports the following:

- 32 vCPU and 1 TB vRAM within the VM
- A 3D virtual card (to support Windows Aero)
- The possibility of connecting USB devices in client mode through vSphere Client
- A USB 3.0 controller
- Smart card reader support
- UEFI BIOS
- A configuration API for the boot order of the BIOS
- E1000e high-performance network card (available only for some operating systems)
- Multicore configuration through the graphic interface (without advanced parameters)

VMs with hardware versions earlier than version 8 can function on ESXi 5.0 hosts but will not have access to all functionality. With version 7, for instance, 32 virtual processors cannot be used. Table 2.5 outlines the compatibility between virtual hardware versions and ESXi host generations, and Figure 2.12 shows the Virtual Machine Version 8 Hardware tab.

Table 2.5 ESXi Hosts and Compatible VM Hardware Versions

	Compatibility with Virtual Hardware			Compatible with vCenter Server Version
	Version 8	Version 7	Version 4	vCenter Server
ESXi 5.0	Create, edit, run	Create, edit, run	Edit, run	vCenter Server 5.0
ESX/ESXi 4.x	Not supported	Create, edit, run	Create, edit, run	vCenter Server 4.x
ESX Server 3.x	Not supported	Not supported	Create, edit, run	VirtualCenter Server 2.x and following versions

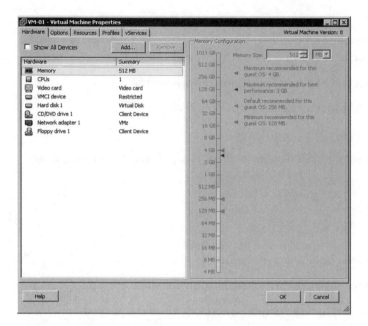

Figure 2.12 Virtual hardware version 8 under vSphere 5.

A VM is encapsulated in files that contain all hardware and software states running within the VM. A VM is composed of the files shown in Figure 2.13.

The following list briefly describes the various files shown in Figure 2.13:

- **vmdk:** Corresponds to a metadata file. The virtual disk description (editable file) provides the link to the .flat-vmdk file.

- **flat-vmdk:** The most important file because it is the VM's virtual disk and contains all the data for the VM: operating system, applications, and so on.

- **vmx:** Contains all configuration information and material parameters for the VM, such as memory size, hard drive size, network card information, and MAC address. It is the first file created when a VM is created.

- **nvram:** Contains the VM's BIOS status.

- **log:** Tracks the VM's activity. Several log files exist, and they are very useful for diagnosing problems. VMware's support services use them. A new log file is created when the VM is shut down and restarted or when the file reaches its maximum size, as defined in advanced configuration options (vCenter's advanced options: log.rotate size and logkeepOld).

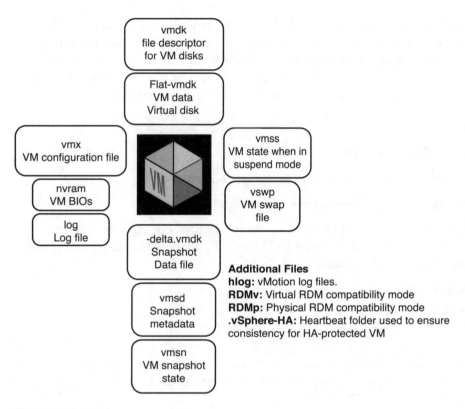

Figure 2.13 VM files.

- **vmss:** Created when a VM is suspended. This file contains the entire content of the active memory. When the VM is put back into service, the content of the vmss file returns to the server's RAM, which creates a work environment identical to the one that existed before the VM was suspended.

- **vswp:** Automatically created whenever a VM starts. This file is used as the VM's memory swap. A VM cannot start if this file cannot be created.

When snapshots are initialized, the following file types are created:

- **-delta.vmdk:** Created and used when taking a VM snapshot. At the moment the snapshot is created, the original vmdk file is quiesced and put into read-only mode. No more data will be written into this original file. For example, 00000#.vmdk contains the metadata associated with the snapshot.

- **vmsd:** Contains snapshot information and metadata, including the name of the associated vmdk and vmsn. A file is created that contains all the information from all snapshots. A vmsn file is created for each snapshot. Filenames follow numeric increments. For example, Snapshotxxx.vmsn contains the state of the snapshot that contains the running VM's status at the moment the snapshot is taken.

Other files:

- **hlog:** Log files for vMotion.

- **RDMv:** Raw device mapping in virtual compatibility mode.

- **RDMp:** Raw device mapping in physical compatibility mode.

- **vSphere HA:** A special folder that includes special files. For example, host-xxx-hb, Poweron, and Protectedlist are special files used by vSphere HA for Heartbeat and for the consistency of protected VMs.

- **mvtx:** For templates.

TIP

Editing these files improperly can render the VM useless afterward. It is best to leave these files as they are. If editing is necessary, making backups beforehand is absolutely essential.

VMware Tools

With VMware Tools, the virtual hardware of the guest OS can be perfectly integrated with ESXi. VMware adds the following components:

- Optimized drivers such as vmxnet, LSI Logic SCSI, and SAS

- SYNC driver to quiesce VMs

- Memory balloon driver (vmmemctl)

- VM Heartbeat

- Time synchronization

- Possibility of shutting down VMs cleanly

- Possibility of adding *dynamic link libraries (DLLs)* to Perfmon

VMware Tools greatly improves graphic display and mouse movement and adds useful features—for example, the option to add scripts after a VM starts up. VMware Tools must be installed on each OS.

Security

The following sections discuss important features related to vSphere 5 security.

vShield Zones

VMware vShield is a suite of security virtual appliances and APIs that are built to work with vSphere, protecting virtualized datacenters from attacks and misuse. vShield Zones consists of a manager that provides an administration interface allowing policy implementation and a virtual appliance that provides security, as illustrated in Figure 2.14. This appliance is automatically integrated into vCenter Server. All activities between the zones and the outside are monitored, and network frames are filtered based on the implemented policy.

vShield Zones is available with Enterprise and Enterprise Plus versions.

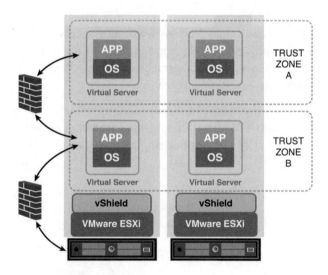

Figure 2.14 vShield Zones.

The vShield suite includes vShield Zones, vShield Edge, vShield App, and vShield Endpoint:

- **vShield Zones:** Provides firewall protection for traffic between VMs. For each Zones firewall rule, you can specify the source IP, destination IP, source port, destination port, and service. VShield Zones is a VM-protection virtual firewall that takes the form of an appliance that is also used to analyze network traffic. With vShield Zones, logical zones can be created, such as *demilitarized zones (DMZs)*, that guarantee Internet traffic is kept separate from the servers' internal traffic. Because of vShield Zones, creating dedicated ESXi servers is no longer a requirement for DMZs. Isolated zones containing several hundred VMs can also be created without the need to manage complex vSwitch and VLAN configurations. The vShield Zones firewall is located at the level of vSwitches using rules that block or allow certain ports or protocols or network traffic.

- **vShield Edge:** Provides network edge security and gateway services to isolate the VMs in a port group, distributed port group, or Cisco Nexus 1000V. vShield Edge connects isolated stub networks to shared uplink networks by providing common gateway services such as *Dynamic Host Configuration Protocol (DHCP)*, *virtual private networking (VPN)*, *Network Address Translation (NAT)*, and load balancing. Common deployments of vShield Edge include the DMZ, VPN extranets, and multitenant cloud environments where vShield Edge provides perimeter security for *virtual datacenters (VDCs)*.

- **vShield App:** An interior vNIC-level firewall that allows you to create access control policies regardless of network topology. vShield App monitors all traffic in and out of an ESXi host, including between VMs in the same port group. vShield App includes traffic analysis and container-based policy creation.

- **vShield Endpoint:** Delivers an introspection-based antivirus solution. vShield Endpoint uses the hypervisor to scan guest VMs from the outside without an agent. vShield Endpoint avoids resource bottlenecks while optimizing memory use.

Components to Monitor

From a security viewpoint, the following ESX components must be monitored:

- Virtualization layer
- Virtual machines
- Network

Virtualization Layer Security

VMkernel is dedicated to supporting VMs. It is not used for any other goal. The VMkernel interface is strictly limited to the APIs used to manage VMs. VMkernel's protection has been reinforced to guarantee its integrity. Disk protection and integrity techniques leverage hardware elements such as the *Trusted Platform Module (TPM)*.

Virtual Machine Security

VMs are isolated from one another. This ensures that several VMs can run simultaneously and securely even if they share physical resources. If a VM crashes or is infected with a virus, other VMs will not be impacted.

Network Security

The network is one of the most sensitive and vulnerable elements in any system. It must be protected. VMs are isolated from one another when it comes to sharing server resources (CPU memory), but they can communicate through the network. As with any physical network, this part of the network must be secured using VLANs, DMZs, and so on. A security policy can also be configured and implemented at the level of the vSwitches' port group.

An Evolved Solution

The VMware solution stack is among the most mature and successful in the industry. Going back to 1998, it has revolutionized the way organizations deploy and manage servers. Beginning with a simple hypervisor, VMware has built a comprehensive stack, going beyond the basic hypervisor. With the many components that comprise a VM, management tools become paramount, and VMware has led the pack in this field.

vSphere 5.0 is a cloud operating system and the foundation for building a virtual Datacenter. It virtualizes the entire IT infrastructure such as servers, storage, and networks grouping these heterogeneous resources and transforming the rigid, inflexible infrastructure into a simple and unified manageable set of elements in the virtualized environment.

With so many features, you might think that the VMware ESXi must have a huge footprint. In ESXi 5, the footprint is only 144 MB. VMware has removed as much of the extraneous code from the hypervisor as possible, reducing the attack surfaces and thus enhancing security. With so much advanced design, it is easy to see why VMware VSphere continues to have a commanding lead in the market.

Chapter 3

Storage in vSphere 5

Storage is usually the most essential component of virtualized architecture, playing a major role in your system's performance and extensibility. It must be able to support the activity of hosted VMs and be upgradeable to meet future needs. In some projects, the time devoted to designing storage architecture can represent up to 60% of all work. Therefore, the best solution must be chosen according to your business constraints, goals, and allocated budget, because costs can vary significantly among the different storage solutions available.

Storage Representation

Because vSphere 5 offers a wide variety of storage options, it is important to know what features are offered and to understand the interactions between traditional storage in the physical world and the integration of vSphere into such an environment (see Figure 3.1).

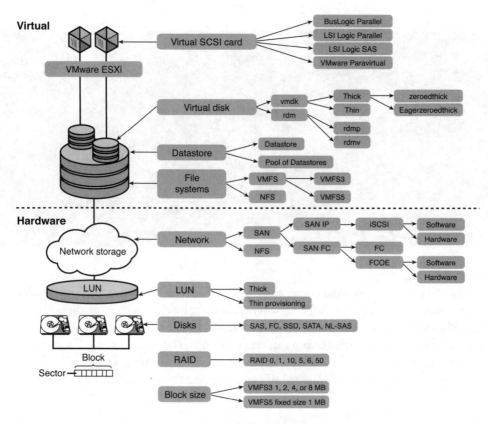

Figure 3.1 How material objects traditionally manipulated by storage administrators (bottom) interact with those manipulated by VMware administrators (top).

Available Storage Architectures

VMware supports several storage protocols, which can make it difficult for companies to know which option best suits their needs. Although this flexibility and freedom can be a good thing, too many options can make decision making difficult or even overwhelming. Although a few years ago, the only viable option for production environments was *storage-area network (SAN) Fibre Channel (FC)*, today the differences between protocols are of less importance, and several criteria must be taken into account. Figure 3.2 shows the supported protocols.

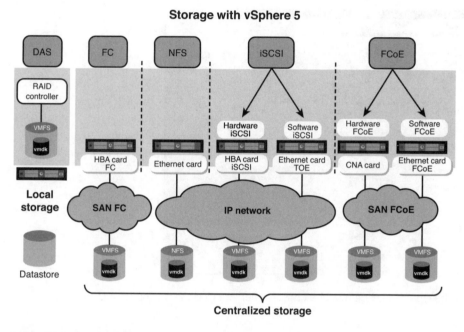

Figure 3.2 Local versus centralized storage architectures.

The following storage options (chosen when creating the datastore in Figure 3.3) are available in virtual environments.

- **Local storage:** Hard drives are directly connected within the server or as *direct-attached storage (DAS)*, which are disk arrays directly attached to the server.

- **Centralized storage:** Storage is external from the server. The following protocols are supported by ESX:

  - *Fibre Channel (FC)*

  - *Internet Small Computer System Interface (iSCSI)* software or hardware initiator

  - *Network File System (NFS)* used by *network-attached storage (NAS)*

  - *Fibre Channel over Ethernet (FCoE)* software or hardware initiator

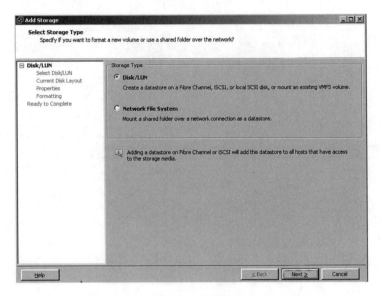

Figure 3.3 The type of storage must be chosen when creating the datastore.

Local Storage

Local storage is commonly used when installing ESXi Hypervisor. When an ESXi server is isolated and not in a cluster, this storage space can be used for operating system image files (provided as ISO files) or noncritical test and development VMs. Because by definition local storage is (usually) not shared, placement of critical-production VMs should be avoided because the service levels are too low. Features such as vMotion, *Distributed Resource Scheduler (DRS)*, *High Availability (HA)*, and *Fault Tolerance (FT)* are not available except when the vSphere Storage Appliance is used.

Centralized Storage

In a centralized architecture, vSphere can be made to work in clusters, increasing service levels by using advanced features such as vMotion, DRS, HA, FT, and *Site Replication Manager (SRM)*. Moreover, these types of architectures provide excellent performance, and the addition of the *vStorage APIs for Array Integration (VAAI)* relieves the host server from some storage-related tasks by offloading it to a storage array.

NAS storage servers are based on a client/server architecture that accesses data at the NFS level. This protocol, called *file mode*, uses the company's standard Ethernet network. Network cards are available in 1 GbE (1 Gbps) or 10 GbE (10 Gbps).

Other protocols provide a direct I/O access (also called *block mode*) between host servers and storage by using SCSI commands in a dedicated network called a *storage-area network (SAN)*. With VMware, the advantage of block mode over file mode is that *Raw Device Mapping (RDM)* volumes can be attributed to VMs. VMware uses the *Virtual Machine File System (VMFS)* in this architecture.

> **NOTE**
>
> In VMware, one notable difference exists between NFS and VMFS. With NFS, the NAS server manages the file system and relies on the ESXi network layer (issues are resolved by network teams), whereas VMFS is managed directly by the ESXi storage layer.

There are different types of SANs, both IP-based SANs and FC-based SANs:

- **SAN IP (called iSCSI):** Encapsulates SCSI commands through the TCI/IP network (SCSI over IP). You can access the iSCSI network by using either a software initiator coupled with a standard network card, or a dedicated hardware *host bus adapter (HBA)*.

- **SAN FC:** Dedicated Fibre Channel high-performance storage network for applications requiring high I/O to access data directly and sequentially. The FC protocol encapsulates the SCSI frames. This protocol has very little overhead because SCSI packets are sent natively. The server uses a Fibre Channel HBA to access the SAN.

- **SAN FCoE (rarely used in 2012):** Convergence of two worlds: IP and FC networks. FCoE uses Fibre Channel technology, but on a converged FCoE network. A *converged network adapter (CNA)* is the type of card used.

As shown in Figure 3.4, SCSI commands are encapsulated in different layers depending on the protocol used. The more layers used, the more overhead at the host level.

> **NOTE**
>
> Companies sometimes ask which protocol is best in a VMware environment. Obviously, this is a difficult question to answer. It is like asking you to pick the best means of travel between two points without having any context. Obviously, the best mode of transportation for going grocery shopping will not be the same as for going on a vacation abroad. Therefore, before answering the question about the best protocol, you need to know the general context as well as information about the infrastructure, the IT team skills in place, the type of applications (critical, noncritical) to virtualize, performance expectations, financial concerns, and so on.

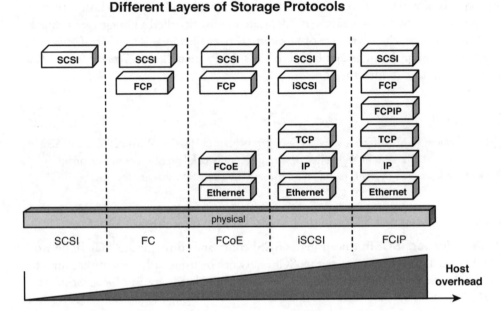

Figure 3.4 Layers of SCSI commands in the different protocols.

Storage Networks

As explained in the preceding section, two networks may be used: the IP Ethernet network (in NAS or iSCSI modes) and the FC network (FC or FCoE).

IP Storage Network

This type of network was not originally designed to offer high-performance storage but rather to carry information between the network's various active elements. Therefore, it is not adapted for applications requiring high performance, such as database applications. The IP network is located at Level 3 of the OSI layer, so it is routable, which favors network interconnectivity over long distances. The FC network is found at Level 2 and, therefore, not routable. Today, throughputs reach 10 GbE, and the future promises 40 GbE and 100 GbE.

The problem with IP networks is that an IP network experiences *packet loss* because of the following factors:

- Signal degradation on the physical line

- Routing errors
- Buffer overflow (when the receptor cannot absorb the incoming flow)

The TCI/IP protocol allows the retransmission of lost packets (if sent data is not acknowledged by the receiver), but this has a dramatic impact on performance.

Another issue is that only a limited quantity of data, called *maximum transmission unit (MTU)*, can be sent in an IP packet. This quantity, called the *payload*, is set at 1500 bytes for an Ethernet packet. Data beyond 1500 bytes must be fragmented before it is sent. Each time a packet is received by the network card, the card sends an interrupt to the host to confirm reception. This adds to the overload at the host and CPU cycle level (called *overhead*). As the number of sent packets increases, routing becomes more complicated and time-consuming.

> **NOTE**
>
> In consolidated virtual environments, the overhead must be taken into account; it should not deteriorate the performance of the host server, which should be entirely dedicated to applications.

To reduce this frame fragmentation, *jumbo frames* were created. These allow the transmission of packets larger than 1500 bytes (up to an MTU of 9000 bytes). The jumbo frames play a significant role in improving efficiency, and some studies have shown reductions of 50% in CPU overhead. The MTU must be activated and compatible from the *beginning to the end* of the chain, including physical switches, cards, cables, and so on.

> **NOTE**
>
> A 9000-byte jumbo frame replaces 6 * 1500 bytes from a standard Ethernet packet, generating five times fewer CPU cycles by the host.

Exercise caution. If a problem occurs, the higher the MTU between the source and the target, the larger the packets to retransmit will be, which decreases performance and increases latency. To make the most of jumbo frames, the network must be robust and well implemented.

IP storage networks have the advantage of being less expensive than SAN FC equipment. Ethernet networks are already in place, so in some cases, less implementation is required, making them easier to use. Furthermore, IT teams have used the technology for several years.

iSCSI in VMware

In the VMware environment, the iSCSI protocol has been supported only since 2006. If deployed in an optimal fashion, this protocol offers very good performance. The IP network is administered by a team other than the storage team.

Advantages: iSCSI has been adopted in many activity sectors because it uses the company's TCP/IP network for access in block mode, without the need to invest in FC equipment. For this reason, it is an ideal solution in certain environments because it is much easier to set up. Using the traditional Ethernet network means greater distances can be covered before requiring special conversion equipment (such as FC to IP converters)—for example, for replication. The skills necessary are network skills rather than advanced storage skills.

Disadvantages: Tests have proven iSCSI is the protocol that uses the most CPU resources. Therefore, monitoring CPU use is important and should be taken into account when provisioning networks.

The following best practices are recommended:

- Using iSCSI is worthwhile only if the architecture can take full advantage of this protocol by activating jumbo frames (MTU 9000), which provides excellent performance. This activation must exist from one end of the chain to the other.

- Using iSCSI HBA cards becomes essential when using 10-GB connections, and links should be aggregated wherever possible for high performance and redundancy in case of failure.

- It is advisable to physically separate the iSCSI storage network from the standard IP network. If this is not possible, streams should be isolated using *virtual local-area networks (VLANs)*.

- Use cards with *TCP/IP offline engine (TOE)* functionality to unload the host from some instructions related to the iSCSI overlay and to reduce the overhead.

- Implement *quality of service (QoS)* by putting the priority on streams. Using vSphere, this can be done using the *Storage I/O Control (SIOC)* functionality.

- Network packet loss is one of the main challenges to achieving good iSCSI network performance. Packet loss can be caused by faulty network configuration or the wrong quality of wiring (for example, using Category 5 cables rather than Category 6 for gigabit links).

NFS in VMware

Network File System (NFS) is a protocol used by NAS and supported by ESX since 2006. It provides storage sharing through the network at the file-system level. *VMware supports NFS version 3 over TCP.* Contrary to what is sometimes believed, tests show good performance if this protocol is implemented properly. Therefore, it is possible to use this protocol under certain conditions for virtual environments. Activation of jumbo frames (MTU 9000) allows the transmission of 8192 (8 KB) NFS data blocks, which are well suited for the protocol. By default, 8 NFS mounts per ESXi host are possible. This can be extended to 256 NFS mounts. If you increase the maximum NFS mounts above the default setting of eight, make sure to also increase the Net.TcpipHeapSize and Net.TcpipHeapMax, as well. The values are in the advanced configuration, and govern the amount of heap memory, measured in megabytes, which is allocated for managing VMkernel TCP/IP network connectivity.

- ESXi 5.0: Set Net.TcpipHeapSize to 32

- ESXi 5.0: Set Net.TcpipHeapMax to 128

NOTE

By default, thin provisioning is the format used when a virtual disk is created on NFS datastores.

Advantages: Like iSCSI, NFS uses the standard TCP/IP network and is very easy to implement without the need for a dedicated storage infrastructure. It is the least expensive solution, and it does not require particular storage skills. Very often, NAS offers de-duplication, which can reduce the amount of storage space required.

Disadvantages: It offers the lowest performance of the described solutions, but it is close to iSCSI's. It makes more use of the host server's CPU than the FC protocol, but less than iSCSI software. Therefore, it could conceivably be used in a production environment with VMs requiring average performance for Tier 2 and Tier 3 applications.

NOTE

With vSphere 5, this protocol does not support NFS boot or the use of RDM.

The following best practices are recommended:

- Use 100 to 400 vmdk files per NFS volume. The maximum possible *logical unit number (LUN)* is 256 for a maximum size of 64 TB per NFS volume. (Manufacturers can provide information about the limit supported by file systems, usually 16 TB.)

- Separate the network dedicated to storage from the Ethernet network by using dedicated switches or VLANs.

- Activate flow control.

- Activate jumbo frames by using dedicated switches with large per-port buffers.

- Activate the Spanning Tree Protocol.

- Use a 10-Gb network (strongly recommended).

- Use full TOE cards to unload ESXi host servers.

- To isolate storage traffic from other networking traffic, use either dedicated switches or VLANs for your NFS and iSCSI traffic

Fibre Channel Network

Essentially, the Fibre Channel network is dedicated to storage that offers direct *lossless* access to block mode data. This network is designed for high-performance storage with very low latency, through advanced mechanisms such as *buffer credits* (a kind of buffer memory used to regulate streams in a SAN). The FC protocol (FC) encapsulates SCSI packets through a dedicated Fibre Channel network. Speeds are 1, 2, 4, 8, or 16 Gbps. FC packets carry a payload of 2112 bytes. This storage network carries data between servers and storage devices through Fibre Channel switches. The SAN, illustrated in Figure 3.5, enables storage consolidation and provides high scalability.

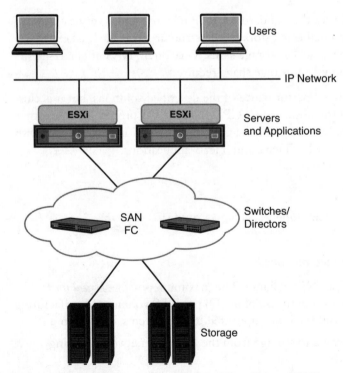

Figure 3.5 Schematic architecture of a Fibre Channel SAN.

SAN FC in VMware

Fibre Channel (FC) is the most advanced of the protocols supported by VMware. This is why it is most often the one used by clients in their production environment.

Advantages: It seems to be a given today that FC is the most high-performing protocol, as well as the one using the least host-server CPU resources when compared to NFS and iSCSI. High performance levels can be reached, and because the technology is lossless, the network is predictive. This protocol works for all popular applications and is ideal for those that are I/O intensive such as databases or *enterprise resource planning (ERP)* applications.

Disadvantages: FC is the most expensive solution because it involves building a specialized storage architecture and requiring an investment in HBA cards, FC switches, *small form-factor pluggable (SFP)* ports, and cables. Moreover, implementing this solution is more complex and requires specialized storage skills. Training is required, and so is learning new terminology to manage the SAN, such as *LUN masking, zoning WWN,* and *fabrics.*

The following best practices are recommended:

- To reduce broken links, insert several HBA cards in each server and use numerous storage array access paths.

- Use load-balancing software, such as native ESXi Round Robin, or EMC PowerPath/Virtual Edition, to optimize path management between servers and storage.

- Use ALUA-compliant storage arrays that are compatible with VMware's VAAI APIs.

- Use the same number of paths between all members of the cluster, and all host servers within a cluster should see the same volumes.

- Comply with the connection compatibility matrix between the members of the ESXi cluster and storage.

> **NOTE**
>
> We have met administrators who connected their servers directly to controller storage arrays to save on the cost of switches! Such a practice cancels the redundancy benefit offered by a FC SAN and is therefore discouraged.

- Use the same speed of switches in all connections to avoid the creation of contention points in the SAN.

> **EXAMPLE**
>
> A company had new blade servers with FC 8-Gb ports. The SAN's core switch was at 4 Gbps. A significant contention appeared on the core switch, which had an impact on all connected elements. The corrective action was to force the new equipment to adopt the fabric speed at 4 Gbps.

- Check firmware levels on FC switches and HBAs, and follow instructions from the storage array manufacturer.

SAN FCoE in VMware

Fibre Channel over Ethernet (FCoE) represents the convergence of various fields: Ethernet for the network (TCP/IP), SAN for storage (SAN FC), and InfiniBand for clustering (IPC). This means a single type of card, switch cables, and management interface can now be used for these various protocols. FC frames are encapsulated in Ethernet frames that provide transport in a more efficient manner than TCP/IP.

FCoE frames carry a payload of 2500 bytes. The goal is to render Ethernet lossless like FC. This is achieved by making the physical network more reliable and by making a number of improvements, especially with regard to QoS. Dedicated equipment is required, as is the activation of jumbo frames (2180 bytes). Congestion is eliminated through stream-management mechanisms.

Because FCoE remains relatively uncommon in 2012, we lack practical experience regarding the advantages and disadvantages of this type of protocol in a VMware environment.

Which Protocol Is Best for You?

In our experience, SAN FC is the protocol administrators prefer for virtual production environments. An estimated 70% of customers use SAN FC for production in VMware environments. The arrival of 10 GbE with jumbo frames, however, allows the easy implementation of a SAN IP infrastructure while maintaining a level of performance that can suffice in some cases. Aside from technical criteria, the optimal choice is based on existing architectures and allocated budgets.

To summarize

- SAN FC should be favored for applications that require high performance (Tier 1 and Tier 2), such as database applications.
- iSCSI can be used for Tier 2 applications. Some businesses use IP in iSCSI for remote data replication, which works well and limits costs.

- NAS can be used for network services such as infrastructure VMs—domain controller, DNS, file, or noncritical application servers (Tier 3 applications)—as well as for ISO image, template, and VM backup storage.

VMFS

Virtual Machine File System (VMFS) is a file system developed by VMware that is dedicated and optimized for clustered virtual environments and the storage of large files. The structure of VMFS makes it possible to store VM files in a single folder, simplifying VM administration.

Advantages: Traditional file systems authorize only a single server to obtain read/write access to a storage resource. VMFS is a so-called *clustered* file system—it allows read/write access to storage resources by several ESXi host servers simultaneously. To ensure that several servers do not simultaneously access the same VM, VMFS provides a system called *on-disk locking*. This guarantees that a VM works with only a single ESXi server at a time. To manage access, ESXi uses a *SCSI reservation* technique that modifies metadata files. This very short locking period prevents I/O on the entire LUN for any ESXi server and for VMs. This is why it is important not to have frequent SCSI reservations, because they could hinder performance.

The SCSI reservation is used by ESXi when:

- Creating a VMFS datastore
- Expanding a VMFS datastore onto additional extends
- Powering on a VM
- Acquiring a lock on a file
- Creating or deleting a file
- Creating a template
- Deploying a VM from a template
- Creating a new VM
- Migrating a VM with vMotion
- Growing a file (for example, a *VMFS)* snapshot file or a thin provisioned virtual disk)
- HA functionality is used (if a server fails, disk locking is released, which allows another ESXi server to restart VMs and use disk locking for its own purposes)

> **NOTE**
>
> One particular VAAI feature, hardware-assisted locking, reduces SCSI reservations. This API unloads locking activity directly through to the storage array controllers.

VMFS-5 Specifications

vSphere 5 introduces VMFS 5 with a maximum size of 64 TB. Table 3.1 outlines the evolution of VMFS from version 3 to version 5.

Table 3.1 VMFS-3 Versus VMFS-5

Functionalities	VMFS-3	VMFS-5
Maximum volume	2 TB	64 TB
Block size	1, 2, 4, or 8 MB	1 MB
Sub-blocks	64 KB	8 KB
Small files	No	1 KB

VMFS-5 offers higher limits than VMFS-3 because the addressing table was redeveloped in 64 bits. (VMFS-3 offered a 32-bit table and was limited to 256,000 blocks of 8 MB [or 2 TB].) With VMFS-5, blocks have a fixed size of 1 MB, and the maximum volume is 64 TB. With VMFS-3, blocks vary in size between 1 MB and 8 MB, which can cause virtual disk maximum size issues if the block size is too low. (For example, 1 MB blocks are limited to 256 GB vmdk files, and the volume must be reformatted using the right size of blocks for a larger file size.) Sub-blocks go from 64 KB to 8 KB, with the possibility of managing files as small as 1 KB.

You should also note the following:

- A single VMFS datastore must be created for each LUN.
- VMFS keeps an event log. This preserves data integrity and allows quick restoration should problems arise.

Upgrading VMFS-3 to VMFS-5

VMFS-3 is compatible with vSphere 5. The upgrade from VMFS-3 to VMFS-5 is supported and occurs without service interruption while VMs are running. Creating a new VMFS volume is preferable, however, because the VMFS-3 to VMFS-5 upgrade carries the following limitations:

- Blocks keep their initial size (which can be larger than 1 MB). Copy operations between datastores with different block sizes will not benefit from the VAAI feature full copy.

- Sub-blocks remain at 64 KB.

- When a new VMFS-5 volume is created, the maximum number of files remains unchanged at 30,720 instead of a maximum of 100,000 files.

- The use of a *master boot record (MBR)* type partition remains, but it is automatically changed to a *GUID partition table (GPT)* when volumes are larger than 2 TB.

Signature of VMFS Datastores

Each VMFS datastore has a *universal unique identifier (UUID)* to identify on which LUN the VMFS datastore is located. This UUID must be unique. If two VMFSs are simultaneously mounted with the same UUID, ESXi does not know on which volume to perform read/write operations (it will send at random to each volume), which can lead to data corruption. vSphere detects this situation and prevents it.

> **NOTE**
>
> The UUID is stored in the header of the VMFS file system and is generated from four variables: the date, time, part of an ESXi MAC address, and LUN identifier in the storage array. This ensures a unique value within the environment and forms part of the VMFS volume's metadata.

When a VMFS LUN is replicated, snapshot, or cloned, the VMFS LUN created is 100% identical to the original, including the UUID. To exploit this new VMFS LUN, it is possible to assign a new signature or to keep the same signature as the original under certain conditions, using the following options (shown in Figure 3.6):

> **NOTE**
>
> Volume signature applies to VMFS file systems in FC or iSCSI, but not to NFS volumes.

- **Keep the Existing Signature:** This option enables the preservation of the same signature and mounting of the replicated datastore. To avoid UUID conflicts, such mounting can be performed only in cases where the source VMFS LUN is unmounted (or removed).

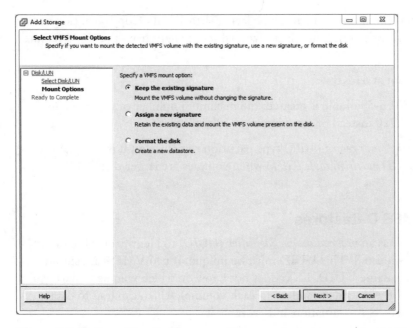

Figure 3.6 Options offered when remounting a replicated or snapshot LUN.

- **Assign a New Signature:** When re-signaturing a VMFS, ESXi assigns a new UUID and name to the LUN copy. This enables the simultaneous mount of both VMFS datastores (the original volume and its copy) with two distinct identifiers. Note that re-signaturing is irreversible. Remember to perform a datastore rescan to update the LUNs introduced to the ESXi.

- **Format the Disk:** This option entirely reformats the volume.

> **NOTE**
>
> Re-signaturing of a VMFS datastore has consequences if the datastore contains VMs. Indeed, each VM's configuration files (vmx, vmsd, and vmdk files) specify on which datastores the VM's virtual disks are located, based on the UUID value. In the case of a volume re-signaturing, the UUID values in these files are no longer correct because they point to the former VMFS with its former UUID. VMs must be re-registered in vCenter to integrate the new UUID, and the datacenter, resource pools, and network mappings must be set up again.

Re-Signature of a VMFS Volume as Part of a DRP

A new UUID is generated when implementing a *disaster recovery plan (DRP)* and in cases where the replicated volume changes signature. The vmx and vmdk configuration files from the VMs recorded on the volume point to the former UUID rather than to the new volume. Therefore, all VMs that are part of the DRP must be manually removed from the vCenter's inventory and re-recorded to recuperate the new UUID. This can be a cumbersome process and can lead to handling errors when these operations are performed manually.

One of the valuable propositions offered by *Site Recovery Manager 5 (SRM5)* is the automation of this workflow to simplify the process and avoid errors. With SRM5, the replicated volume is re-signatured on the backup site, and configuration files are automatically referenced with the proper UUID, pointing the VMs to the new replicated volume. Each protected VM is associated with the virtual disks assigned to it.

> **NOTE**
>
> Manual operations are further complicated when RDM volumes are used because the RDM's VMFS pointer no longer exists. SRM also allows the automatic remapping of these volumes with new reinventoried VMs.

Technical Details

Within the environment, a VMFS volume is represented in the following ways:

- By its UUID (for example, 487788ae-34666454-2ae3-00004ea244e1).

- By a network address authority (NAA) ID (for example, naa.5000.xxx). vSphere uses NAA ID to detect the UUID with which the LUN ID is associated.

- By a label name seen by ESXi and a datastore name seen by vCenter Server (for example, myvmfsprod). This name is provided by the user and is only an alias pointing to the VMFS UUID, but it makes it easier to find your way.

- By a VMkernel device name, called *runtime name* in vCenter (for example, vmhba1:0:4).

When re-signaturing a VMFS, ESXi assigns a new UUID and a new label name for the copy and mounts the copied LUN like an original. The new associated name adopts the format type snap—for example, *snapID-oldLabel*, where *snapID* is an integer and *oldLabel* is the datastore's former name.

Besides snapshots and replication, other operations performed on a datastore are seen by ESXi as a copy of the original and, therefore, require action from the administrator:

- **LUN ID change:** When changing a LUN ID, vSphere detects that the UUID is now associated with a new device.

- **Change of SCSI type:** For example, going from SCSI-2 to SCSI-3.

- **Activation of SPC-2 compliance for some systems:** For example, EMC Symmetrix requires this activation.

Rescanning the Datastore

After each storage-related modification at the ESXi or storage level, it is necessary to rescan storage adapters to take the new configuration into account. This allows updating of the list of visible datastores and related information.

Rescanning is required each time the following tasks are performed:

- Changing zoning at the SAN level, which has an impact on ESXi servers

- Creating a new LUN within the SAN or performing a re-signature

- Changing the LUN masking within the storage array

- Reconnecting a cable or fiber

- Changing a host at the cluster level

By default, VMkernel scans LUNs from 0 to 255. (Remember, the maximum number of LUNs that can be introduced to a host is 256.) To accelerate the scanning process, it is possible to specify a lower value in the advanced parameters: Disk.MaxLUN (for example, 64 in Figure 3.7).

Disk.MaxLUN	64
Maximum number of LUNs per target scanned for	
Min: 1	Max: 256

Figure 3.7 Performing a datastore scan.

> **NOTE**
> You can also start a rescan of datastores by right-clicking the datacenter, cluster, or folder containing the relevant hosts.

Alignment

Alignment is an important issue to take into account. Stacking up various layers can create nonaligned partitions, as shown in Figure 3.8. Contrast this with an example of aligned partitions, shown in Figure 3.9.

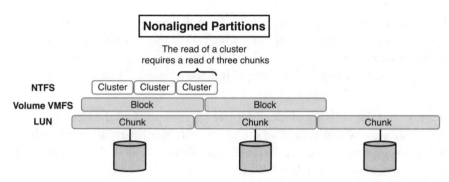

Figure 3.8 Nonaligned partitions.

The smallest unit in a RAID stack is called a *chunk*. Under it is the VMFS, which uses 1-MB blocks. Above it is the formatted NTFS using blocks of 1 KB to 64 KB (called the *disk cluster*). If these layers are not aligned, reading a cluster can mean reading two blocks overlapping three chunks on three different hard drives, which can offset writing and, thus, decrease performance.

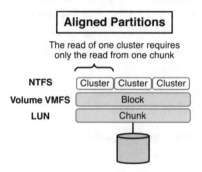

Figure 3.9 Aligned partitions.

When the partition is aligned, a cluster should read a single block, itself aligned with a chunk. This alignment is crucial, and in a VMware environment, nonalignment can cause a 40% drop in performance.

In a Microsoft environment, Windows Server 2008 is automatically aligned, whereas older operating systems must be aligned using the Diskpart utility. See the software publisher's instructions.

Increasing Volume

Volume Grow allows the dynamic extension of an existing VMFS without shutting down the VMs (up to 32 extensions). When a physical storage space is added to a LUN, the existing datastore can be extended without shutting down the server or the associated storage. This complements storage array options, which allow the dynamic extension of LUNs. Extending the storage space of a virtual disk (vmdk) is also possible in persistent mode without snapshots, using *Hot VMDK Extend*. It is recommended that extensions be put on disks with the same performance.

The vmdk extension and the visibility of the disk's free space depend on the OS mechanism and its file system. Depending on the OS version, third-party tools might be required to extend a system partition, as is the case with Windows 2003. To find out more, refer to VMware's Knowledge Base: KB 1004071.

Can a Single Large 64-TB Volume Be Created to Host All VMs?

With vSphere 5, the maximum size for a LUN VMFS-5 is 64 TB. Theoretically, a single, very large 64-TB volume could be created. Because the storage arrays integrate VMware's APIs (VAAI), they offer excellent volume-access performance. However, *we do not recommend adopting this approach*, for the following reasons:

- Separating environments is absolutely essential; production, testing, receipt, and backup should each have its own dedicated environment and LUN. It is important not to mix I/O profiles when these are known (random versus sequential access, for example) and not to balance the load based on the VMs' activities (even though Storage DRS allows load balancing).

- During migrations, because migrating a large volume is more complex than migrating several small volumes, which can be performed in stages.

- When a large volume gets corrupted, the impact is more significant than if the volume is smaller, containing fewer VMs.

Because of the preceding issues, creating separate LUNs is the preferred approach. It also makes replication easier (for example, by allowing protection to apply only to the critical environment).

Best Practices for VMFS Configuration

The following best practices are recommended:

- Generally, you should create VMFS volumes between 600 GB and 1 TB and use 15 to 20 active vmdks per volume (no more than 32). (A VM can have several active vmdks.)

- For environments that require high levels of performance, such as Oracle, Microsoft SQL, and SAP, the RDM mode is preferable.

- VMware recommends the use of VMFS over NFS because VMFS offers the complete set of capabilities and allows the use of RDM volumes for I/O-intensive applications.

- To avoid significant contentions, avoid connecting more than eight ESX servers to a LUN.

- Avoid placing several VMs with snapshots on the same VMFS.

- Avoid defining the DRS as aggressive because this will trigger frequent VM migration from one host server to another and, therefore, frequent SCSI reservations.

- Separate production LUNs from test LUNs, and store ISO files, templates, and backups on dedicated LUNs.

- Align vmdk partitions after the OS is configured for new disks.

- Avoid grouping several LUNs to form a VMFS because the different environments cannot be separated (the production environment, test environment, and templates), which increases the risk of contentions, with more frequent reservations.

- Avoid creating one VMFS per VM because it increases the number of LUNs and makes management more complex while limiting expansions to 256 LUNs or 256 VMs.

Virtual Disk

Just like a traditional hard drive, the virtual disk contains the OS, applications, and data. A VM's virtual disk is represented by a vmdk file or by an RDM volume.

VMDKs

The vmdks are the most important files because they are the VM's virtual disks, so they must be protected and secured. In vSphere 5, the vmdk's maximum size is 2 TB (more precisely, 2 TB minus 512 bytes). Two files make up a virtual disk: a descriptor bearing the extension .vmdk, and a file containing data, using the extension –flat.vmdk, which you can see in the command-line interface (see Figure 3.10) or in the graphical user interface (see Figure 3.11).

- The vmdk file corresponds to a metadata file, which is the virtual disk's description (editable file in some support maintenance needs). This file provides the link to the –flat.vmdk file and contains information regarding the UUID. (See the section "Re-Signature of a VMFS Volume as Part of a DRP," earlier in this chapter.)

- The -flat.vmdk file corresponds to the virtual disk with its content.

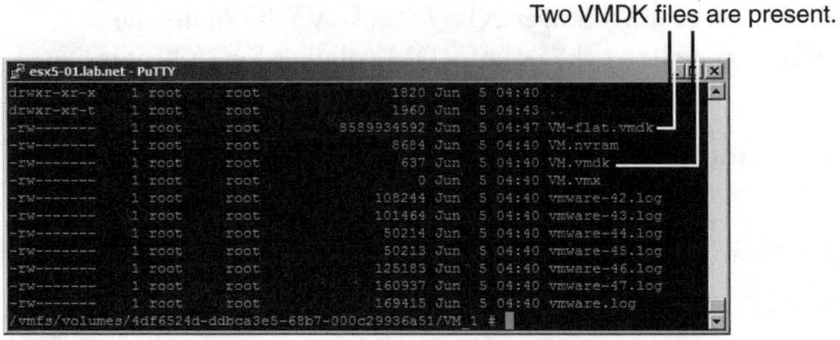

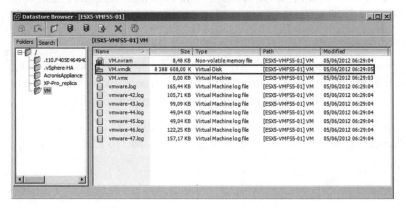

Two VMDK files are present.

Figure 3.10 Command-line interface showing the vmdk files.

Figure 3.11 vCenter's GUI showing a single vmdk file, the same size as the virtual disk.

Disk Types

When a VM is created, the following disk types can be used: *thick disk* (*lazy zeroed* or *eager zeroed*) or *thin disk*, depending on the option you select, as shown in Figure 3.12. Table 3.2 compares the advantages of these disk types.

Table 3.2 Disk Types and Their Respective Advantages

	Advantage	When to Use
Zeroed thick	Creation is faster, but performance is lower for the first writes.	Standard when creating a VM.
Eager zeroed thick	Longer to create, but performance is better during the first writes.	Cloning a VM or deploying a VM from a template uses this mode.
Thin	Very rapidly created, but write performance is not as good as in other modes.	The NFS datastore uses this mode by default.

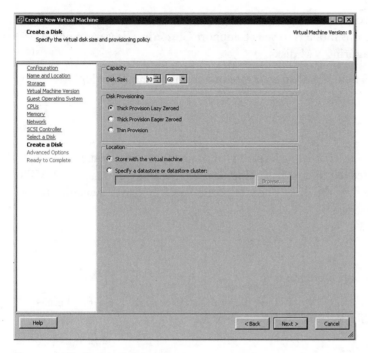

Figure 3.12 Optional disk types.

Thick Disks

Thick disks are easier to administer because, after they are provisioned, verifying the space available for the VM is no longer required. However, this means additional costs because the disk space is not optimized. This type of disk supports the *Fault Tolerance (FT)* feature.

With a thick disk, the size of the vmdk file is equal to the size of the disk configured when creating the VM.

Thick disks have two formats:

- **Lazy zeroed (also called zeroed):** This is the default format. All disk space is allocated, but the data previously written at disk level is not deleted. Existing data in the storage space is not deleted but remains on the physical disk. Erasing data and zeroing out blocks (formatting) is done only when first writing on the disk, which somewhat deteriorates performance. This performance degradation is greatly reduced by the VAAI feature Block Zero (utilizing the SCSI command write same).

- **Eager zeroed:** All disk space is reserved; data is entirely deleted from the disk, and blocks are zeroed out (formatted) when the disk is created. Creating such a disk takes longer, but security is improved because previous data is removed and deleted. Compared with zeroed thick, it offers much better performance when writing on the disk.

The thick disk format is recommended for applications that require high levels of performance. A simple way to use this mode is to select Support Clustering Features Such As Fault Tolerance when configuring VM disks.

It is always faster to create a new VM than to create one from a clone or to deploy a template.

Thin Disks

Some studies show that 40% to 60% of disk space is allocated but never used. In cases where the thin disk option (called thin provisioning) is used, the reserved space on VMFS equals the space actually used on the disk. The size of this space increases dynamically so that storage space is optimized.

EXAMPLE

A 20-GB file is created, but only 6 GB are used.

With thin disks, the space taken up by the vmdk file in the storage space is 6 GB, whereas with thick disks, the vmdk file uses 20 GB of storage space.

In thin mode, performance is inferior because the space is allocated dynamically upon request and disk blocks must be zeroed out. Thin disks are useful for avoiding wasted storage space, but they require particular care and supervision to ensure that there is no shortage of storage space. The Out of Space API allows proactive monitoring and alerting to prevent this situation.

NOTE

Using a thin LUN is very useful when replication is implemented because the first synchronization replicates only the data used on the disk. For a thick LUN, all data must be replicated, even if the blocks are empty. Initial synchronization is greatly reduced with a thin LUN.

NOTE

Avoid using storage array based thin provisioning in conjunction with vmdk disks in thin mode because keeping things straight becomes very difficult, and it's easy to make interpretation errors.

You can convert a disk from thin to thick by using either of the following methods:

- Use the Inflate option in the Datastore Browser.
- Use Storage vMotion to change the disk type to thick, as shown in Figure 3.13.

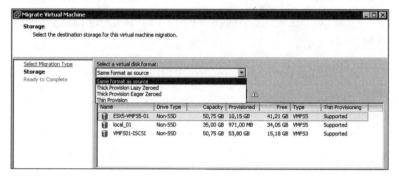

Figure 3.13 Using Storage VMotion interface to change disk type.

Modes

There are three modes for virtual disks, as follows:

- **Independent persistent:** All disk writes by the VM are actually written on disk (in the vmdk file). Even after rebooting, the modifications are preserved. This mode offers the best performance.

- **Independent nonpersistent:** All changes made since the VM was started up are destroyed when it is shut down. Modifications are written in a file that logs all changes at the VM's file system level. In this mode, rebooting the VM means going back to a reference VM. Performance is not as good.

- **Snapshot:** This enables the return to a previous state.

> **NOTE**
>
> Following security rules and associated good practices, avoid nonpersistent disks. When the VM is rebooted, these make it impossible to analyze the logs because everything is put back into its initial state. This prevents investigations and corrective actions in case of security problems.

Raw Device Mapping

Using the *Raw Device Mapping (RDM)* format, raw storage volumes can be introduced to ESX servers. This mode is mainly used in the following situations:

- When a Microsoft Cluster (MSCS or Windows Server Failover Clustering under Windows 2008 Server) is used (the only supported mode)

- When array-based snapshots are taken

- When introducing volumes directly to VMs for high performance (database-type)

- When introducing big SAN volumes to a VM (from 300 TB), avoiding the long P2V volume conversion to vmdk

RDM takes the form of a file (a kind of pointer) stored in a VMFS datastore that acts as a proxy for the LUN volume.

Figure 3.14 illustrates the difference between vmdk and RDM.

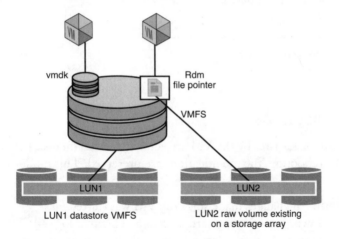

Figure 3.14 vmdk versus RDM format.

The RDM format exists in two modes: RDMv (virtual compatibility mode) and RDMp (physical compatibility mode).

RDMv Disks

The maximum size of an RDMv disk is 2 TB (precisely, 2 TB minus 512 bytes). RDMv is mainly used for large volumes. Beyond 300 GB, introducing dedicated LUNs to the VM can be interesting. Indeed, the vmdk is a file that can be easily moved, but when it is a large file, moving it can be more complex. In this case, the better practice is to introduce the raw volume and use storage array functionalities to move volumes.

RDMv creates a file on the VMFS that acts as a proxy between the VMFS and the LUN in direct link with the VM. It allows the hypervisor to intercept I/O and logs them at need. RDMv authorizes VM snapshots (but not storage array snapshots) as well as the creation of clones and templates.

RDMp Disks

The maximum size of RDMp disks is 64 TB. This type of disk does not allow the hypervisor to intercept I/O. *This means that VM snapshots cannot be taken* (but array-based snapshots are possible), and creating clones or templates is not possible.

In general, RDMp disks are used to introduce to test servers the same data that is in the production databases, using the storage array snapshot functionality. They are also used for MSCS clustering. When using MSCS, the shared disks must not share the virtual controller of the OS.

Some companies might be hesitant about migrating their applications to virtual environments. With RDMp, the change can be done slowly and confidently because the company is free to return to a physical environment if tests are not conclusive in the virtual environment. For applications not officially supported in a virtual environment (for example, older versions of Oracle), RDMp can be used to provide a simple means of replicating the problem in a physical environment that is supported by the software publisher.

RDMp disks cannot be backed up like traditional VMs. The capabilities offered by the two modes are summarized in Table 3.3.

Table 3.3 RDMv Versus RDMp Disks

RDM Type	vMotion	Storage vMotion	Filename	VM Snapshot	Snapshot at Storage Array Level
Rdmv	Yes	Yes	rdm.vmdk	Yes	Not recommended
Rdmp	Yes	Yes	rdmp.vmdk	No	Yes

OVF Format

Current virtual disk formats are vmdk (used by VMware) and *Virtual Hard Disk (vhd)* (used by Microsoft Hyper-V and Citrix XenServer).

Open Virtual Machine Format (OVF) is not a virtual disk format; it is a file format whose particularities facilitate interoperability between the various virtualization and hypervisor platforms. An OVF file includes parameters and metadata such as virtual hardware settings, prerequisites, and security attributes. Provided OVF packages are not limited to one VM and can contain several. An OVF file can be encrypted and compressed.

The OVF template is made up of the following files:

- **MF:** A manifest file, serving to verify the integrity of the OVF template and determine whether it was modified.
- **OVF:** An XML file containing the information on the virtual disk.
- **vmdk:** A virtual disk in VMware, but this file can use a different format to facilitate the interoperability of hypervisors. VMware specifications authorize different types of virtual disks.

> **NOTE**
>
> To simplify moving and manipulating various items for the export of OVF files, it is possible to use the *Open Virtualization Appliance (OVA)* format that groups multiple files into a single file. An OVA file is identical to a TAR file and can actually be renamed to use the .tar extension instead of the .ova extension so that the contents can be seen using a typical archive application.

You can download preconfigured virtual appliances containing an OVF operating system and application solution from https://solutionexchange.vmware.com/store/category_groups/19.

The Datastore

In VMware, the storage space is conceived as a *datastore*. The datastore is a virtual representation of the storage resources on which VMs, templates, or ISO images are stored. The datastore hides the complexity of the different technologies and storage solutions by offering the ESX server a uniform model no matter what storage has been implemented. Datastore types are VMFS and NFS.

> **NOTE**
>
> VMware's best practices recommend the proper separation of datastores used to store templates or ISO images from the datastores used for VMs. We also recommend monitoring the available space of datastores. These must always have at least 25% to 30% available space. This space is required for snapshot or backup operations or for VM swaps. Lack of space can have significant negative consequences and can have an impact on the global performance of the virtual environment.

A *datastore cluster*, also called a *pool of datastores* (POD), is a collection of datastores grouped to form a single entity as illustrated in Figure 3.15. When a datastore cluster is created, Storage DRS can be used.

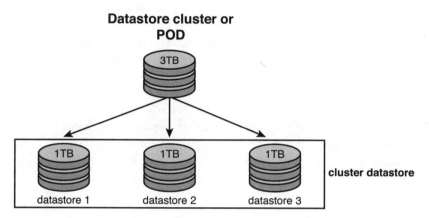

Figure 3.15 Pool of datastores (POD).

A datastore cluster can consist of volumes from different storage arrays (in terms of performance and volume), and different VMFS can be mixed (VMFS-3 and VMFS-5), but this is not generally recommended. The mix of VMFS and NFS volumes in a datastore cluster is not supported.

Storage vMotion

Storage vMotion allows the hot migration of VM virtual disks between two different storage spaces. All files forming the VM migrate from one datastore to another in the same storage array or in another storage array without service interruption. The storage arrays can be from different manufacturers.

NOTE

vMotion migrates a VM from one physical server to another but without moving the files that make up the VM. Storage vMotion moves virtual disks. These two operations cannot be run concurrently on the same VM unless that VM is powered off.

When to Use Storage vMotion

Storage vMotion is used for preventive maintenance operations for storage arrays. It can also be very useful when purchasing a new storage array because it does not require service interruption. Migration is performed very easily, in a fully transparent manner. This relieves administrators from this task, often a cumbersome and sensitive one in a traditional physical environment. Storage vMotion allows the administrator to switch storage array manufacturers and to migrate VMs without the need for a complex compatibility matrix.

> **NOTE**
>
> Using Storage vMotion when there is little storage-level activity is preferable. Before performing migrations with Storage vMotion, it is necessary to confirm that sufficient storage bandwidth exists between the source and destination ESXi servers.

How Storage vMotion Works

A number of improvements were made to Storage vMotion with vSphere 5. Several technologies have been used in the past. In vSphere 4.1, Dirty Block Tracking is used to copy disk blocks between source and destination: full copy, followed by the sending of modified blocks only to the target. (Dirty Block Tracking is a form of *Changed Block Tracking [CBT]* mode.) Issues with this technique were the duration of the switch to the target VM and the malfunction risk in cases of significant I/O load in the source VM. In vSphere 5, as shown in Figure 3.16, Storage vMotion makes a full copy of the VM and then uses a mirror driver to split write-modified blocks between the source and destination VMs.

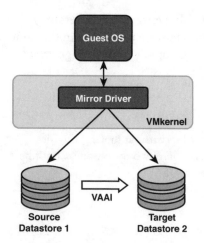

Figure 3.16 Storage vMotion using a mirror driver.

This I/O mirroring is preferable to a succession of disk copies because it has the advantage of guaranteeing migration success even if the destination VM is slow. Migration will be shorter and more predictable.

The following occurs when using Storage vMotion:

1. The VM's working folder is copied to the destination datastore.

2. An image of the VM, called a *shadow VM*, starts on the destination datastore by using the copied files. The shadow VM is paused.

3. Storage vMotion activates a driver (called a *mirror driver*) to write a mirror of the blocks already copied to the destination.

4. The copy of the VM's disk files to the destination datastore is completed while the I/O is being mirrored.

5. Storage vMotion pauses the source VM and transfers the source VM being executed to the shadow VM.

6. The old folder and the VM's disk files are deleted from the source datacenter.

> **NOTE**
>
> The original file is deleted only after the destination file is correctly written and an acknowledgment is sent, which ensures the operation succeeded.

Storage vMotion, available in the Enterprise version, works with VMs that have snapshots and also supports the migration of linked clones.

Storage DRS

Storage DRS (SDRS) allows the automation of the choice of datastore to use for VMs. It makes for more balanced performance and more efficient storage space. This frees up time for administrators, who no longer have to spend time choosing which datastore to use. To function, datastores are grouped in datastore clusters.

SDRS takes care of the following operations:

- Initial placement of a VM
- Balancing the load between datastores according to the following factors:
  - The use of storage space
  - The I/O load based on latency

Initial placement occurs when a VM is created, moved, or cloned. Based on the space used and I/O charge of the cluster's datastores, SDRS provides a particular datastore to store the vmdk.

Datastore Load Balancing

The load balancing is performed every 2 hours for used space and every 8 hours for the I/O load based on the history of the last 24 hours. As shown in Figure 3.17, SDRS makes migration recommendations when a datastore passes the thresholds defined by the user based on the percentage of disk space used (80% by default) and/or the I/O latency (15 ms by default).

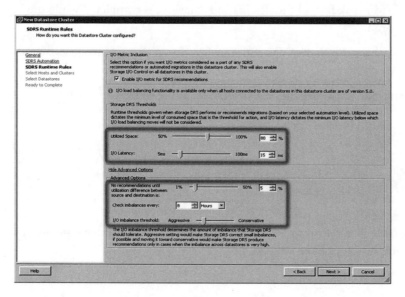

Figure 3.17 SDRS interface showing load balancing information.

Several levels of automation are possible:

- Manual (default).

- Automatic.

- Planned (scheduled). The planning mode is interesting during a backup period, for example; it is not necessary to move the virtual disks. It is therefore possible to disable SDRS during the backup operations.

- Datastore maintenance mode. A datastore's *maintenance mode* removes all vmdks from the datastore and distributes them to the cluster's other datastores.

At this point, you might ask, "How does SDRS detect the datastores' I/O load?"

SDRS uses the SIOC functionality and an injector mechanism to choose the best target datastore to use. The injector is used to determine each datastore's characteristics by randomly "injecting" I/O. This allows it to determine the response time and latency associated with each datastore.

Affinity Rules

As illustrated in Figure 3.18, several affinity rules can be applied:

- **Intra-VM vmdk affinity:** All the same vmdk VMs are placed on the same datastore.

- **Intra-VM vmdk anti-affinity:** This rule can be applied to ensure that the vmdks are placed on different datastores. This rule is useful, for instance, to separate a database VM's log disks from its data disks. The rule applies to all or part of the disks within a VM.

- **VM-VM anti-affinity:** Different VM are placed on separate datastores. This offers redundancy for VMs in the event of failure of a datastore.

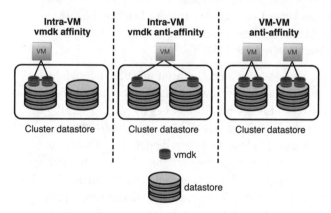

Figure 3.18 Affinity rules.

The current limitations of SDRS are as follows:

- SDRS is not supported with SRM.
- SDRS works only with hosts using ESXi5 or later.

Profile-Driven Storage

Profile-Driven Storage preserves the compliance of VMs with the defined storage needs. This functionality eliminates initial placement errors and simplifies day-to-day management for administrators by automating these tasks. Administrators create profiles that contain the characteristics of the storage. These can be enforced using *vSphere Storage storage-detection APIs (VASA)* or associated with indicators defined by the user (for example, Gold, Silver, Bronze).

A VM's profile is associated during provisioning, creation, migration, cloning, and so on. If the VM is placed in a storage space offering the capacities defined in the VM's storage profile, such storage is deemed compliant. Profile-Driven Storage complements SDRS for initial placement and the automatic migration of vmdk.

Storage I/O Control

Resource sharing creates new challenges. Noncritical VMs should not monopolize available resources. Disk share addresses only part of the issue because sharing is established only with regard to a single ESXi host and is used only when contention occurs at the ESXi host level. This latter scenario is not relevant because VMs located on another ESXi server can use a larger share while being less of a priority. Figure 3.19 illustrates storage sharing with and without *Storage I/O Control (SIOC)*.

For the management of I/O resource allocation to be efficient, it must be independent from the VM's location. The issue must be addressed by sharing the datastore's access resources at the level of the ESXi cluster. This is what SIOC does by placing sharing (QoS) at the cluster level instead of at the ESX level. SIOC monitors the I/O latency of a datastore. When latency reaches a threshold (set at 30 ms by default), the datastore is deemed *congested* and SIOC intervenes to distribute the available resources following sharing rules defined in each VM. Lower-priority VMs have reduced I/O queues. Sharing occurs if and only if contentions appear in storage I/O for access to datastores. Using SIOC guarantees that the most important VMs will have adequate resources no matter what happens, even in the case of congestion.

Using this QoS regarding VM access to the datastore, administrators can confidently consolidate the environment. Even in times of high activity, the most critical VMs will have the necessary resources.

SIOC activation is found in the properties dialog (see Figure 3.20) of the datastore. Note that at this time, SIOC does not support datastore with multiple extents and RDM disks.

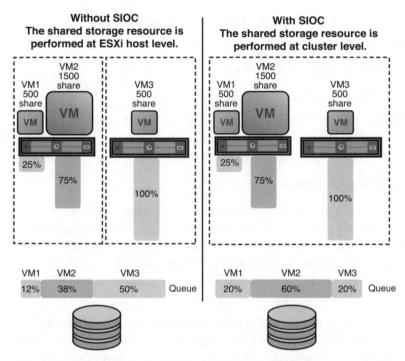

Figure 3.19 Storage sharing with and without SIOC.

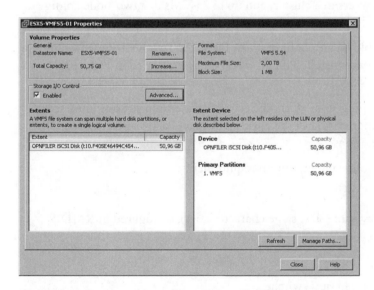

Figure 3.20 Datastore properties dialog with SIOC enabled.

VMware recommends different threshold values for different disk types:

- **Fibre Channel:** 20 ms to 30 ms
- **Serial Attached SCSI (SAS):** 20 ms to 30 ms
- **Solid State Drive (SSD):** 10 ms to 15 ms
- **Serial ATA (SATA):** 30 ms to 50 ms

vSphere Storage Appliance

vSphere Storage Appliance (VSA) is an appliance designed for *small to medium businesses (SMBs)* (20 to 35 VMs), allowing access to shared storage at a lower cost by using advanced features such as HA, DRS, DPM, FT, and vMotion. The appliance, available only for vSphere 5, is deployed as a VM on each ESXi server (distributed as a 3-GB OVF file). VSAs occupy the available space on the local disks of ESXi servers and show an NFS volume replicated by the ESXi server.

The replication of local storage on another ESXi server ensures redundancy if a host server is out of service. When a VSA node is out of service, the VSA Manager switches IP addresses and shared storage to the replicated VSA. This is done without service interruption for that datastore's VMs.

VSA supports 2 or 3 ESXi servers in a cluster, and up to 25 VMs in a two-node configuration or up to 35 VMs in a three-node configuration.

Therefore, there are two deployment configurations for VSA: Two ESXi servers with one VSA and the VSA cluster service installed on vCenter, or, as illustrated in Figure 3.21, three ESXi servers with one VSA.

VSA Manager (installed as a plug-in in vCenter Server) is the administrative interface of the VSA cluster. It enables monitoring of the cluster's state and allows maintenance and VSA-node replacement operations.

The VSA appliance has the following minimum requirements:

- 6 GB RAM
- 4, 6, or 8 identical disks (same size, same characteristics), configured in RAID 5, RAID 6, or RAID 10
- 4 1-GB network cards
- 2 VLANs configured on physical switches

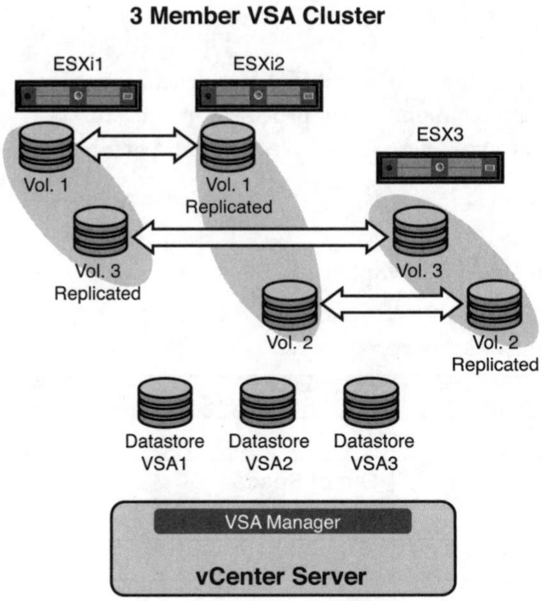

3 Member VSA Cluster

Figure 3.21 VSA deployment configuration.

Because vCenter Server provides VSA management, it must be placed outside the VSA cluster—either in a VM outside the cluster or on a dedicated physical server. Note that this is the only case in which VMware recommends putting vCenter Server on a physical server.

Installing the appliance is rather simple and quick (approximately 10 minutes) and requires no particular storage skill.

VMware Storage APIs

The APIs provided by VMware allow administrators and publishers to extend the functionality of vSphere 5.

vStorage API for Array Integration

The *vStorage API for Array Integration (VAAI)* is a set of application program interfaces allowing interoperability between VMware and storage array manufacturers to communicate with VMware in a smarter manner. Some tasks can be offloaded to the storage array, which lightens the load of ESXi hosts.

> **NOTE**
> Processor manufacturers have already integrated Intel VT and AMD V instructions into their chips to reduce high-consuming CPU interceptions. What processor manufacturers have done for servers, VAAIs do for storage arrays. These APIs now seem indispensable to obtain high levels of consolidation.

Table 3.4 lists the VAAI in vSphere 4.1 and VAAI 2 in vSphere 5.

Table 3.4 VAAI Functionality: vSphere 4.1 Versus vSphere 5

VAAI vSphere 4.1	VAAI 2 vSphere 5
Block	
Hardware Assisted Locking	Out of Space
Hardware Accelerated Zero	Space Reclaim
Hardware Accelerated Copy	
NAS	
Not available	Full Clone
	Extended Stats
	Space Reservation

Following is a brief description of each of the features listed in Table 3.4:

- **Hardware Assisted Locking:** Without the API, SCSI reservations are done at the global LUN level. With the API, the work is done at the block level instead of the LUN level, which causes fewer issues related to SCSI reservations and reduces VM startup time, in particular for virtual desktop infrastructure (VDI) projects.

- **Hardware Accelerated Zero:** Without the API, when creating a datastore, the "zero write" is done by the server, which sends SCSI commands to the storage array. With the API, a single command is initiated by the ESX server, and the storage array is responsible for repeating the operation and informing the ESX server when the operation is finished. This reduces traffic between the ESXi server and the storage array.

- **Hardware Accelerated Copy:** Without the API, copy operations are performed from the ESX server toward the storage array. With the API, data is moved within the array by the storage array without going through the server. This reduces the load of the ESXi server and the time required for data migration.

In vSphere 5, new primitives have been defined for VAAI 2:

- **Dead Space Reclaim:** Allows the recovery of spaces that are no longer used when a virtual disk is deleted or after the migration of a virtual disk from one datastore to another by using Storage vMotion on a provisioned thin LUN. ESXi 5.0 transmits the information about the freed-up blocks to the storage system via VAAI through commands, and the storage system recovers the blocks.

- **Thin Provisioning Out of Space API:** Guards against storage-space problems on thin LUNs.

  - **Thin Provisioning LUN Reporting:** Enables the identification of the storage array use in vCenter.

  - **Quota Exceeded:** Displays an alert in vCenter when a capacity threshold is passed within a datastore.

  - **Out of Space Behavior:** The VM determines whether the space is available before the write. If storage space is full, an alert message is displayed in vCenter and this VM is paused (while the other VMs continue running).

The following primitives are defined for NAS VAAI storage:

- **Full-File Clone:** Enables cloning and snapshot operations of vmdk files to be performed by the NAS in a cold manner, similar to VMFS block cloning (Full Copy).

- **Extended Stats:** Enables the visibility of consumed spaces on NFS datastores.

- **Space Reservation:** Allows the creation of vmdk files in thick-provisioning mode for NAS storage.

vSphere Storage API: Storage Awareness

The *vStorage API for Storage Awareness (VASA)* is a storage-detection API. It allows the visualization, straight from vCenter, of the information related to storage arrays, such as replication, RAID type, compression, de-duplication, thin or thick format, disk type, snapshot state, and performance (IOPS/MBps). Among other things, the vStorage API is used for Profile-Driven Storage.

Multipathing

Multipathing can be defined as a solution that uses redundant components, such as adapters and switches, to create logical paths between a server and a storage device.

Pluggable Storage Architecture

Pluggable Storage Architecture (PSA) is a collection of APIs that allows storage manufacturers to insert code directly into the VMkernel layer. Third-party software (for example, EMC PowerPath VE) can thus be developed to offer more advanced load-balancing functionalities in direct relation to their storage array's technology. VMware, however, offers standard basic multipathing mechanisms, called *native multipathing (NMP)*, divided into the following APIs: *Storage Array Type Plug-in (SATP)*, which is in charge of communicating with the storage array; and *Path Selection Plug-in (PSP)*, which provides access to load balancing between paths.

As shown in Figure 3.22, VMware offers three PSPs:

- **Most Recently Used (MRU):** Selects the first path discovered upon the boot of ESXi. If this path becomes inaccessible, ESXi chooses an alternate path.

- **Fixed:** Uses a dedicated path designated as the preferred path. If configured otherwise, it uses the path found at boot. When it can no longer use this path, it selects another available path at random. When it becomes available again, ESXi uses the fixed preferred path again.

- **Round Robin (RR):** Automatically selects all available paths and sends the I/O to each in a circular fashion, which allows basic load balancing. PSA coordinates NMP operations, and third-party software coordinates the *multipathing plug-in (MPP)* software."

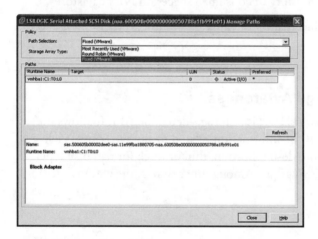

Figure 3.22 PSPs offered by VMware.

The NMP Round Robin path-selection policy has a parameter known as the I/O operation limit, which controls the number of I/Os sent down each path before switching to the next path. The default value is 1000; therefore, NMP defaults to switching from one path to another after sending 1000 I/Os down any given path. Tuning the Round Robin I/O operation limit parameter can significantly improve the performance of certain workloads (such as *online transaction processing [OLTP]*). In environments that have random and OLTP workloads, setting the Round Robin parameter to a lower number yields the best throughput, but lowering the value does not improve performance as significantly as it does for sequential workloads. For these reasons, some hardware storage companies recommend that the NMP Round Robin I/O Operation parameter should be lower (can be set to 1).

Third-party software solutions use more advanced algorithms because a limitation of Round Robin is that it performs an automatic distribution without taking into account the actual activity at path level. Some software establishes dynamic load balancing and is designed to use all paths at all times rather than Round Robin, which uses only a single path at a time to bear the entire I/O burden.

Modes

Access to data stored on shared storage space is fundamental in a virtual environment. VMware strongly recommends implementing several access paths to the LUN. Two paths is a minimum, but VMware recommends using four. Multipathing reduces service interruptions by offering a redundancy of access paths to the LUNs. When a path is not available, another is used—without service interruption. These switch mechanisms are called *multipath I/O (MPIO)*.

In VMware, as shown in Figure 3.23, storage can adopt various modes:

- **Active/active:** At a given moment, a LUN is connected to several storage controllers at the same time. The I/O can arrive from several controllers simultaneously.

- **Active/passive:** At a given moment, a single controller owns one LUN (owned LUN). No other controller can send I/O to this LUN as long as it is linked to a controller.

- **ALUA:** Access to a LUN is not direct (nonoptimized) but occurs in an asymmetrical manner, going through the secondary controller.

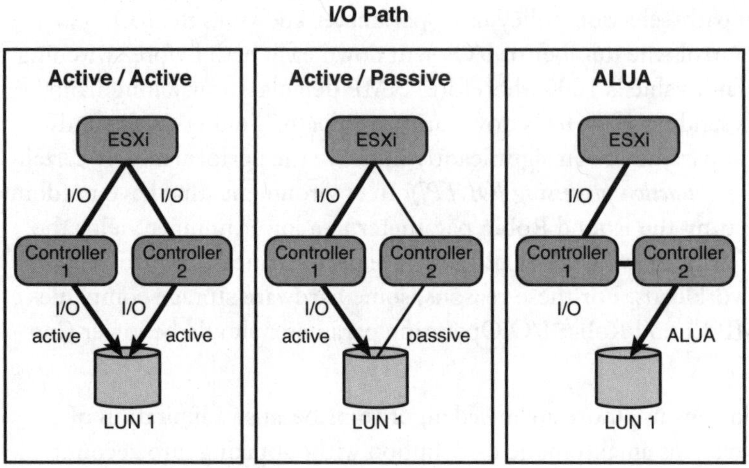

I/O Path

Figure 3.23 Storage modes.

Disk Technology Considerations

This section examines a number of the factors to consider when deciding on the disk technology to use in your environment.

Supported Disk Types

As you have seen, storage architecture is important, and the disk technology plays an important part. ESXi supports a variety of disks, including SSD, SAS, FC, SATA, NL-SAS, IDE, USB, and SCSI.

Many options are available, making it possible to adapt the technology according to several criteria. As shown in Table 3.5, in terms of disk technology, many parameters are to be considered: speed expressed in revolutions per minute and in *I/O per second (IOPS)*, as well as bandwidth transfers.

Table 3.5 Average Speed Parameters for Disk Types (May Vary)

Disks	RPM	IOPS
SSD	N/A	3000
SAS	15 K	180
SAS	10 K	130
NL-SAS	7.2 K	100
SATA	5.4	50

Solid-State Drives (SSDs) are high-performance drives composed of flash memory. These disks are nonmechanical. They are less likely to experience failures, they consume less energy, and they heat up much less than traditional disks. Their access time is low, with very high IOPS (3000 IOPS). They are ideal for reading but not well adapted to a large quantity of writes.

These disks are typically used for log files (for example, for databases). They are often used to extend the cache memory of controllers. (EMC calls them Fast Cache disks, and Netapp calls them Flash Cache disks.) In a VMware environment, these high-performance disks are ideal for storing the swap memory of VMs. They are also very useful for absorbing the charge when activity spikes appear—for example, in a VDI environment, when all VMs boot simultaneously. (This phenomenon is called a *boot storm*.) Disk sizes currently available are 100 GB, 200 GB, and 400 GB. Soon, 800 GB will also be available.

Serial Attached SCSI (SAS) disks replace Fibre Channel disks. These disks are directly connected to the controller, point to point. Revolution speeds are high—10,000 RPM or 15,000 RPM. They are ideal for applications with random access, and they can process small-size I/O of 8 bytes to 16 bytes, typically databases. The stream is bidirectional. Current disk sizes are 300 GB, 600 GB, and 900 GB.

Today, SAS disks are best adapted to virtual environments, and they offer the best price–performance ratio. Although FC disks are still widely found in production environments, the trend is to replace them with SAS disks.

Near-Line SAS (NL-SAS) disks use the mechanics of SATA disks mounted on SAS interfaces. Their advantage over SATA is that they transmit data in full duplex. Read and write can be performed simultaneously, contrary to SATA, which allows only a single read or write at a time. These disks offer features that allow the interpretation of SCSI commands, such as command queuing (to reduce read-head movements), and they provide better control of errors and reporting than SATA disks.

Serial-ATA (SATA) disks allow the management of a large capacity—2 TB, 3 TB, and soon 4 TB. They are recommended for the sequential transfer of large files (for example, backups, video files), but are not suitable for applications with elevated random I/O-like databases (for example, Oracle, Microsoft SQL, MySQL). They are unidirectional and allow a single read or write at a time. Depending on storage array manufacturers, SATA may or may not be recommended for critical-production VMs. Find out from the manufacturer. SATA disks are always well-suited for test VMs or for ISO image, template, or back-up storage.

RAID

Table 3.6 lists recommendations for RAID types and associated traditional uses.

Table 3.6 RAID Types and Traditional Uses

	Write	Read	Use	Protection
RAID0	Excellent	Excellent	Real-time workstation	None (striping)
RAID1	Excellent	Excellent	DB log file, operating system, ESXi Hypervisor	Mirror
RAID5	Good	Very good	DB, ERP, web server, file server, mail	Parity
RAID6	Average	Very good	Archiving, backup, file server	Double parity
RAID10	Excellent	Excellent	Large DB , application servers	Striping + mirror

Storage Pools

In a physical environment, a LUN is dedicated to a server and, thus, to a specific application. In this case, parameters can be set to adapt RAID levels to the application, either sequential or random. This method is not well adapted to a virtual environment. Indeed, because of the dynamic nature of a virtual environment, keeping the same LUN-attribution logic based on the application becomes difficult. VMs are mobile and move from one datastore to another. RAID levels risk not remaining the same. Instead of using dedicated RAID levels, some manufacturers suggest using storage pools. This method is preferable because it offers excellent performance and simplifies management.

Automatic Disk Tiering

Only 20% of a LUN's data is frequently accessed. Statistics also show that 80% of data is unused after two weeks. Through automatic tiering, frequently used data is automatically placed on high-performance SSD or SAS disks, while less frequently used data is stored on lower-performance disks such as SATA or NL-SAS.

Performance

In virtual environments, monitoring performance is complex because of resource pooling and the various layers (for example, applications, hypervisor, storage array). Speeds measured in IOPS and bandwidths in MBps depend on the type and number of disks on which the datastore is hosted. Storage activity should be monitored to determine whether waiting queues form on either of these criteria (*queue length*). At the hypervisor or vCenter level, the most reliable and simplest performance indicator for identifying contentions is the device access time.

Access time through all HBAs should be below 20 ms in read and write. Another indicator that should be monitored and that shows a contention by highlighting an activity that cannot be absorbed by the associated storage is the *Stop Disk* value. This value should always be set to 0. If its value is higher than 0, the load should be rebalanced. There are usually two causes:

- VM activity is too high for the storage device.

- Storage has not been properly configured. (For example, make sure there is no zoning issue, that all paths to storage are available, that the activity is well distributed among all paths, and that the storage cache is not set to forced flush.)

Additional Recommendations

Following are additional recommendations that can improve disk performance:

- Using solid-state cache allows a significant number of I/O to disk. The cache serves as leverage because the major part of the read and write I/O activity occurs in the cache. Databases require very high I/O operations in 4-byte, 8-byte, or 16-byte random access, while video-file backup servers require high speeds with large block sizes (32, 64, 128, or 256 bytes).

- Sequential access and random access should not be mixed on the same disk. If possible, I/Os should be separated by type (read, write, sequential, random). For example, three VMs hosting one transactional DBMS-type database should each have three datastores:

  - One datastore for the OS in RAID 5. Separating the OS means a VM can be booted without drawing from the database's available I/Os from RAID 5.

  - One datastore for the RAID 5 database if the read/write ratio is 70%/30%. If not, the RAID type should be changed. A database generally uses 70% of random read-type transactions.

  - One datastore for logs in RAID 1 because writes are sequential (or RAID 10 for large databases with a high write rate).

Device Drivers

Figure 3.24 displays the standard SCSI controllers that ESXi makes available to the guest OS.

Among the available options, BusLogic offers a greater compatibility with older-generation operating systems. LSI Logic Parallel offers a higher performance on some operating systems, but a driver must be added.

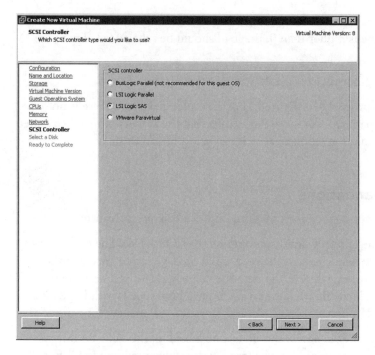

Figure 3.24 Standard SCSI controller options.

The VM VMware Paravirtual device driver is used mainly for heavy workloads. It directly accesses the virtualization layer. This driver is said to be paravirtualized because it interprets requests from the guest OS and sends them directly to the hypervisor. This reduces request interceptions by the *Virtual Machine Monitor (VMM)*, which improves performance. This option works only with Windows Server 2003, Windows Server 2008, and RHEl 5.

Another available controller, VMDirectPath I/O, is a storage I/O driver that allows direct access to the physical device without going through ESXi's virtualization layer to benefit from all the driver's native functionality and performance within the VM.

Storage Is the Foundation

In any architecture, having a strong foundation is key, and this is especially true in virtualization. Many options are available, allowing virtualization to thrive in remote offices or the highest-performance data center. VSphere 5 raises the bar by providing additional array awareness, ensuring that the hypervisor can communicate with the storage. vSphere can use that information intelligently, moving VMs off a poorly performing volume. With so many options, you might think that the configuration will be very difficult, but vSphere provides the tools to ensure that the configuration is optimal.

Chapter 4

Servers and Network

When most IT professionals think about virtualization, the first thing that comes to mind is often the server. The complexity of the server, as well as its criticality, make it the first thing, but a *virtual machine (VM)* on a server without network connectivity rarely serves its intended purpose. Servers can seem daunting, but with the information provided in this chapter, you'll be up to speed in no time. Networks are often the domain of a network team, but as a virtualization professional, you'll need to converse with them effectively. This chapter helps you with understanding the servers and network components that are required in any virtualization solution.

ESXi Servers

Servers consist of thousands of parts, but often only three are commonly referenced in virtualization. Storage, which is discussed in Chapter 3, is where the data and configuration resides. Memory is where the data that is actively being used resides, and is often the most precious of the available resources. CPU is the last major component, and ESXi has complex and efficient scheduling algorithms to maximize the efficiency of the processor resources.

Memory Management

Because memory is often the most constrained resource, ESXi can perform several resource-saving operations to ensure that you can take advantage of the server hardware optimally. Many of the memory management techniques that ESXi employs are exclusive to it, allowing the VMware hypervisor to do more with limited memory than other solutions.

Memory Overcommitment

The resource sharing offered by virtualization has benefits over traditional architectures, notably in the management of ESXi host server memory. It is possible to have more memory in configured virtual machines than there is physical memory (called RAM); this is called *memory overcommitment*. Memory overcommitment enables a high level of server consolidation, and is illustrated in Figure 4.1.

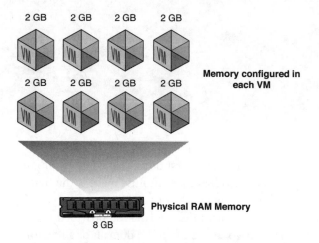

Figure 4.1 With memory overcommitment, it is possible to have eight virtual machines configured with 2 GB of memory each, on a server with only 8 GB of physical RAM, and with no performance loss.

When memory overcommitment is used, ESXi must use techniques to reclaim the memory space from one or several VMs. These techniques are known as *transparent page sharing (TPS)*, *ballooning*, *swap*, and *memory compression*.

Transparent Page Sharing

When an ESXi host runs multiple VMs with the same operating system, it is quite probable that some memory pages will be identical. The TPS process scans the memory. If it finds identical pages, it keeps a copy and directs the VMs using this page before freeing up the duplicate page. This is done in a completely transparent manner for the OS, which is not aware it is sharing a memory page with other VMs, as depicted in Figure 4.2.

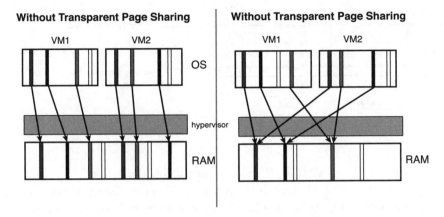

Figure 4.2 Memory pages (with and without transparent page sharing).

EXAMPLE

Imagine 10 VMs with a 1-GB memory made from the same template. After all the memory boots, the memory pages are identical.

Without TPS, the space occupied by these ten VMs is 10 * 1 GB = 10 GB.

With TPS, only 1 GB of space is used, which saves 9 GB. This technique leads to considerable gains in memory space.

Ballooning

Ballooning is taking memory from a VM that does not need it and giving it to a VM that does need it when using memory overcommitment.

Ballooning takes advantage of the following principle: In a production environment, only a percentage of memory is used intensively—the active memory necessary for the system to function properly. The rest of the memory (*idle memory*) is used very little. Because memory is shared, this idle memory can be reclaimed and made available for other VMs. vSphere takes advantage of this unused memory through ballooning.

In the example shown in Figure 4.3, 2 GB of memory is consumed, while only 25% of the memory is active. The rest was allocated when the machine booted but remains unused. In a traditional environment, it doesn't matter, but in a shared-resource environment, the unused memory can be reclaimed and put at the disposal of other VMs. This is what ballooning does.

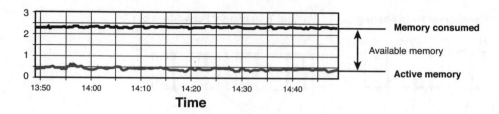

Time

Figure 4.3 Idle memory available for ballooning.

How does ballooning work? When VMware Tools is installed, a balloon driver (vmmemctl) is placed in the VM. This driver has no outside interface; it communicates directly with ESXi privately. When the ESXi server wants to reclaim memory, it instructs the driver to inflate, which increases the pressure put on the VM. The guest OS calls up its own memory-management algorithms to free up the memory pages that are less used (those in idle mode), as illustrated in Figure 4.4.

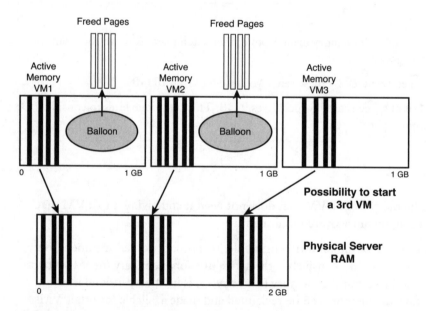

Figure 4.4 When a third VM is started, the other VMs' balloon drivers inflate and increase pressure on those VMs, freeing up idle memory pages.

When ballooning is used, ESXi must decide to inflate the balloon driver in some VMs to reclaim memory. But which VM will free up memory?

This is where the *share* notion comes in. Share is a notion of relative importance or priority regarding other VMs. There are four levels: low, medium, high, and custom, using a 1:2:4 ratio or a custom ratio. ESXi reclaims memory in priority from VMs with share set to low, to give memory in priority to VMs with share set to high. Memory with share set to high is reclaimed only as a last resort.

EXAMPLE

An ESXi server has 4 GB of RAM. The two VMs are configured with 4 GB each; VM1 is set to high (ratio 4) and VM2 is set to low (ratio 1).

Given the share settings, the proportions are calculated as follows:

VM1 = 4/5 x 4 GB, including 3.2 GB taken from the RAM

VM2 = 1/5 x 4 GB, including 800 MB taken from the RAM

If a third VM with share set to high (ratio 4) is added, the result would be as follows:

VM1 = 4/9 x 4 GB = 1.77 GB

VM2 = 1/9 x 4 GB = 444 MB

VM3 = 4/9 x 4 GB = 1.77 GB

The main limitation of the share setting is the lack of criteria regarding the use of active memory. Therefore, it is likely a VM with share set to high will accumulate inactive memory, while a VM with share set to low can be penalized if it uses a large quantity of active memory.

ESXi solves this problem with the introduction of the *idle memory tax*. This tax has a simple task: reclaiming idle memory in priority, whatever the VM's share level may be. The concept is that an idle page will be taxed, while an active page will not. This book does not go into detail about the calculations for this idle memory; what is important to understand is that ESXi uses a probability approach on samples of memory pages. It does so directly, without intervening within the VMs' operating systems. Each VM is sampled individually at a configurable interval. By default, ESXi samples 100 pages every 30 seconds.

By default, the idle memory tax parameter is set to 75%, which corresponds to 75% maximum reclamation of unused memory.

EXAMPLE

An ESXi server has 4 GB of RAM. Each VM is configured with 4 GB of memory (with memory shares set to normal). There are two VMs—one has intense memory activity, the other does not.

> VM1 = Active directory with 1 GB of active memory (3 GB idle)
>
> VM2 = SQL with 3 GB of active memory (1 GB idle)
>
> Because share is set to normal, each VM receives a portion of 50%, or 2 GB each. VM1 has 1 GB available.
>
> Idle memory tax authorizes the hypervisor to reclaim up to 75% of VM1's inactive memory (specifically 75% of 1 GB, or 750 MB).
>
> With idle memory tax, VM1 = 1.25 GB and VM2 = 2.75 GB.

A VM can be protected by forbidding ballooning from reclaiming its memory. To do this, the VM must be configured with a reservation level identical to the configured memory.

Swap

When a VM starts up, a swap file is created with the extension .vswp. A VM can be started only if this file can be created and is available (which means attention should be paid to the available storage space).

ESXi uses this swap file in cases where overcommitment is used and the balloon driver cannot reclaim memory from other VMs. In this case, it uses the disk as memory. Note that this technique should *never* be used, given how much performance is affected by disk access. The only advantage of this swap is that the VM does not crash if memory becomes insufficient.

FOR YOUR INFORMATION

The hard drive access time is measured in *milliseconds (ms)* (one-thousandth of a second), and memory access time is measured in *nanoseconds (ns)* (one-billionth of a second), which is 1,000,000 times faster. This means that if memory takes 1 second to access information, the hard drive will take 11.5 days (1,000.000 / (60 s x 60 min x 24 h).

The swap file has the following features:

- Its extension is .vswp.

- The file size equals configured memory size minus reservation.

- By default, the file is placed in the folder where the vmx configuration file is found. (This can be modified in the memory's advanced options.)

- The file is deleted as soon as the VM is shut down (and deletion can be prohibited).

- A VM cannot start if there is not enough storage file to create the file.

Memory Compression

Before the hypervisor decides to swap its pages on the hard drive, there is an interme-
diate level: memory compression. ESXi compresses pages and stores them in a protected
memory space. Access to compressed memory is faster than disk access without too much
performance loss. When a virtual page must be swapped, ESXi first attempts to compress
it on 2-KB blocks or smaller.

> **NOTE**
>
> In vCenter's advanced parameters, it is possible to define the maximum size of the
> compression cache and/or to deactivate memory compression.

Sizing

To benefit from a good level of consolidation, memory overcommitment must be used.
It is possible to start from the following sizing principle. A basic rule for sizing is to have
between at least 4 GB and 8 GB of RAM per physical core.

> **EXAMPLE**
>
> A server with a total of 12 cores should have at least between 48 GB and 96 GB of RAM.

To determine the number of VMs that can operate, several approaches are possible:

- For an optimized approach, notably for test, development, and preproduction applications, follow this rule: *The sum of memory configured in VMs can be double the physical
RAM in the server.*

> **EXAMPLE**
>
> A server with 32 GB of RAM can have 32 VMs configured with 2 GB of memory each (or
> 64 VMs with 1 GB each).

- For a conservative approach (for sensitive applications), transpose the same amount
of memory used in the physical environment to determine the amount of memory
required on the ESXi server and then add 10%.

EXAMPLE

A server with 32 GB of RAM can have 30 VMs configured with 1 GB of memory each.

Following are some best practices to keep in mind:

- Memory swap must be avoided. However, using SSD disks to store swap files is a good practice to reduce performance degradations.

- Favor TPS, which prevents performance degradations. For optimum exploitation, use VMs of the same type (Windows or Linux) on the same server. Use templates to create VMs; this provides a common base.

- If activity is high, make sure all VMs have enough memory. If ballooning activity is high and the guest OS performs swaps, memory-resource problems arise.

NOTE

Some environments (for example, SAP) use memory intensively and recommend not using memory overcommitment. In this case, use a reservation equal to the size of the configured memory.

- Configure VMs with values that represent the activity; do not oversize or undersize the amount of memory.

The Processor

Before explaining how it works, we will define some terminology used:

- 1 *central processing unit (CPU)* = 1 physical processor = 1 socket.

- 1 physical core = 1 core within a physical processor.

- *Hyperthreading* involves creating two logical instances for each physical core.

- A *logical CPU (LCPU)* corresponds to the number of logical CPUs available (within the ESXi server) and configurable for VMs. The maximum supported is 160 LCPUs per ESXi server.

> **EXAMPLE**
>
> Two physical processors with 6 cores and hyperthreading activated correspond to 24 LCPUs. In theory, this allows the configuration of a VM with 24 vCPUs or 4 vCPUs with 6 vCores. However, good practice dictates not going over 70% to 80% of available LCPUs on the ESXi for a single VM. In this case, with 24 LCPUs, a maximum of 18 vCPUs should be configured for the VM.

- A *vCPU* is a virtual CPU configured in the VM.
- A *vCore* is a core within a vCPU.

In vSphere 5, it is possible to configure a VM with up to 32 vCPUs and to have up to a total of 2048 vCPUs per ESXi host. It is also possible to configure the number of vCores within a vCPU, but the host has a limit of 25 vCPUs per physical core.

> **NOTE**
>
> It can be interesting to configure at the vCore level because some operating systems and applications are based on the number of vCPUs (not on the number of vCores). For example, a VM can be configured with 1 vCPU and 4 vCores rather than 4 vCPUs because it does not affect anything in terms of performance but leads to savings on licenses. It also provides freedom from certain limitations in terms of the maximum number of processors for some operating systems. For instance, Windows 2008 Server Standard is limited to 4 vCPUs (and 256 LCPUs).

When creating a VM, the number of virtual sockets and cores per virtual socket must be entered, as shown in Figure 4.5.

Processor Management

Instructions from the virtual processor of the guest OS (called *vCPU*) are intercepted by the VMM transmitted to the ESXi VMkernel. At regular intervals, VMkernel dynamically distributes the VMs' workload among the server's different processors (or cores, in the case of a multicore processor). VM instructions thus migrate from one processor (or core) to another based on each processor's workload. The processor is the only server component that is not masked by the virtualization layer. The guest OS sees the type and model of the physical processor found in the server on which it runs. Figure 4.6 illustrates this concept.

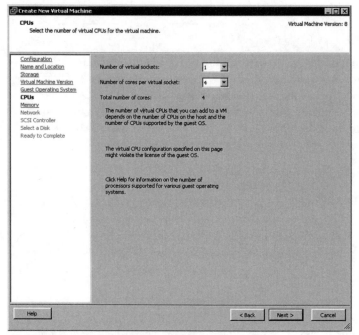

Figure 4.5 Selecting the number of virtual CPUs.

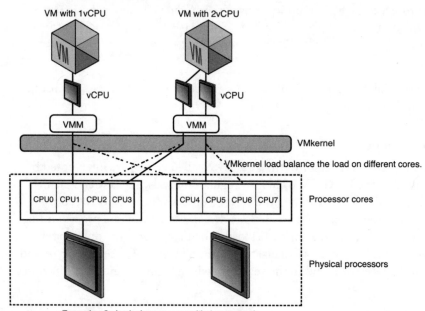

Figure 4.6 Processor management, with four virtual processors (cores) and two physical processors.

Multicore and Virtualization

Studies by Intel have shown that increasing frequency leads to a 13% gain in performance for a 73% increase in power use. However, by adding a core and decreasing the cores' frequency by 20%, performance can be increased by 70% while increasing power use by only 2%. If two more cores are added, total power consumption increases by only 6%, while performance increases by 210%!

Using multicore leads to considerable power-use reductions and provides very good performance. Virtualization is one of the technologies that best exploits the possibilities offered by multicores because ESXi can manage a core like a physical processor.

This makes it worthwhile to have a large number of cores to reach significant consolidation rates. Today, some processors have six cores, but in a few years, it is likely that processors will have dozens, if not hundreds, of cores and will reach even more significant consolidation levels.

Symmetric Multiprocessing and Virtual SMP

Symmetric multiprocessing (SMP) and *virtual SMP (vSMP)* involve an operating system addressing several different processors simultaneously by parallelizing execution tasks (this is called *multithread*), which allows the balancing out of the workload among processors. In theory, this might seem very interesting; in practice, a few precautions must be taken.

A server with several physical processors can exploit the SMP and benefit from it if the application was developed to manage this parallelism of execution tasks. In practice, however, with the exception of a few database-type applications (Microsoft SQL, Oracle, IBM DB2, SAP) and business and scientific applications, there are very few multithread applications. Applications must be redeveloped if they were not initially designed this way.

> **NOTE**
>
> With an older version of ESX (ESX 2) a VM configured with two vCPU requires that both processors must be available at the same time to manage the task (called CPU scheduling). With more recent versions of ESXi (version 3, 4 and 5), VMware introduced relaxed co-scheduling, which allows a two vCPU VM to be scheduled, even though there were not two physical CPU available at the same time. Despite this, it is always important to not assign more vCPUs than necessary to a VM.

In certain cases, using vSMP can even hinder performance because a VM configured with two vCPUs needs both processors to be available at the same time to manage the task. In a shared environment, this entails a risk of contention.

As a general rule, before using SMP, it is best to consult the software manufacturer.

vCPU

The guest OS works with virtual processors called vCPUs. In vSphere 5, a VM can be configured with 1 to 32 vCPUs that can exploit SMP. (Note that the guest OS must also be able to support SMP.)

If several applications run on the same server, it is possible to configure the VM with several vCPUs. This improves performance because programs can run simultaneously on different processors. In practice, system prerequisites (for example, OS, service packs) can make the various applications incompatible, making their cohabitation impossible. Moreover, this configuration increases the risk of conflict in memory management.

For these reasons, in the very rare cases where applications are specifically developed or if several applications should run in the VM, it is preferable to limit the number of vCPUs in VMs.

> **NOTE**
>
> Windows 2003 Server and earlier uses a different HAL (Hardware Abstraction Layer) depending on how many CPUs are in the system. For a single vCPU, Uni-Processor (UP) is used. For multiple processors, Symmetric Multiprocessing (SMP) is used. Windows automatically changes the HAL driver when going from UP to SMP. It can be very complex to go from SMP to UP, depending on the OS and version. So, it's best way to start with one vCPU and adds vCPUs as needed if performance is poor with only one vCPU. If you reduce from multiple vCPU to one vCPU, you will still have the multiprocessor HAL in the OS. This can results in slower performance than a system with correct HAL and consume more CPU. Windows 2008 Server is not affected by this problem, because the same HAL for UP and SMP is used.

Hyperthreading

Hyperthreading involves creating two logical core instances on a physical processor or core. Execution tasks are thus parallelized within the core, making them more efficient. While this functionality had vanished from previous-generation processors, Intel Nehalem processors have reintegrated it.

For more information about performance results, visit www.vmware.com/products/vmmark/results.html.

Virtualization Techniques

To be able to use different operating systems simultaneously on the same hardware, hypervisors use several different techniques: full virtualization, paravirtualization, and hardware-assisted virtualization.

To understand how these three techniques work, you must understand the architecture of x86 processors.

As illustrated in Figure 4.7, the architecture of x86 processors offers four privilege levels (Ring 0 to Ring 3, where Ring 0 = kernel mode and Ring 3 = user mode).

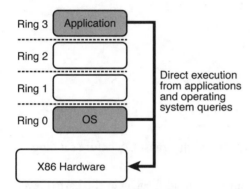

Figure 4.7 x86 privilege levels.

Execution levels, or rings, define the execution privileges of programs. The lower the level at which a program is installed, the more control it has over the system. The OS has the highest control level; it has direct access to resources by being executed in Ring 0.

Applications run in Ring 3, the highest. They cannot modify what is being executed on lower numbered rings. An application cannot stop the OS, but the OS can stop an application.

Rings 1 and 2 define privileges of lower importance than those of Ring 0.

In this type of architecture, how can a hypervisor be placed between the hardware and the OS, designed to be executed in Ring 0?

This challenge was overcome thanks to the techniques of full virtualization and paravirtualization.

Full Virtualization

VMware was first to solve this issue in 1998 by developing a technique called *binary translation*. With binary translation, the hypervisor can be placed in Ring 0, and the operating systems are moved to a higher numbered level (Ring 1), which provides them with more privileges than applications (Ring 3), as illustrated in Figure 4.8.

Because operating systems are designed to be run in Ring 0, they regularly check that this is where they reside because some instructions can be executed only if they have Ring 0 as their source or destination. ESXi uses binary translation by intercepting some requests, which deceives the guest OS as to the place they really occupy within the system.

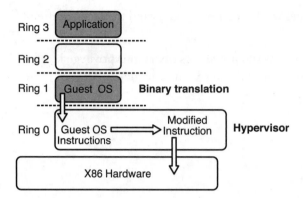

Figure 4.8 Binary translation example.

Binary translation modifies some instructions coming from the guest OS before sending them to physical processors for treatment.

The advantage of using this technique is that it requires no modification at the kernel level (node) of the guest OS because binary translation occurs at the level of the processor's binary code.

Advantages: The host OS is unaware that it is virtualized and no modification of the OS is required. This enables compatibility with many operating systems.

Disadvantages: Binary translation requires additional work on the CPU's part (called *overhead*).

Paravirtualization

Developed by Xen (among others), paravirtualization is another technique for using multiple operating systems. It involves modifying the guest operating systems (the node layer: the kernel) to allow them to run somewhere other than in Ring 0, as illustrated in Figure 4.9.

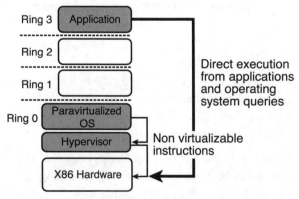

Figure 4.9 Paravirtualization example.

The guest operating systems are aware of their virtualization and modify certain low-level instructions before sending them to the hardware. Therefore, there are no instruction interceptions and no binary translation.

This paravirtualization technique is effective, but it requires the modification of the guest OS, which is not always possible, notably with some versions of Windows. It simplifies the task performed by the hypervisor, which has privileges for certain sets of processor and memory instructions.

Advantages: Performance comes very close to that of a purely physical environment.

Disadvantages: It is rather complex to implement because the kernel must be modified. Compatibility with the OS is very low.

> **NOTE**
>
> VMware has introduced certain aspects of the paravirtualization technique by using para-virtualized drivers. These specific drivers (developed by VMware) are aware of the virtualization layer and communicate more easily with the hypervisor. They are added by VMware Tools for certain guest operating systems, thereby improving performance.

Hardware-Assisted Virtualization

To simplify the hypervisor's task while avoiding placing the OS in a ring that is not designed for such a purpose or modifying the kernel of the OS, Intel processors with Intel VT and AMD processors with AMD-V introduce a new mode of execution called *hardware-assisted virtualization*.

It provides a root level that corresponds to rings below 0, and a normal level that corresponds to the former Rings 0 to 3, as illustrated in Figure 4.10. The privileged level accesses hardware directly. This allows direct reception of some instructions from the guest OS, which limits binary translation work.

The hypervisor functions in root mode with the highest level of control. Guest operating systems function in Ring 0. They occupy the space for which they were designed.

There is no need to modify the guest OS or, in most cases, to use binary translation. (Binary translation is, however, still required for some sets of instructions.)

This new root level considerably reduces overhead. This evolution of the instruction set also makes the sharing of physical resources between VMs more fluid.

Thanks to the hardware assistance within the processor, x86 architecture is free from a number of technical hurdles and provides virtual-environment performance coming very close to that of the native environment (90% to 95% depending on circumstances).

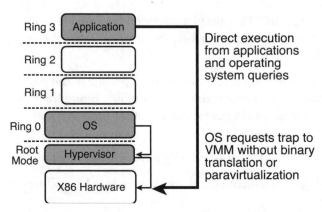

Figure 4.10 Hardware-assisted virtualization.

CPU Indicators

Many indicators are available. In vCenter Server, two visible indicators are particularly interesting: CPU usage and CPU ready time.

CPU Usage (Average)

This indicator, available at the server, VM, or resource pool level, determines the percentage of time the CPU is used (see Figure 4.11).

This value should be monitored and gives indications if a VM monopolizes an important proportion of CPU time. It is important to monitor the use of the ESXi's physical processors (pCPU), because they should not go beyond 75% on average.

CPU Ready Time

A very interesting indicator that is less known is *ready time*. In a virtual environment with shared resources, several VMs can use the physical CPU simultaneously. The resource manager within VMkernel allocates CPU time based on VM requests and decides on which core the VM should run. Some VMs must wait before attention from the physical CPU. Ready time is the amount of time a VM waits before it can be run by a CPU.

> **NOTE**
>
> If a processor's core is overloaded, the resource manager favors leaving the VM on the same core so that its data on the CPU cache can be used; this generates a short CPU ready time. The manager can decide to migrate the VM to another core, however, if the waiting time is too long.

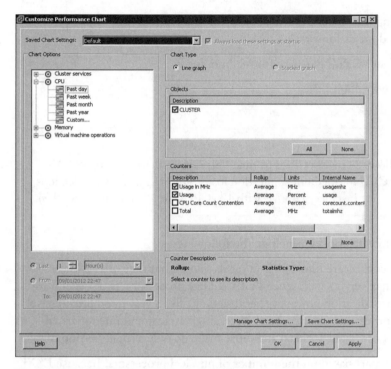

Figure 4.11 CPU performance chart settings.

Although it is normal for a server to accumulate ready time, the value should be monitored so that it does not exceed the following:

- 10% for one vCPU, or 2000 ms

- 20% for two vCPUs, or 4000 ms

- 40% for four vCPUs, or 8000 ms

This value is not the only one to take into account, but it must be regularly monitored. It is a good indicator of eventual configuration problems (improper use of Scheduling Affinity, vSMP, or VMs with an inappropriate Share or Limit setting) and of the improper placement of some VMs within the infrastructure.

Good Practices

How many VMs can there be per ESXi host server? This is a difficult question because the answer depends on environment and application load. There are a few points of reference, however. The number of VMs that can run on a server depends on the number of cores (not taking hyperthreading into account) available within the ESXi server. Globally, capacity planning can be done as follows:

- Between two and four vCPUs per core for medium loads

- One vCPU per core for high loads

EXAMPLE

A server with 12 cores allows 24 to 48 vCPUs to run. This is equivalent to 24 to 48 VMs configured each with 1 vCPU for medium application loads. For high-activity applications, this represents 12 vCPUs (for instance, 12 VMs with 12 vCPUs, or 3 VMs with 4 vCPUs).

Other good-practice options to consider include the following:

- Uniprocessors (one socket) are interesting in terms of cost, but they offer a lower consolidation rate than servers with several CPUs. Dual processors (two sockets) are the most used for virtualization nowadays because they offer a very good price/consolidation ratio. Quad processors (four sockets) offer a high attachment rate to virtualization. Octo processors (eight sockets) and more make up only a small portion of sales.

- Licensing is done in part based on the number of physical processors. Because ESXi can manage a core like a physical processor, processors with the highest number of integrated cores should be favored.

- It is important to place VMs based on their morphology and activity.

- Studies have shown that activating hyperthreading improves performance for applications that know how to manage multithreading.

- Because some applications reap no benefit from several vCPUs, VMs should be configured with a minimum of vCPUs. Consult manufacturers for recommendations.

- Faster frequency processors improve performance. For some workloads, however, a larger cache can improve performance. Consult software manufacturers for additional recommendations.

Moving VMs with VMotion

vMotion is the technology invented by VMware to migrate a functioning VM from one ESXi host server to another in a fully transparent manner. The OS and application running in the VM suffer no service interruption.

How vMotion Works

When migrating using vMotion, only the status and memory of the VM—with its configuration—moves. The virtual disk does not move; it stays in the same shared-storage location. Once the VM has migrated, it is managed by the new host. vMotion can function only with a centralized storage architecture (such as SAN FC, SAN FCoE, iSCSI, or NAS) or with vStorage Appliance.

When vMotion is triggered, the active memory is transferred through the network to the destination host in steps (see Figure 4.12):

1. vCenter Server confirms the VM is in a stable state.

2. The VM's memory status and its content are transferred to the destination server through the VMkernel port. vMotion takes a series of memory snapshots and successively transfers these snapshots to the destination server.

3. After the copy is complete on the destination server, vCenter Server unlocks and suspends the source VM so that the destination server can take control of it by performing an on-disk lock.

4. Because the network layer is also managed by VMkernel, vMotion ensures that after the migration, the VM's network identity—like its MAC address and SSID—is preserved. Active network connections are also preserved.

5. The VM continues its activity on the destination host.

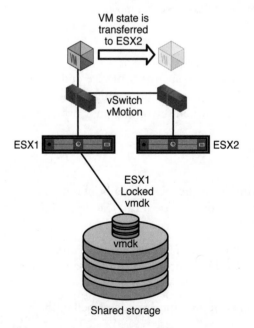

Figure 4.12 vMotion framework.

6. The VM runs on ESX1. Its vmdk virtual disk is found in the shared storage. vCenter triggers the migration of the VM to the destination server. The VM's status is copied onto the second server (see Figure 4.13).

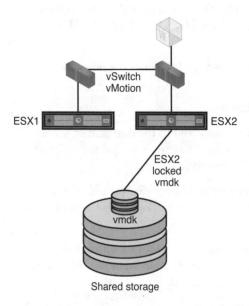

Figure 4.13 After the VM's status is copied, the ESX1 server removes on-disk locking and the ESX2 server locks the vmdk for its own use. The vmdk virtual disk does not move during migration.

When to Use vMotion

vMotion is mainly used for planned maintenance operations, such as firmware updates or when adding components (for example, memory). It makes it possible to migrate VMs to another server, perform the maintenance operation and, when the operation is over, bring the VMs back to the initial server.

Requirements and Best Practices

- vMotion generates SCSI reservations and thus locks the LUN for a brief moment. For this reason, it should not be used too frequently because it can lead to performance loss at the disk-access level.

- It is important to avoid spending too much time using vMotion on processors with overly different sets of instructions. It is best to choose processors of the same generation and family whenever possible.

- To function properly, vMotion needs a number of prerequisites, described in the following sections.

Storage

vMotion can work only if there is a shared storage array accessible by both servers—source server and destination server.

Network

vMotion requires at least a one gigabit network card. All source and destination host servers must be configured with a dedicated VMkernel port group. When performing a migration, vCenter Server assigns VMs to the port group based on the name given. This is why using consistent port group names among hosts is important.

> **NOTE**
>
> In vSphere 4, only a single GbE network card could be configured for vMotion. This limit has been removed in vSphere 5, and it is possible to have up to 16 1-GbE cards and 4 10-GbE cards for vMotion. This also reduces the time required to migrate a VM, notably for VMs with intense memory activity. The number of concurrent vMotion instances supported per host is 4 on a GbE network and 8 on a 10-GbE network.

The CPU plays the most restrictive part in a vMotion event. Instruction sets can vary depending on the processor type, model, and generation, so compatibility among different processors should be verified. VMware puts in a great deal of effort to provide improved compatibility between processors. *Enhanced vMotion Compatibility (EVC)* enables the masking of some differences. This offers more compatibility between servers with different generations of processors. (See VMware's Knowledge Base: KB 1992 and KB 1003212.)

> **NOTE**
>
> ESXi5 introduces version 8 of virtual hardware. This version is not compatible with versions earlier than ESXi5, so VMs with virtual hardware 8 can migrate only to ESXi5 host servers or later.

To support vMotion, the virtual hardware versions of the VMs must be compatible. For security reasons, it is possible to activate encryption when making a transfer using vMotion (in vCenter's advanced options).

Enhanced VMotion Compatibility

Because each generation of processors carries several new functionalities, EVC ensures all host servers within a cluster offer the same instruction sets for VMs, guaranteeing compatibility among processors from different generations for vMotion.

To do so, EVC uses *baselines*. A baseline enables the definition of a set of functionalities supported by all processors within the cluster. The baseline is the common denominator for all processors.

ESXi works directly with Intel VT Flex Migration and AMD-V Extended Migration processors and technologies to show only common instruction sets and hide those that could create compatibility issues. (To find out which baselines and instruction sets are masked, see VMware s Knowledge Base: KB 1003212.)

EVC does not hinder performance and does not affect the number of cores or the size of the cache. The only possible degradation surrounds some instructions (for example, SSE 4.2) that will not be used.

> **NOTE**
>
> To use EVC, all hosts in the cluster must use processors from the same vendor (Intel or AMD) and have the NX/XD functionality activated in the BIOS.

Once EVC is activated in a cluster, all host servers are automatically configured to correspond with the defined baseline. Host servers that do not have the prerequisites cannot be part of the cluster.

Distributed Resource Scheduler

Distributed Resource Scheduler (DRS) is a method of automating the use of vMotion in a production environment by sharing the workload among different host servers in a cluster.

DRS collects information about the use of the cluster's host servers and makes recommendations for the placement of VMs to improve workload distribution. When a server is part of a cluster and DRS is activated, recommendations can arise in two cases:

- **Initial placement:** Initial placement occurs when the VM boots.

> **NOTE**
>
> DRS and *High Availability (HA)* can be used jointly. When HA restarts VMs, DRS with initial placement recommends the best host server to use within the cluster.

- **Load balancing:** When VMs are running, DRS optimizes resources by distributing the VMs' workload among the cluster's different servers. This migration can be performed automatically or manually (after validation by the administrator) following defined criteria.

NOTE

It is possible to use the *Fault Tolerance (FT)* functionality with DRS when vMotion's improved compatibility function (EVC) is activated.

DRS Rules

In an ESXi cluster with DRS is enabled, it is possible to set rules to always keep VMs together on the same server (affinity rule), to always run VMs on different servers (anti-affinity rule), or to always have VMs running on specific servers (host affinity).

Figure 4.14 shows the Type settings, which are then described in the list that follows.

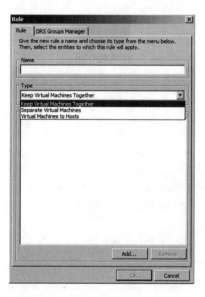

Figure 4.14 Setting DRS rules.

- **Keep Virtual Machines Together:** Allows the implementation of *VM affinity*. This option ensures that VMs stay together on the same server within the ESXi cluster when VMs are migrated using DRS. The main advantage of this setting has to do with performance considerations between VMs (such as when a server is linked to a database). Communication between VMs located on the same host is extremely rapid because it occurs inside the ESXi server (without going through the external network).

- **Separate Virtual Machines:** Allows the implementation of *VM anti-affinity*. This option ensures that VMs are located on different ESXi servers. This configuration is mainly used for high-availability considerations (for example, with a Microsoft MSCS cluster or Windows Server Failover Clustering for Windows 2008). Using this rule, VMs are on different physical servers. If one VM breaks down, this ensures the application is clustered on another VM. Anti-affinity rules should not be used to manage performance, they should focus on availability.

- **Virtual Machines to Hosts:** Allows the placement of VMs on specific host servers. With *host affinity*, the host on which the VM will run can be specified. This enables the fine-tuning of the relation between the VMs and the host servers within a cluster. Part of a cluster can be dedicated to VMs.

The possible settings are as follows:

- Must Run on Hosts in Group

- Should Run on Hosts in Group

- Must Not Run on Hosts in Group

- Should Not Run on Hosts in Group

NOTE

The Must Run parameter implies that the instruction is mandatory and directly impacts the use of vSphere HA and vSphere DPM. Table 4.1 lists the benefits of both Must parameters with vSphere HA.

vSphere HA skips some affinity (or anti-affinity) rules while positioning VMs after a host failure. This does not apply to Must Run and Must Not Run parameters that are systematically run by HA.

Table 4.1 Must Parameters and vSphere HA

DRS			
Type	**Affinity**	**Anti-Affinity**	**Respected by vSphere HA?**
VM-VM	Keep VMs together	Separate VMs	No
VM-Host	Should run on hosts in group	Should not run on hosts in group	No
	Must run on hosts in group	Must not run on hosts in group	Yes

Automation

vSphere DRS migrates VMs in a more or less automatic manner depending on the parameters defined. vSphere DRS is activated to do the following:

- Redistribute CPU or memory load between servers ESXi hosts in the cluster.

- Migrate VM when a server is placed in maintenance mode.

- Keep VMs together on the same server host (affinity rule) or separate VMs on two different host servers (anti-affinity rule).

As shown in Figure 4.15, there are different levels of automation:

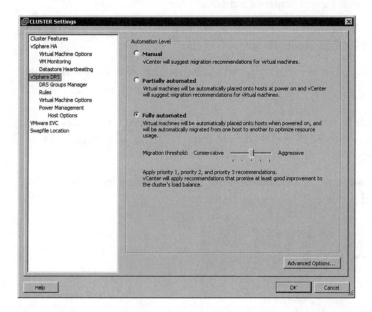

Figure 4.15 Automation levels.

- **Manual:** DRS makes recommendations but will not place VMs on host servers without validation from the administrator.

- **Partially Automated:** Initial placement is done automatically by DRS, but the migration of functioning VMs will be performed only after the administrator validates recommendations in vCenter.

- **Fully Automated:** Initial placement and the migration of functioning VMs are performed automatically. This automatic migration is based on a threshold corresponding to five levels of recommendations: conservative (5 stars) to aggressive (1 star):

  - **Level 1:** Conservative, 5 stars—Migration will occur only if the rules are respected or if the host is placed in maintenance mode.

  - **Level 2:** 4 stars—Migration will occur only if the first level is met or if migration brings about significant improvements.

  - **Level 3:** 3 stars—Migration will occur only if the first two levels are met or if migration brings about good improvements.

  - **Level 4:** 2 stars—Migration will occur only if the first three levels are met or if migration brings about moderate improvements.

  - **Level 5:** Aggressive, 1 star—Migration will occur only if all recommendations from Levels 1 to 4 are met or if it brings about a little improvement.

The conservative setting leads to fewer migrations and will be triggered only in cases where the affinity rule is not respected. Level 5 leads to more frequent VM migrations between the cluster's servers.

In certain cases, some VMs can have an automation level that is different from the automation level defined at the cluster level, as illustrated in Figure 4.16.

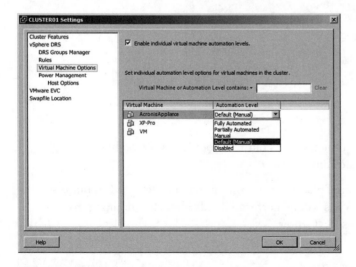

Figure 4.16 Administrators can also specify automation at the VM level.

Possible choices are as follows:

- Fully Automated
- Partially Automated
- Manual
- Disabled

vSphere Distributed Power Management

The *Distributed Power Management (DPM)* functionality allows a reduction in the power used by the datacenter's server by placing the VMs on servers in such a way as to have the minimum number of host servers running. DPM is coupled with DRS to move VMs from servers that are used very little in order to reduce the number of functioning servers, thus reducing power use—both in power supply and for air-conditioning needs.

DPM uses remote server power-on technologies such as *Intelligent Power Management Interface (IPMI)* or remote-access cards such as *Integrated Lights-Out (iLO)* or the Wake-on-LAN functionality.

ESXi can also take advantage of advanced processor functions such as Intel Enhanced SpeedStep or AMD PowerNow! to adapt the frequency of the processors based on actual needs.

Network

As illustrated in Figure 4.17, network management in vSphere 5 is done through one of two technology options:

- vSphere Standard Switch (also called vSS) is a simple-to-configure virtual switch that is managed independently on each ESXi host. vSS is simple to use, but in large-scale environments it increases the workload of administrators because every configuration modification must be replicated on each ESXi. Another disadvantage of vSS relates to VM migration using vMotion. Because the VM's network status is reinitialized, monitoring and troubleshooting are more complicated.

- vSphere Distributed Switch (vDS) is a distributed switch offering centralized uniform management on a set of ESXi servers (maximum 350 per vDS). It also ensures a certain configuration and security consistency when moving VMs between servers. vDS provides centralized management on a set of servers, which simplifies operations. Unlike a vSS, during a vMotion, VM network status is maintained.

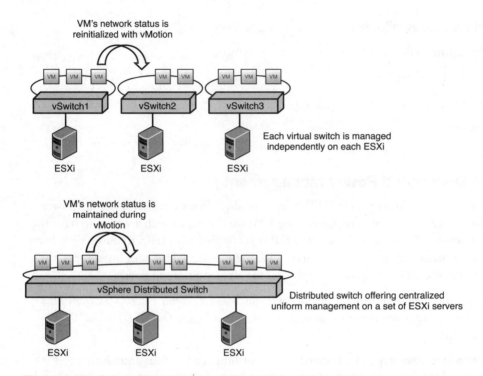

Figure 4.17 vSphere 5's standard and distributed switch options.

Other third-party solutions exist, such as Cisco Nexus 1000V. This is a distributed switch technology that has advanced functionalities and provides unified Cisco management for the physical and virtual environments. It can be useful for large-scale environments.

> **NOTE**
> With vSS or vDS virtual switches, the network team has no direct view of the internal configuration of the vSwitches because they are managed directly by the VMkernel. Nexus 1000V allows network teams to take control of the entire network configuration and apply it to the VMs.

IBM also has a distributed virtual switch, called the System Networking Distributed Virtual Switch 5000V. Both the Cisco Nexus 1000V and the IBM DVS 5000V build upon vDS, so they require the vSphere 5.0 Enterprise Plus license.

vSphere Standard Switch

vSS operates on Layer 2 (like a Layer 2 virtual switch) within the VMkernel and enables the linkage of the physical network components to the virtual network components. ESXi does not take charge of the vMotion migration of VMs between hosts in different broadcast domains.

> **NOTE**
>
> When designing network architecture, if you want to use features such as vMotion or DRS, it is necessary to place the hosts in the same Layer 2 VLAN.

Virtual switches bring about an impressive flexibility of use because it is possible to easily create advanced network architectures such as the following:

- *Demilitarized zones (DMZs)*

- VLANs (ESXi supports 802.1Q VLAN tagging, VLAN ID between 1 and 4095.)

- VMs completely isolated from the company's network or connected to different networks

It is possible to have several networks use the same vSwitch or to create several different vSwitches for each network.

VM Communication with Network Elements

Figure 4.18 shows a schematic representation of the different elements of the physical and virtual network.

Each VM possesses one or several Ethernet virtual network cards, called a *vNIC*. Each vNIC has a MAC address, an IP address (vSphere 5 supports IPv4 and IPv6), and a connection to a vSwitch.

> **NOTE**
>
> By default, vSphere automatically generates one MAC address per vNIC in the VM. This value starts with 00:0C:29 followed by 3 bytes generated by VMware's algorithm. A MAC address can be manually defined in the following range: 00:50:56:00:00:00 to 00:50:56:3F:FF:FF.

Through the vNIC, VMs connect to the vSwitches, which have two aspects: one virtual, the other physical.

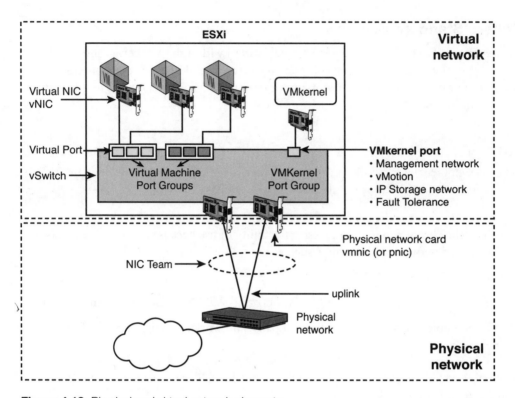

Figure 4.18 Physical and virtual network elements.

On the vSwitch's virtual network side, there are virtual ports and port groups. VMs connect their vNIC to the virtual ports (that can be thought of as virtual RJ-45 ports) of the vSwitch associated with a port group, which usually corresponds to a virtual LAN (VLAN) or a specific port group. Each vSwitch can have up to 1016 active virtual ports (plus 8 ports reserved by the VMkernel for its own use).

As shown in Figure 4.19, two connection types can be used to define a port group: Virtual Machine and VMkernel.

NOTE

The notion of *port group* exists only in virtualized environments. It allows the implementation of a policy regarding security, network segmentation, and traffic management. It also serves to improve availability and optimize performance.

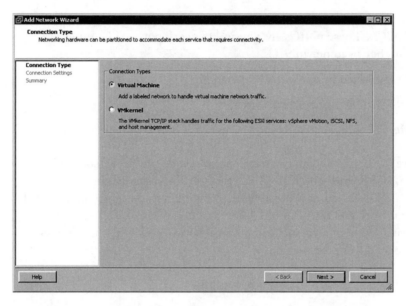

Figure 4.19 Connection types.

VMkernel

This connection is used for network management, vMotion traffic, IP storage network, or FT. The VMkernel port requires an IP address and at least one physical network card. This type of port is also used to manage the ESXi server and communicate with a user interface (such as vSphere Client).

> **NOTE**
>
> The management port and the vMotion and FT ports must be located in different subnetworks and distinct VLANs.

Virtual Machine

This connection is used by VMs to connect to the physical environment and to communicate to one another. In the case where no network card is connected, the network is completely isolated from outside the server and communication between VMs will occur at the VMkernel level (internal to the ESXi host).

On the vSwitch's physical network side, there are physical network cards called *uplinks* (or *pNICs*, for *physical NICs*). These pNICs are physical network ports. When they are connected to a vSwitch, they become vmNICs.

A vmNIC link can be established in a vSwitch in two modes:

- **Active adapter:** Used by the standard switch.

- **Standby adapter:** Becomes active as soon as an active adapter breaks down.

As illustrated in Figure 4.20, the vSwitch can have one or several physical associated network cards (up to 32-GbE cards and 8 10-GbE cards per ESXi server). In cases where several network cards are associated, it is possible to group them into a single logical card to offer redundancy and workload distribution. (This is called *NIC teaming*.) It is also possible to have a vSwitch without an associated physical network switch, thus creating a network completely isolated from the outside.

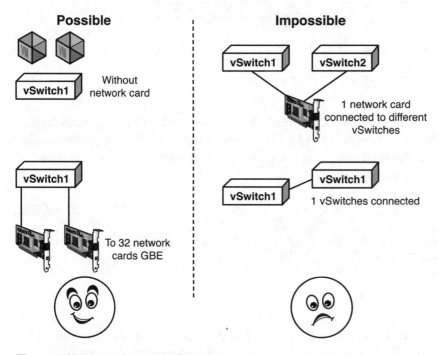

Figure 4.20 Network card configurations.

When two VMs from an ESXi server are connected to the same vSwitch, network traffic between them is routed locally and uses no bandwidth from the external physical network.

Several cards can be put onto the same vSwitch. A physical network card (uplink) cannot be connected to several different vSwitches and one vSwitch cannot be linked to another vSwitch, which eliminates the potential for bridge loops.

ADVICE

Once pNICs are assigned, they bear vmNIC IDs from 0 to n. If two network ports are integrated onto the motherboard and one dual-port PCI card, numbering can be predicted before activating the physical server to provide integration teams with prewiring plans. The vmNICs are numbered based on their PCI ID. This means the motherboard's port 1 will be vmNIC 0, port 2 will be vmNIC 1, and so on. It is worth looking at the schematics of the motherboard to insert network cards in a way that increases redundancy within the frame and thus compensate for the failure of a motherboard's riser or internal bus, which eliminates a *single point of failure (SPOF)*.

Setting Up the Virtual Machine Port Group

As shown in Figure 4.21, when creating a VM port group, it is necessary to enter the port group name and, optionally, the VLAN ID (between 1 and 4095). After it is created, the vSwitch's port group policy must be configured.

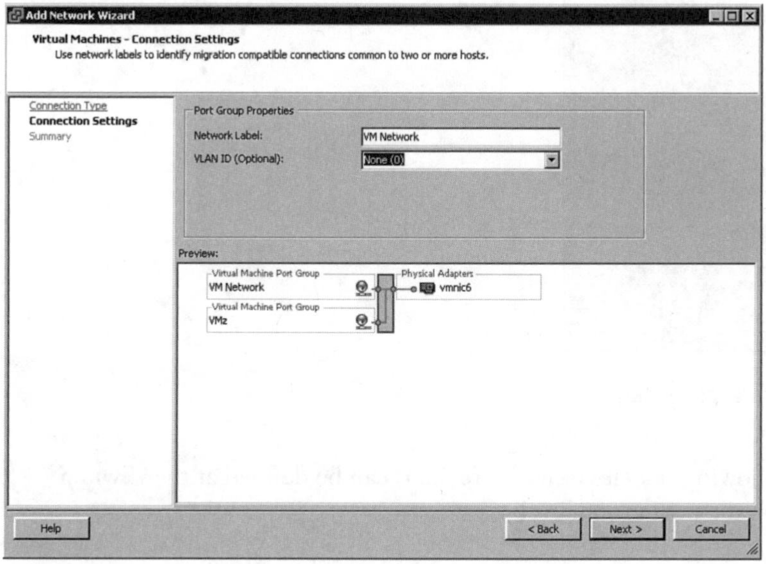

Figure 4.21 Port group property settings.

NOTE

A VLAN allows the sharing of a physical network and its logical segmentation to reduce network equipment needs (for example, the number of switches or network cards). This also decreases the use of multiple physical subnetworks. Furthermore, VLANs offer better traffic management, network flow separation, and isolation between networks. The interconnection of two physical switches is done through *trunking*, which allows the VLANs to exist on many trunked switches.

Settings must be configured as follows:

- **General:** This setting allows the configuration of the number of available ports within the vSwitch (8 to 4088 ports) and *maximum transmission unit (MTU)* (1280 to 9000). See Figure 4.22.

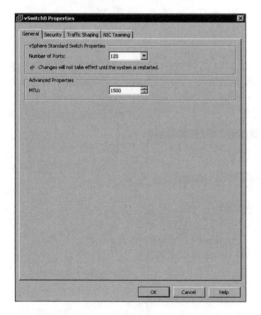

Figure 4.22 vSwitch general properties.

- **Security:** The following policies (see Figure 4.23) can be defined at the vSwitch level and can reach the port group level:

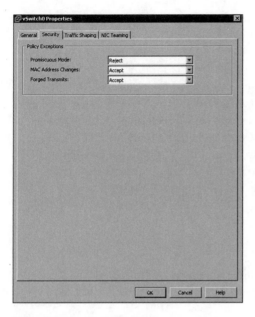

Figure 4.23 vSwitch security properties.

- **Promiscuous Mode:** This mode (by default set to Reject) forbids a vNIC within a VM from observing the network traffic of the vSwitch to which it is connected. For security reasons, activating this mode is not recommended. However, VMs can be dedicated to network monitoring (for example, to detect intrusions). In this case, activating this functionality is worthwhile.

- **MAC Address Changes and Forged Transmits:** When a VM is created in vSphere, two MAC addresses exist—initial and effective.

The initial MAC address is generated by vSphere in the range 00:50:56:00:00:00 to 00:50:56:3F:FF:FF (or 00:0C:29, modifiable in the vmx file). The guest OS has no control over this MAC address.

The effective MAC address is the one used to communicate with the network's other elements. By default, the two addresses are identical. It is nevertheless possible to force another MAC address, placing it manually in the guest OS (in the network card's advanced settings). It is possible to authorize or forbid a difference between the MAC address in the vmx configuration file and the MAC address in the guest OS using the MAC Address Changes and Forged Transmits settings. The MAC Address Changes setting relates to incoming traffic while Forged Transmits relates to outgoing traffic. For example, if MAC Address

Changes is set to Reject and both MAC addresses are not identical, incoming traffic is forbidden.

- **Traffic Shaping:** This setting (see Figure 4.24) enables bandwidth limitation at the switch level for outgoing traffic. By default, it is deactivated. In the case of vDS, traffic shaping relates to incoming and outgoing traffic.

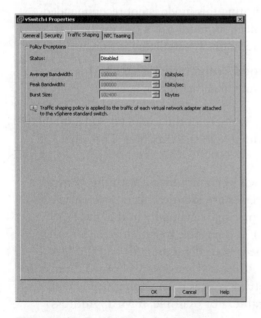

Figure 4.24 Traffic shaping properties.

- **NIC Teaming:** NIC teaming (see Figure 4.25) is the grouping of several physical network switches attached to a vSwitch. This grouping enables load balancing between the different pNICs and provides Fault Tolerance if a card failure occurs.

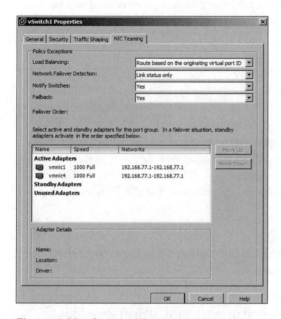

Figure 4.25 vSwitch NIC teaming properties.

Also, note that on the NIC Teaming properties page, load-balancing options are available. *Load balancing* is a load distribution based on the number of connections, not on network traffic. In most cases, load is managed only for outgoing traffic, and balancing is based on three different policies:

- **Route based on the originating virtual switch port ID (default):** In this configuration, load balancing is based on the number of physical network cards and the number of virtual ports used. With this configuration policy, a virtual network card connected to a vSwitch port will always use the same physical network card (vmNIC). If a physical network card fails, the virtual network card is redirected to another physical network card.

EXAMPLE 1

Ten VMs are connected to a vSwitch with five physical network cards. With NIC teaming, the load is as follows: Two VMs will be connected to each physical network card.

EXAMPLE 2

If five VMs are connected to a vSwitch with six physical network cards, the five VMs are connected to five different physical network cards and one physical network card will be used only if one of the five cards fails. It is important to note that port allocation occurs only when a VM is started or when a failover occurs. Balancing is done based on a port's occupation rate at the time the VM starts up.

NOTE

When speaking of teaming, it is important to understand that if, for example, teaming is created with two 1-GB cards, and if a VM consumes more than one card's capacity, a performance problem will arise because traffic greater than 1 GB will not go through the other card, and there will be an impact on the VMs sharing the same port as the VM consuming all resources.

- **Route based on source MAC hash:** This principle is the same as the default but is based on the number of MAC addresses.

- **Route based on IP hash:** The limitation of the two previously discussed policies is that virtual networks use the same physical network card. IP hash-based load balancing uses the source and destination of the IP address to determine which physical network card to use. Using this algorithm, a VM can communicate with several different physical network cards based on its destination. This option forces the configuration of the physical switch's ports to EtherChannel. Because the physical switch is configured similarly, this option is the only one that also provides inbound load balancing.

- **Network Failover Detection:** The two possible settings are Link Status Only and Beacon Probing.

  - **Link Status Only:** Enables the detection of failures related to the physical network's cables and switch. However, be aware that configuration issues are not detected.

  - **Beacon Probing:** Allows the detection of failures unseen by link status by sending Ethernet broadcast frames through all network cards. These network frames authorize the vSwitch to detect faulty configurations and force the failover if ports are blocked. According to VMware's best practices, it is recommended to have at least three cards before activating this functionality.

Setting Up the VMkernel Port

The configuration of the VMkernel port offers the same settings as the VM port group with the addition of the IP addressing configuration and the definition of its use. As shown in Figure 4.26, choices are vMotion, Fault Tolerance Logging, Management Traffic, and iSCSI Port Binding.

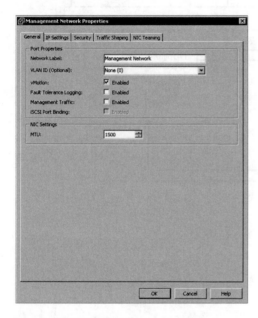

Figure 4.26 VMkernel port settings.

vSphere Distributed Switch

vDS works with dvSwitches configured and managed by vCenter Server. Whereas a standard vSwitch manages the network for a single host server, a distributed switch works for all associated ESXi host servers. vDS guarantees a consistent network configuration when VMs are migrated from one ESXi server to another using vMotion, as illustrated in Figure 4.27. This allows the unified management of the network by addressing the datacenter's ESXi servers in a homogenous manner. The dvSwitch possesses one or several dvPortGroups, allowing the application of a networkwide policy. The distributed port groups are created in a unique location (vCenter), and all host servers inherit the same configuration.

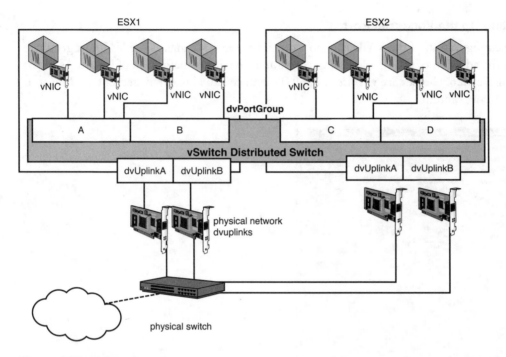

Figure 4.27 vDS configuration.

NOTE

When a VM is migrated using vMotion, the statistics of distributed ports and their associated policies are preserved. This simplifies debugging and troubleshooting operations.

NOTE

vDS allows the implementation of quality of service through *Network I/O Control (NIOC)*.

The dvUplinks provide an abstraction layer for the physical network cards (vmNICs) of each host. The policy applied to the dvSwitches and dvPortGroup is applied to the dvUplinks (no longer to each network card found in each host). Therefore, each network card is associated to a dvUplink.

vDS also allows the management of how VMs are bound to ports. This can be done in three ways:

- **Static binding:** This allocates a port to a VM when the VM connects to the distributed port. Static binding increases security and provides network teams with more troubleshooting possibilities. For example, it will allow a VM undergoing vMotion migration to keep its traffic statistics and default frames, if any, when it moves from one ESXi host to another because the switch's port "moves" with the VM.

- **Dynamic binding:** This allocates a port to a VM when the VM is first powered up after being connected to the distributed port. Dynamic binding has become obsolete in ESXi 5.0.

- **Ephemeral binding:** No port binding (dynamic) occurs.

vDS also permits the use of *private VLANs (PVLANs)*. PVLANs allow the isolation of the traffic between VMs in the same VLAN. This provides added security between the VMs on the same subnetwork. PVLAN is very useful on DMZ when servers need to be accessible from both inside and outside the company.

Contrary to vSS, which only supports traffic shaping for outgoing traffic (egress), vDS supports traffic shaping for incoming and outgoing traffic (ingress and egress).

vSphere 5 supports NetFlow with vDS. NetFlow allows the collection of information on stream traffic between the source and destination. This provides administrators with the possibility of viewing network communications between the VMs. This can help in detecting intrusions, profiling, or any other malicious process. All data is sent to a NetFlow collector.

vDS Architecture

As shown in Figure 4.28, a vDS contains the *control plane* and the *I/O plane*. These two elements are separate.

- vCenter Server manages the control plane, which is in charge of the configuration of vDS, distributed ports, uplinks, and NIC teaming and coordinates port migration.

- The I/O plane is hidden and implemented like a standard vSwitch within the VMkernel on each ESXi host. Its role is to manage streams. An I/O plane agent (VMkernel process) runs on each host and is responsible for communication between the control plane and the I/O plane.

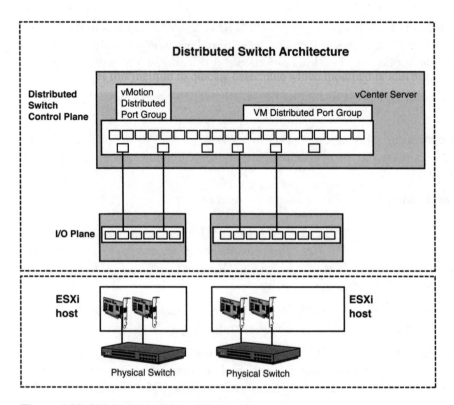

Figure 4.28 Distributed switch architecture.

Network I/O Control

Just like SIOC for storage, *Network I/O Control (NIOC)* allows the implementation of *quality of service (QoS)* for the network. It provides network traffic management and control over network I/O with vDS. For each type of traffic and each group of VMs, the administrator can define share, limit, and QoS priority rules at the following levels:

- VMs
- Management network
- iSCSI
- NFS
- FT
- vMotion
- User defined
- vSphere replication

> **NOTE**
>
> NIOC is very useful in consolidated 10-GB network infrastructures because it allows the sharing and limiting of different types of traffic.

Virtual Network Cards

The following virtual network cards can be configured within a VM:

- **vlance:** Emulates a PCNet32 card and offers the best compatibility for a 32-bit guest OS.

- **E1000:** Emulates an Intel 82545EM Gigabit Ethernet card compatible with the most recent guest OS, such as Windows 2008 Server.

- **E1000e:** Evolution of the E1000 card, available with virtual hardware version 8.

- **vmxnet, vmxnet2, and vmxnet3:** Offer the best performance and support jumbo frames. (These cards are available only when VMware Tools is installed.)

For more information, refer to VMware's Knowledge Base: KB 1001805.

Cisco NEXUS 1000V

Cisco Nexus 1000V is a virtual network appliance that integrates into VMware's virtual datacenter. This appliance enables the extension of the network policies defined for the datacenter related to VLAN, security, filtering, and so on to all VMs within a server. The appliance provides an interface to provision, monitor, and administer the physical and virtual networks through the virtual network using standard Cisco management tools used by existing network teams. Figure 4.29 illustrates the Cisco Nexus architecture.

As shown in Figure 4.29, the Cisco Nexus 1000V distributed vSwitch is made up of two elements: the *Virtual Supervisor Module (VSM)* and the *Virtual Ethernet Module (VEM)*.

- **VSM:** This is the module (deployed in the form of a virtual appliance) that allows the command-line configuration of the virtual switch. It can be doubled to ensure HA. (Switching from the active VSM to the back-up VSM is called *switchover*.) Each VSM supports up to 64 VEMs.

- **VEM:** This is the component that is integrated between the physical network card and the virtual network card in the VM. It replaces VMware vSwitches and is responsible for sending packets to the correct location. It is installed onto each ESXi host and configured through the VSM. A *data plane agent (DPA)* receives the information from vCenter.

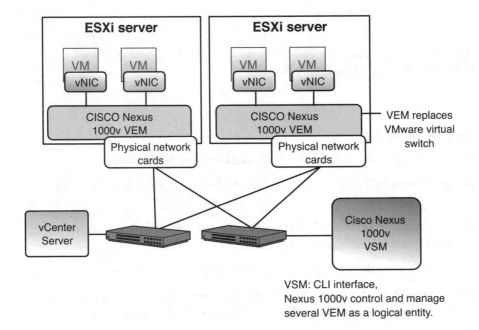

Figure 4.29 The Cisco Nexus architecture.

The VEM component communicates with the VSM through three distinct channels:

- **Management:** This channel used by the ESXi servers and the vCenter Server. The VSM uses this channel to speak with the vCenter and make port groups visible so VMs can connect to them. The management channel sends configuration data from the vCenter to the VEM during installation, in a format called *opaque data*.

- **Control:** This is the communication channel between the VSM and the VEM. It enables the unmasking of the VEM modules, configuration, and synchronization of the second VSM. Heartbeat packets are sent between the two VSMs (by default every two seconds with a six-second timeout). NetFlow streams are also sent from the VEMs to the VSMs.

- **Packet:** This channel allows information to go from the network to the VSM for analysis.

> **NOTE**
>
> Leaving the management network on a standard vSwitch can be worthwhile to avoid cutting off the branch on which you are sitting, so to speak, in case of configuration error. Control and packet channels can remain on the dVS.

Provisioning and Good Practices

The network can become a bottleneck in a virtual architecture. It is strongly advised to use the maximum number of network cards, especially now that they cost so little, given their usefulness. Following this recommendation will help ensure that the virtual infrastructure can automatically manage the failure of any physical element without any production incident occurring. A minimum of four network cards is recommended.

Also, use multiple quad-port network cards and distribute them among different PCI ports and risers if there are enough PCI slots available. (A simple standard configuration will already use a minimum of two ports for management, two for vMotion, two for IP storage, and two for VMs.)

ADVICE

When implementing a virtualization project, it is necessary to alert network teams regarding the number of ports that will be required to integrate the ESXi server into the datacenter. This virtualized infrastructure initially consumes many ports (for the time required to decommission old physical machines). It is sometimes necessary to begin with only some of the network ports (two minimum, for redundancy purposes) until ports are freed up on machines that will migrate to VM form. Time is needed for ordering and integrating new switches, and delays must be anticipated because they can have a considerable impact on the project's progress.

Following are some additional recommended best practices:

- For security reasons, separate vSwitches must be created for the management network, the storage network, and VMs' network traffic.

- The management port can be configured with one dedicated vSwitch and two physical network switches or, alternatively, with two dedicated vSwitches and one physical network switch per card, but the latter requires two IP addresses (recommended for HA detection).

- For the VM port group, use the maximum number of network cards. (Using two gigabit network cards is a required minimum.)

- The average traffic and bandwidth for a VM is 7 MBps, which generally allows eight to ten VMs per gigabit card. This is, of course, an average; it depends on workload as well as the application itself.

- For the VMkernel port, use two network cards for vMotion. For iSCSI or NFS, use a minimum of two network cards.

- Configure the network in a manner that is consistent among a cluster's different ESXi servers.

Applications in a Virtualized Environment

Within companies, we find applications with varying levels of criticality. Some servers—such as database servers—are critical because they contain information essential to the company's business needs. Databases are often part of a multitier application. They are the reference in managing work processes, notably in SAP environments.

For a long time, virtualization was used for test, development, and receipt servers within the environment. Today, the adoption curve shows the generalization of virtualization for all types of servers and application loads. Because vSphere 5 VMs support up to 32 vCPUs, 1 TB of memory, 1,000,000 IOPS, and 36 Gbps for the network, they easily meet the performance requirements of the very vast majority of applications—more than 95% according to VMware. There is no longer any obstacle to migrating to a virtualized environment for critical applications, as the vast majority of applications can be virtualized without any problem.

Some applications, however, have very precise requirements that must be taken into account so these can be integrated into a virtualized environment in the best possible way.

Oracle and SQL Databases

- CPU virtualization adds only a small amount of overhead. At the host level, enable hyper-threading

- Memory set reservations to avoid memory overcommitment. Size the memory suggested by DBA Administrator. Refer to the manufacturers' recommendations for the number of vCPUs and memory within the VM.

- Network: Use the VMXNET3 paravirtualized NIC. VMXNET3 is optimized for virtual environments and designed to provide high performance

- Storage: Create dedicated datastores to service database workloads. Enable jumbo frames for IP-based storage using iSCSI and NFS, align VMFS properly, use Paravirtualized SCSI adapters for Oracle data files with demanding workloads. Applications requiring high levels of performance can be put onto dedicated datastores with dedicated logical unit numbers (LUNs) and can keep certain basic rules, such as not mixing types of I/O disks.

- For databases that generate random read type I/O, use RAID 5 or 5/0 for databases with a read/write ratio (R/W) of 70%R/30%W.

- Log files will follow a sequential write profile, use RAID 1 or 1/0 for logs. It is preferable to work with disks in Raw Device Mapping (RDM) mode,but VMDK disks can be also used.

NOTE

When I/O are mixed, disk heads move too much and latency develops, which hinders performance.

Refer to the manufacturers' recommendations for the number of vCPUs in the VM and for memory. Consideration must be given to the fact that several types of VMs can be mixed within the environment. Therefore, it is crucial to implement QoS for some critical VMs, notably for databases.

Are Oracle Databases Supported in vSphere 5?

For a long time, the support of Oracle databases in virtualized environments was very confusing and subject to interpretation. Officially, Oracle databases are supported (by Oracle) in VMs only as of the 11G version (precisely 11.2.0.2). Any previous version is officially not supported.

For earlier versions, however, when an incident is reported to Oracle support and the problem is known to Oracle, technical support will provide an appropriate solution. If the problem is not known to Oracle, technical support reserves the right to ask to replicate the problem on physical hardware to prove it is not related to the virtualization layer. In practice, only a few cases require replication in a physical environment.

Oracle Licensing in VMware

Attention must be paid to the licensing mode of Oracle databases in a virtualized environment; licensing is based on all processors on which VMs can function. In an ESXi cluster, the VM can potentially function on any cluster server, which means a license is required for all processors in the cluster.

EXAMPLE

In the case of an ESXi cluster with three nodes and two CPUs per node, Oracle licenses will be required for six CPUs. However to decrease Oracle licensing costs, administrators can use a host affinity earlier in this chapter) to isolate the vMotion domain of Oracle workloads and only license the host server on which that workload has an "affinity" to be run on.

To find out more about licensing, see the following article: http://bartsjerps.wordpress.com/2011/11/09/oracle-vmware-licensing-cost-savings.

Exchange

With Exchange 2010, a VM with 32 vCPUs greatly exceeds the highest configuration levels required by Microsoft; for a simple role, 12 CPUs are required, and for multiple roles, 24 CPUs are required.

For Exchange 2007, for instance, it is possible to create several VMs (configured with 12 GB and 2 vCPUs), each supporting 2000 users. This means a physical server can have up to 16,000 mailboxes (8 VMs, each supporting up to 2000 mailboxes). In a physical environment, a single physical server does not support more than 8000 mailboxes. Increasing a server's capacity cannot be leveraged to increase the number of mailboxes within the same server.

SAP

Because SAP applications use a great deal of memory, VMware recommends not using memory overcommitment. To force this, a reservation must be made for the VM using the same value as the memory configured in the VM. The memory must be sized based on the memory actually used.

A sizing tool is available at http://service.sap.com/sizing. This allows the determination of Server Agent Plugin Synchronization (SAPS) prerequisites. The sizing model is the same whether the environment is physical or virtual.

Some other considerations for SAP applications:

- The configuration of VMs in several vCPUs enables the use of the multithreading features of applications if they offer such support (which is usually the case). This leads to an increase in performance.

- Regarding storage, it is possible to mix RDM and vmdk disks in a SAP environment and to prefer one LUN mapping for each VM, to avoid I/O contentions.

- Using the vmxnet driver in VMs is recommended for improved performance.

- The SAP Central Services component is a good choice for protection using the vSphere FT functionality in a VM with one vCPU.

Active Directory

Active Directory (AD) works very well in a VM. An important point to consider, however, is the synchronization with the time clock. All Active Directory activities (for example, changing passwords, replication services, and so on) depend on the time at which these operations must occur. Kerberos is at the heart of any Active Directory authentication request. It demands the AD client clock be synchronized through the time synchronization service. The implementation of Kerberos tolerates a maximum discrepancy of five minutes.

This dependency on time can cause issues in a VM. When a VM is functioning, it requires CPU cycles, and time heartbeats are provided to the VM. If a VM has no activity, however, it solicits no CPU cycles from the host server. The host server provides none, and the VM lags behind the time (because time heartbeats are not sent to the VM by the physical host). A phenomenon called *timekeeping* occurs, and the VM experiences a time discrepancy.

Two methods can be used to solve this issue:

- Using Windows Time services
- Using VMware Tools

To find out more, refer to VMware's Knowledge Base: KB 1318 and KB 1006427.

The following best practices are recommended with AD:

- Do not pause AD VMs.
- Do not take snapshots of AD VMs because this can cause corruption and hinder performance.
- Use vSphere HA; because it has priority over all other VMs in the infrastructure, it has to be set to high priority.
- Configure the VM with one vCPU with a vmxnet3 virtual network card.
- Keep the PDC emulator as a physical server.

Microsoft Cluster Service in a vSphere 5 Environment

Microsoft Cluster Service (MSCS) clustering services can be preserved between two VMs within the virtualized environment. Note, however, that MSCS functions only with disks using the RDMp mode (*storage-area network Fibre Channel [SAN FC]* or iSCSI, but not *Network File System [NFS]*). Snapshots and clones cannot be used due to the use of RDMp disks.

Can MSCS be replaced by vSphere HA? In theory, no, because granularity is different. MSCS monitors an application and restarts it if it functions in HS, while vSphere HA monitors physical ESXi servers and reboots VMs in cases where the server is down (even if it is possible to also detect a crashed OS or application in some cases).

Some companies, however, have abandoned MSCS because the implementation of clustering makes the full use of it cumbersome. (For example, scripts must be developed, each OS update must be tested.) Moreover, MSCS requires the protected application to be *cluster aware*, and only a few applications are, whereas vSphere HA works for any type of VM (legacy application). Note that with both vSphere HA and MSCS, in the case of a failure, the application will experience an outage but will start back up automatically.

Some companies prefer implementing vSphere HA. It does not provide the same detection granularity, but it is easier to manage on a day-to-day basis.

> **NOTE**
>
> Some companies consider that if the OS becomes corrupted, vSphere HA is no longer useful. This is true, but restoring a VM can be done much faster than rebuilding a physical machine. If a company considers this restoration time as excessive, implementing MSCS clustering is recommended.

Transforming the Datacenter

Virtualization has transformed the datacenter, allowing unprecedented flexibility in x86 computing. Memory over commitment allows more VMs to run on a host, and vSphere offers technologies like ballooning to help maximize the ability to overcommit memory. The ability to manage VMs in an enhanced way goes beyond memory, and also is available for CPU and network resources. vSphere provides for more than just enhanced management, and can improve the availability of VMs by allowing them to move between physical ESXi hosts. This allows for in-service hardware upgrades and the ability to manage performance by distributing VMs. With multiple options for network switching, it is important to work closely with your organizations network experts to make the right choices.

With so many capabilities, almost any application can be run in a vSphere 5 VM. Microsoft SQL, Oracle, Exchange, SAP, and Active Directory are commonly deployed in virtual machines, and with the right planning, can perform even better than their physical counterparts.

Chapter 5

High Availability and Disaster Recovery Plan

Application availability is essential for the proper functioning of a company's IT system. Implementing a secure hardware architecture that leverages the advanced features of vSphere 5 helps to reach high levels of service and rapid business recovery if disaster strikes the production site.

General Comments

Following this introductory section, this chapter is divided into two main parts. The first discusses local high availability within the datacenter. The second part discusses the disaster recovery plan and business continuity when a production site no longer functions following a major event. This chapter describes advanced features (such as vSphere HA [High Availability], vSphere FT [Fault Tolerance], and SRM5 [Site Recovery Manager 5]) and how they interact with the infrastructure's components.

Recovery Point Objective/Recovery Time Objective

In the area of data protection, the key factors are the *recovery point objective (RPO)* and the *recovery time objective (RTO)*, which determine the various possible solutions and choices for post-failure recovery.

RPO corresponds to the maximum quantity of data that can be acceptably lost when a breakdown occurs. Daily backup is the technique generally used for a 24-hour RPO. For an RPO of a few hours, snapshots and asynchronous replication are used. An RPO of 0 involves setting up a synchronous replication mode and corresponds to a request for "no data loss."

RTO corresponds to the maximum acceptable duration of the interruption. The time required to restart applications and put them back into service determines the RTO. Tapes located at a protected remote site can be used for a 48-hour RTO. For a 24-hour RTO, restoration can be performed from tapes at a local site. For an RTO of four hours or less, several complementary techniques must be implemented—for example, clustering, replication, VMware HA-specific techniques, FT, SRM, and storage virtualization.

Virtualization simplifies some processes that allow reduced RTOs. RTO depends on the techniques implemented and strongly hinges on the restart of applications and application consistency when the production site comes to a grinding halt. If application consistency is not guaranteed, RTO varies and is difficult to predict.

Of course, every company wants solutions that ensure no data loss and the restart of production as quickly as possible when a problem occurs. Yet it is no secret: The lower the RPO and RTO times, the more costly the solutions are to implement. This is why it is crucial to involve managers and executives to determine the desired RTO and RPO based on business needs and constraints.

Another consideration is *business impact analysis (BIA)*, which quantifies the actual value of data for the company. Often, investments are made to protect the wrong data (which may be important for the administrator but not necessarily for the company), and crucial data is insufficiently protected. A collective decision by stakeholders will determine the level of risk taken based on the solutions chosen.

The *service-level agreement (SLA)* is a contract that specifies service levels. It is a formal and binding agreement concluded between a service provider and its client. When such an agreement is entered into, RTO and RPO factors come into play.

Information Availability

The information system is essential to company operations. It allows users to be productive and have efficient means of communication (for example, mailbox, collaborative tools, and social networks) at their disposal. The information system provides the business applications that enable business activities. The unavailability—even partial unavailability—of a service can lead to significant, even unrecoverable, income loss for a company.

STATISTIC

According to the *National Archives and Records Administration (NARA)*, 93% of companies losing their datacenter for 10 days or more following a major breakdown have gone bankrupt during the following year.

To protect the company, it is crucial to implement measures that reduce service interruptions and allow the return to a functioning system in the event of a major incident on the production site.

As shown in Figure 5.1, the greatest portion of periods of unavailability (79%) comes from planned maintenance for backup operations, hardware addition, migration, and data extraction. These are predictable but can, nevertheless, cause service unavailability. Other types of unavailability relate to unpredictable events that cannot be anticipated and whose consequences can be dramatic if reliable measures and procedures are not implemented.

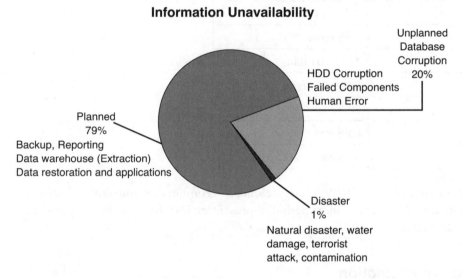

Figure 5.1 Predictable and unpredictable causes of system unavailability.

Data availability is calculated as follows: $IA = MTBF / (MTBF + MTTR)$.

- **IA:** Information availability.

- **MTBF:** Mean time between failure, the average time before a system or component experiences failure.

- **MTTR:** Mean time to repair, the average time required to repair an out-of-service component. (MTTR includes the time spent detecting the bad component, planning a technician's intervention, diagnosing the component, obtaining a spare component, and repairing the system before putting it back into production.)

Information availability is measured as a percentage, and it answers business needs for a set period. The greater the number of nines in the decimal percentage value, the higher the availability. In general, high availability starts at 99.999%.

Table 5.1 shows the relation between the availability (in the number of nines) and the unavailability period it represents per year.

Table 5.1 Unavailability Durations Based on Availability Percentages

Availability	Unavailability Per Year
98%	7.3 days
99%	3.65 days
99.8%	17 hrs 31 min
99.9%	8 hrs 45 min
99.99%	52.5 min
99.999%	5.25 min
99.9999%	31.5 sec

A system with an availability of 99.999% represents a maximum downtime of 5.25 minutes annually. Note that this is a very short period, representing less than the time required to reboot a physical server!

Infrastructure Protection

Protection of the information system (see Figure 5.2) can be put into two categories: *local availability* on a site, and defined *business continuity* processes that follow when a major incident occurs on the production site.

To sustain local high availability, you can use the following to prevent service interruptions when a component breaks down:

- Hardware redundancy to eliminate a *single point of failure (SPOF)*
- Clustering systems to return applications to productivity in case of a server failure
- Data securing through backup to prevent data loss, or replication mechanisms to compensate for the loss of a storage bay
- Snapshots, used to quickly return to a healthy state if an application becomes corrupt

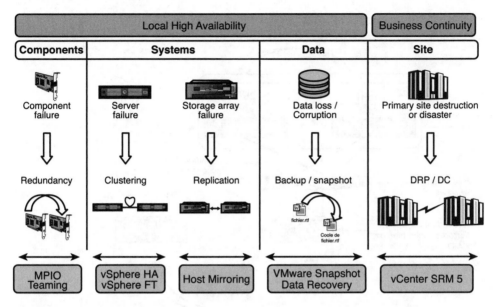

Figure 5.2 Infrastructure components.

For business continuity, a *disaster recovery plan (DRP)* can be implemented to quickly return a production site to a functioning state when a major event occurs. By having in place a DRP, a *business continuity plan (BCP)*, and an IT contingency plan on a backup site, you can handle such events when they occur within the production datacenter.

Local Availability

This section describes strategies and processes that can support local availability protection.

SPOF Removal

A SPOF can render the information system unavailable if it breaks down. Infrastructure virtualization leads to consolidation on a reduced number of pieces of equipment. Because this hardware hosts a large number of *virtual machines (VMs)*, it becomes highly critical. One piece of hardware failing could cause the interruption of several VMs, which can have dire consequences for the information system. Hardware redundancy can help prevent such an eventuality. To reduce service interruptions in a virtualized environment, a best practice is to make all hardware redundant, as in the example shown in Figure 5.3.

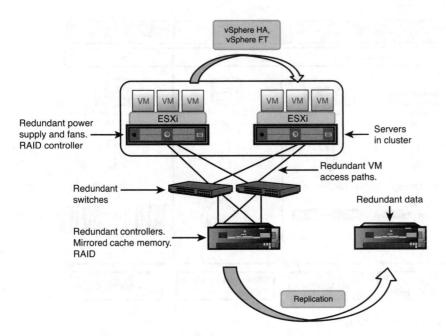

Figure 5.3 Hardware redundancy model.

Important considerations when planning for hardware redundancy include the following:

- Hard drives are the most important components to protect because they contain data and are frequently accessed. To make up for hard drive breakdowns, RAID technologies must be used.

- Power supplies and fans are susceptible to overheat and break down. Redundant power supplies and fans compensate for these problems.

- Although not common practice, memory can be secured with mirroring techniques.

- Network cards can be secured by using the IEEE 802.3ad protocol to aggregate links.

Because the processor and motherboard contain no mechanical parts, they are less likely to malfunction. Nevertheless, these are critical components that can be secured through hardware solutions such as NEC's Fault Tolerant or Stratus Server Systems, whose architecture makes the motherboard redundant. To get around breakdowns, software solutions can be implemented, such as clustering (Microsoft MSCS/WSFC) or using vSphere FT or vSphere HA to offer high availability.

In a well-designed *storage-area network (SAN)* architecture, all components are made redundant: *host bus adapter (HBA)* cards, *Fibre Channel (FC)* physical switches, and storage array controllers. Access to data can be secured by implementing redundant access paths, using a process called *multipathing* or *multipath I/O (MPIO)* that is native in vSphere and allows an automatic switch when a connection breaks down.

Within the storage array, some array manufacturers provide mirrored cache memory, redundant controllers, and multiple disk access paths within the array.

High Availability

High availability is defined by a set of mechanisms that ensure the local service continuity of one or more vital applications within a company. With virtualization, thanks to vSphere's advanced features, it is much easier to provide a 99.000%-level continuity of service than in a physical environment.

What Is a Cluster?

Basically, a cluster is a group of resources connected to one another to form a single logical entity.

The goal is to provide one of the following:

- High availability through technologies such as IBM PowerHA for IBM AIX, HP Serviceguard for HP UX, Veritas Cluster Server, SUN Cluster, Microsoft MSCS, and Oracle RAC

- Calculation (called *high-performance computing*)

A cluster in vSphere is a grouping of several ESXi servers (up to 32 ESXi hosts and 3000 VMs per cluster) with shared resources, allowing high availability and workload distribution through features such as vSphere HA, *Distributed Resource Scheduler (DRS)*, or FT.

vSphere 5 also introduces the concept of a *datastore cluster*, a grouping of datastores (up to 32 datastores and 9000 virtual disks per datastore cluster), allowing the use of Storage DRS to distribute the VM workload based on their I/O activity and available space.

TIP

Within a cluster, best practice is to make the ESXi uniform with regard to hardware (for example, identical configuration of processors, memory) and software (for example, identical versions, same level of patches). This simplifies daily management and allows the use of advanced features such as vMotion and FT in an optimal fashion. If servers are not totally identical, ensure that the cluster's processors are of the same generation. After using Update Manager, verify that all updates were performed on all cluster members.

> **RECOMMENDATION**
>
> A cluster can contain a maximum of 32 ESXi host servers. In our experience, it is best to place eight ESXi hosts to a cluster. Using more than eight hosts makes management more complex (for example, maintaining compatibilities or updating hardware). Using fewer than eight hosts provides less flexibility and fewer possibilities with regard to workload distribution and availability.

vSphere HA

When an ESXi host server breaks down, the VMs protected by vSphere HA (High Availability) are automatically restarted (15 or 18 seconds after detection on the cluster's other ESXi servers). All servers that are part of an HA cluster must have access to the same shared storage space. Service interruption and application unavailability are reduced because the restart occurs automatically without intervention from an administrator.

> **NOTE**
>
> If this unavailability period is too long, it is possible to reduce unavailability to 0 by using vSphere FT (Fault Tolerance).

vSphere HA Components

vSphere HA was completely rewritten for vSphere 5 and many improvements were made to refine the distinction between a host server's actual breakdown and a simple network problem. HA no longer depends on *Domain Name System (DNS)* servers, and it works directly with IP addresses.

There are three essential components of vSphere HA:

- The *Fault Domain Manager (FDM)* replaces the former Legato *Automated Availability Manager (AAM)*. This agent's role is to communicate with the cluster's other host servers about the server's available resources and the state of VMs. It is responsible for heartbeat mechanisms, the placement of VMs, and the restart of VMs in relation to the hostd agent.

- The hostd agent is installed on the host server. The FDM communicates directly with hostd and vCenter. For HA to function properly, this agent is required. If the agent does not function, the FDM puts all HA functions on hold and waits for the agent to be operational again.

- vCenter Server is in charge of the deployment and configuration of FDM agents on the cluster's ESXi hosts. vCenter provides the configuration modification information within the cluster to the server elected master (for example, when adding a host to the cluster).

NOTE

If vCenter is unavailable, vSphere HA is autonomous and ensures the restart of VMs. Without vCenter, however, it is not possible to modify the cluster's configuration.

NOTE

There are no agents to install within the VM's guest OS to make vSphere HA function.

Master and Slaves

When creating a vSphere HA cluster, the FDM agent is deployed on each of the cluster's ESXi servers. One server is elected *master* of the cluster, and the rest are *slaves*. The master's role is to monitor the state of hosts forming the cluster and detect incidents. The master holds the list of VMs protected by HA. It is responsible for placing the VMs within the cluster and restarting them if a host server breaks down. It also verifies that the VMs are actually restarted, and it exchanges information directly with vCenter.

If the master host server fails or is restarted, another master is elected. The election of a master occurs upon the first activation of vSphere HA in a cluster, and a new election occurs when the master:

- Fails

- Is isolated from the network or partitioned

- Is disconnected from vCenter

- Is put into maintenance or standby mode

- Has a reconfigured HA agent

The choice of a new master is made based on which server has the largest number of connected datastores, and, in the case of a tie, which server has the highest managed object ID.

The slaves keep their VMs' state up-to-date and inform the master of changes. Slaves also monitor the master's health by sending heartbeats, and they take part in electing a new master when the current one fails. If a master fails, the slaves are responsible for restarting the master's VMs.

NOTE

In vSphere 4, an HA cluster worked with five primary hosts; all others were secondary. This created important limitations when blade servers were used. Indeed, in a case where the five primary nodes resided on the same chassis, losing a chassis made HA nonfunctional because no primary node was available and no VM restart was possible.

Another limitation of the five primary hosts occurred when using HA in a stretched cluster between two datacenters. Because there was a maximum of five primary hosts and one did not know where they were elected, a maximum of four ESXi per datacenter had to be used to ensure that at least one primary host was available on the other datacenter to restart VMs. Therefore, the cluster was limited to eight hosts. With the master/slave concept, this limit vanishes; if the master fails, another master is elected, no matter where it is located.

Heartbeat

As shown in Figure 5.4, the HA cluster's FDM agents communicate with one another through a private exchange called a *heartbeat*.

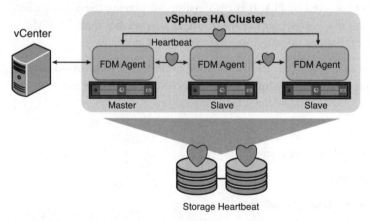

Figure 5.4 FDM agents communicating via heartbeats.

The term *heartbeat* refers to a mechanism that can determine whether a server is still functioning. Each slave server sends a heartbeat to the master server; the master also sends a heartbeat to each slave server. This occurs every second. When the master server no longer receives a heartbeat from a slave, it means there is a network communication breakdown, not necessarily that the slave server has failed. To verify whether the slave server is still functioning, the master checks its "health status" using two methods:

- It sends a ping *Internet Control Message Protocol (ICMP)* to the slave server's management IP address.

- It performs an exchange at the datastore level (called *datastore heartbeat*), as illustrated in Figure 5.5.

The second communication channel leads to a distinction between a slave that is isolated on the network and one that has completely crashed.

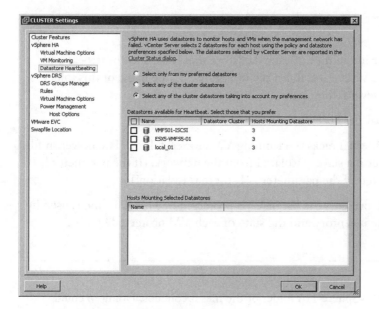

Figure 5.5 Datastore heartbeat options.

The datastore heartbeat works by using the metadata of the VMFS volume, called the *heartbeat region*, which is updated regularly. To allow the regular update of this region, a host needs an open file in the volume. Therefore, as shown in Figure 5.6, HA creates a specific file with the following format: host-number host-hb.

Each host has a dedicated file on the datastore. On NFS volumes, each host writes in the *host-xxx-hb* file every five seconds. To validate the operation, the master verifies this file is available.

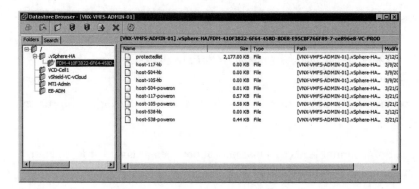

Figure 5.6 vSphere HA heartbeat files.

vSphere HA creates a folder in the root of each datastore that is used for heartbeat and the consistency of protected VMs. As you can see in Figure 5.7, the name of this folder is .vSphere-HA, and in it are several files:

- **host-*xxx*-hb files:** For the heartbeat datastore.

- **host-*xxx*-poweron files:** Tracks the running VMs for each host. The poweron file also informs the master if a slave is isolated from the network. (If the parameter is 0, it means it is not isolated; if the parameter is 1, there is isolation.)

- **protectedlist file:** Represents the list of VMs protected by HA. This file is used by the master to store the inventory and the state of each VM protected by HA.

TIP

Do not delete or modify the .vSphere-HA folder or the files it contains. Doing so could make HA unusable.

Different States

When the master can no longer communicate directly with the FDM agent of a slave server but the heartbeat datastore answers, the server is still functioning. In this case, the slave host is considered isolated, or partitioned, from the network.

A server is declared isolated if it no longer receives the master's heartbeat and the master cannot ping the management address. A scenario in which several hosts in a cluster are isolated but can communicate among themselves through the management network is called a *network partition*. When this happens, a second host is elected master within the same partitioned network. There can be several segments, each partition having a master.

For example, there can be three partitions with three different masters. When communication is reestablished, one master remains and the rest become slaves again.

When a host is isolated, HA forces the VMs to stop based on the defined parameter—Power Off or Shut Down (if VMware Tools is installed)—and initiates the reboot of the VMs on the cluster's other host servers. This behavior can be modified, and the VMs can be kept running, by selecting Leave Powered On (option shown in Figure 5.7). This allows the VMs to continue functioning.

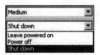

Figure 5.7 HA Cluster Isolation Responses.

RECOMMENDATION

In an IP storage architecture (iSCSI or NFS), it is preferable not to use the Leave Powered On option. A phenomenon known as *split brain* can occur, meaning a VM can be started simultaneously on two hosts, which can trigger corruption. In vSphere 5, however, this risk is reduced because HA automatically stops the original VM when a split-brain situation is detected.

If no communication is established between the master and a slave (heartbeat network and heartbeat datastore), the latter is declared as having failed. The HA mechanism triggers the restart of VMs on another host server.

If the slave server is the one that has failed, the sequence is as follows:

1. T0: The master no longer receives a heartbeat from the slave.

2. After 3 seconds, the master sends a heartbeat datastore for 15 seconds.

3. After 10 seconds, if there is no answer from the heartbeat network and datastore, the host is declared unreachable. The master pings the slave server's management server for 5 seconds.

There are two possible scenarios:

- If the heartbeat datastore is not configured, the host is declared dead after 15 seconds, and reboot of the VMs is initiated according to defined parameters.

- If the heartbeat datastore is configured, the host is declared dead after 18 seconds, and reboot of the VMs is initiated according to defined parameters.

If the master fails, the sequence is different because a new master must be elected before reboot of the VMs can be initiated:

1. T0: Slaves no longer receive the master's heartbeat.

2. After 10 seconds, the election of a new master is initiated by the slaves.

3. After 25 seconds, the new master is elected. (The choice is based on which host has the largest number of datastores.) It reads the *protectedlist* file containing all VMs protected by HA.

4. After 35 seconds, the new master initiates the reboot of all VMs on the protectedlist file that are not running.

Restart Priority

When the HA mechanism is triggered, vSphere HA follows a specified order to restart VMs. VMs are rebooted based on the VM restart priority, shown in Figure 5.8. Possible values are High, Medium (default), Low, and Disabled.

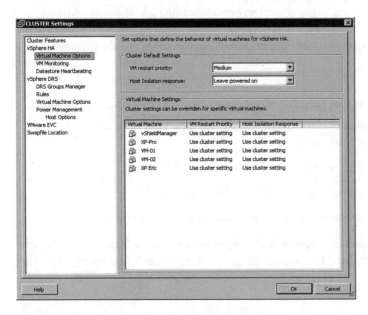

Figure 5.8 Selecting VM restart priority levels.

The reboot order is very important because some services must be restarted before others. A domain controller, for example, must be booted first. VMware recommends setting the restart priority to High for VMs providing the most important services.

NOTE

vSphere HA will not issue more than 32 concurrent power-on tasks on a given host. If a host fails, which contained 33 virtual machines and all of these had the same restart priority, only 32 power on attempts would be initiated. Regardless of success or failure of the power-on tasks, once one is complete, vSphere HA will then issue the power-on to the 33rd virtual machine.

VMs with a High value have boot priority over the others. If a VM is disabled, it is not rebooted when the host fails. If the number of host failures exceeds the admission control specification, VMs with a Low priority setup might not be able to restart because they do not have the necessary resources.

VM and Application Monitoring

The VM Monitoring settings (see Figure 5.9) determine whether a VM is nonfunctional by using a heartbeat exchange between the host server and the VM's VMware Tools feature. This exchange is performed every 30 seconds. If the exchange does not occur, the VM is restarted.

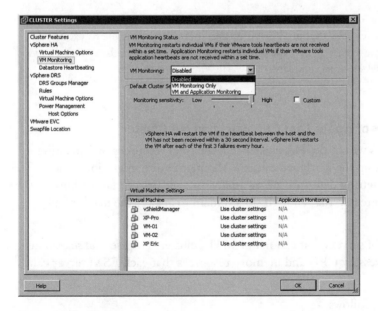

Figure 5.9 VM Monitoring settings.

NOTE

When an application crashes in the VM or a VM's network card is deactivated, the VM is not rebooted because the heartbeat exchange is internal and does not detect this type of incident. However, if the guest OS crashes, VM monitoring detects it, and the VM is restarted.

To detect the crash of an application on a guest OS, vSphere 5 provides an application-recognition API (a new module of vSphere HA). It allows the development of monitoring solutions for the health of an application and to have HA reboot the VM if necessary. It is possible for a VM to function but for the running application to be nonfunctional. Selecting VM and Application Monitoring in the CLUSTER Settings dialog enables VMs to reboot if the heartbeat for the application is not received.

Neverfail (vAppHA) and Symantec (Application HA) use this API. This provides a simple solution to increase service levels for critical applications by favorably replacing clustering solutions that are cumbersome to manage on a day-to-day basis. This also allows the management of applications that are not cluster aware.

NOTE

To monitor and reboot applications that are cluster aware, it is always possible to use Microsoft *Microsoft Cluster Server (MSCS)*-type clustering within the VM. (Using *Raw Device Mapping physical [RDMp]* disks is a prerequisite.)

Determining the Number of Hosts That Can Fail in an HA Cluster

When one or several servers within the HA cluster fail, the total resources of remaining servers must be able to pick up the workload of the VMs that require migration. The Current Failover Capacity setting determines how many host servers can fail within the HA cluster while guaranteeing that enough slots remain to answer the needs of all functioning VMs.

To determine the number of servers that can fail in an HA cluster, HA uses *slot sizes*. The slot size determines the necessary CPU and memory resources that each ESXi server can receive.

The slot size is calculated as follows:

- For the CPU, it is the highest value of VM reservation that is part of the cluster. (If there is no reservation, this value is set to 32 MHz by default, but this can be modified in the advanced settings das.vmCpuMinMHz file.)

NOTE

In vSphere 4, the default value for slot size was 256 MHz.

- For memory, it is the highest reservation value of the VMs functioning in the cluster. (If there is no reservation, this value is set to the highest memory overhead of VMs.)

When the slot size is determined, HA determines the number of available slot sizes on each server. The maximum number of slots is equal to the number of resources on the host server divided by the CPU and memory slot size. The lowest value is kept. (See the example shown in Figure 5.10.)

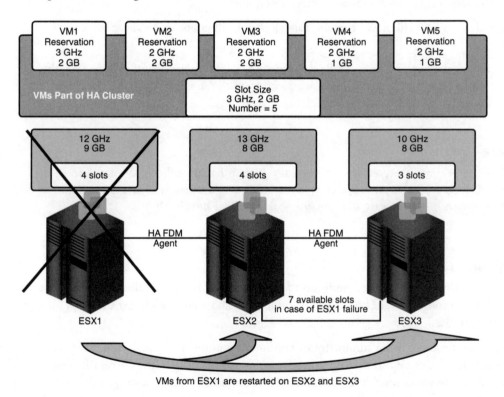

Figure 5.10 Slot size example.

EXAMPLE

As shown in Figure 5.11, five VMs are running (corresponding to five necessary slots in the cluster). The highest reservation value for the CPU is 3 GHz and 2 GB for memory. Slot size is thus 3 GHz and 2 GB.

The number of available slot sizes for the ESX3 server is as follows:

CPU = 10 GHz / 3 GHz = 3

Memory = 8 GB / 2 GB = 4

Therefore, the number of available slots for ESX3 = 3.

If ESX1 fails, ESX2 and ESX3 can manage seven slots.

If ESX1 and ESX3 fail, ESX2 contains four slots and will not be able to handle the workload.

In this case, the cluster's current failover capacity is 1. This means that if a server fails, the two remaining servers can take on the workload from all running VMs in the HA cluster.

NOTE

A VM might contain a reservation value that is higher than the other VMs. This can alter the slot size calculation. A maximum value can be set for the processor and memory in advanced options settings for das.slotCpuInMHz and das.slotMemInMB.

Admission Control

When creating an HA cluster, configuring the number of tolerated failures among host servers is recommended. (The maximum value of the host failures cluster tolerates setting can be 31 nodes.)

There is no problem if the administrator configures a number less than or equal to the current failover capacity. If the configured number is greater than the current failover capacity, admission control intervenes and either authorizes or forbids certain actions based on the defined parameter.

When admission control is activated, VMs cannot be powered on if they violate availability constraints. To ensure that all VMs have enough resources to reboot, actions to start a VM, migrate a VM to a host server, or increase the CPU or memory reservation of a VM are prohibited.

When admission control is deactivated, VMs can be powered on even if they violate availability constraints.

New VMs can be started even if the total of slots available prevents dealing with all the VMs to be migrated. In this case, VMs boot in the cluster's available slots based on the VM restart priority. The risk is that some VMs may not find an available slot.

EXAMPLE

This example refers back to the previous example:

Three ESXi servers each with available slots.

Five VMs run in the HA cluster.

Current failover is one.

If admission control is activated, it is possible to start a maximum of two extra VMs (seven slots available) while guaranteeing the load of all VMs. If the VMs' admission control is deactivated, it is possible to start more than two, but in this case nothing guarantees that all VMs will have enough slots available within the cluster to be able to boot.

NOTE

vSphere HA goes into alert mode if the number of VMs (slots, to be precise) exceeds the value of the Current Capacity Failover setting. If admission control is deactivated, vSphere HA goes into normal mode.

Best Practices

The following are recommended best practices when using vSphere HA:

- Using HA lowers consolidation rates because resources must be reserved. Therefore, HA should be used only for truly critical applications.

- VMware recommends not using vSphere HA in clusters where Storage vMotion or Storage DRS is used intensively.

- To increase the strength of vSphere HA, putting several physical network cards (a minimum of two) for the management network on separate physical network switches is recommended.

vSphere Fault Tolerance

vSphere *Fault Tolerance (FT)* is a level above vSphere HA. It offers very high availability while protecting VMs from a host server failure. This means that even if a server suddenly stops, there is no service interruption, no data loss, and no loss of connectivity.

FT hardware solutions are made by manufacturers such as NEC and Stratus. These companies offer servers in which all components are redundant (even the motherboard and processors). A chipset built in to these servers uses the lockstep principle, enabling primary and secondary modules to run the same set of instructions simultaneously on both independent motherboards. This ensures service continuity even if a component fails. These servers are used for very critical applications that must never stop. vSphere FT adapts this very high availability technology to virtual environments. FT functions only with shared storage, and requires a specific network configuration.

How vSphere FT Works

vSphere FT makes a carbon copy of a given VM. As shown in Figure 5.11, everything that occurs in this VM, called the *primary VM*, is mirrored in a VM called the *secondary VM*.

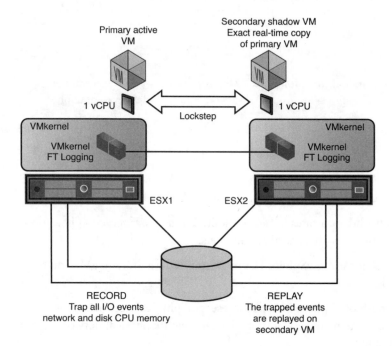

Figure 5.11 How fault tolerance works.

vSphere FT uses the vLockstep Record/Replay technology, which captures all events from the active primary VM—CPU instruction sets, memory state, I/O—and sends them to a passive secondary VM on another host server. This technology records executed tasks and restores them.

If the primary host server fails, the secondary VM that holds the same instruction sets as the primary VM can take over activities in a fully transparent manner without service interruption or data loss.

All information and logs are sent and received through VMkernel's dedicated port for FT: VMkernel FT Logging (vmklogger).

What You Need to Know About vSphere FT

To make use of FT, guest operating systems are standard; there is no kernel modification to make and no special patch to install. FT is activated at the VM level. An FT VM and its copy cannot run on the same host server. FT uses anti-affinity rules to guarantee that the two VMs (primary and secondary) will never be on the same host. This is to prevent losing both VMs at once if an ESXi server fails.

The major constraint at this point is that FT is limited to VMs with a single vCPU. However, there is a lot of critical applications where 1 vCPU is sufficient. Let's take some examples of use cases for vSphere FT:

- Small to medium instances of SQL Server or Exchange

- Web and File servers

- Manufacturing and Custom Applications

- SAP ECC 6.0 System based on SAP NetWeaver 7.0 platforms.

- BlackBerry Enterprise Server: 1 vCPU BES can support 200 users, 100-200 emails/day

Furthermore, this technology is resource intensive; the VM's capacity is consumed twice (on the source ESXi and on the target ESXi machine hosting the second VM). A high-performance dedicated network is required. If several VMs are used, a 10-GB network is recommended, which is still pricey. If the target ESXi machine suffers from contention and its performance is deteriorated, this will have an impact on the performance of the source VM, which will also slow down. The latency between the two processors must be monitored. To avoid deteriorating the performance of production VMs, factors such as the distance between the two servers, bandwidth, and activity must be taken into account.

Another constraint related to this functionality is that FT cannot currently be used with VMs that have snapshots. This limitation means backups cannot be performed by using the *vStorage APIs for Data Protection (VADP)* (such as VMware Data Recovery and similar software) because they use VM snapshots in their backup processes. (See the section on VADP backups in Chapter 6, "Backups in vSphere 5.") To back up an FT VM, FT must first be disabled, then the backup must be made, and then FT must be reenabled when the backup process is completed.

Note that vSphere FT can be used with vSphere DRS when vMotion's improved compatibility (EVC) function is activated.

Following are additional factors to keep in mind when using vSphere FT:

- Processors must be compatible with one another to support FT and the guest OS. (To find out which processors and guest OS support VMware FT, see VMware's Knowledge Base: KB 1008027.)

- A minimum of two gigabit network cards is required (10GbE cards are recommended): one for FT Logging and one for vMotion.

- All ESXi host servers must have the same patch and version levels.

- The mode of virtual disks must be set to Thick Eager Zeroed or RDMv (virtual compatibility only).

- Using Storage vMotion is not possible. If the virtual disk needs to be migrated, the FT functionality must be stopped, the disk migrated, and FT reactivated.

- Using FT on a VM with linked clones is not possible.

- To ensure redundancy and maximum Fault Tolerance protection, VMware recommends that you have a minimum of three hosts in the cluster. In a failover situation, this provides a host that can accommodate the new Secondary VM that is created.

Business Continuity

Business continuity (BC) is a set of processes and activities allowing the preparation and implementation of procedures to guarantee the availability of information when events occur. The *disaster recovery plan (DRP)* and IT contingency plan also come into play.

The BC aims at ensuring the company's survival after a disaster affecting the IT system. Its goal is to restart the business as quickly as possible (ideally without service interruptions), with minimal data loss.

In case of a major crisis or a large-scale crisis affecting an IT center, the DRP ensures that the infrastructure is rebuilt and that the applications supporting a company's operations are restarted. With a DRP, no infrastructure is shared with the target platform, thus preserving complete independence. The site is usually located more than 30 miles (50 km) away from the production site. Users have guidelines and access to a backup site where they can work if the main site no longer exists or is no longer accessible. Communication is switched to the backup site by redirecting routing or public addresses to the backup site, which takes over production.

The IT contingency plan is similar to a DRP but allows only local recovery on the same LAN. In general, electrical infrastructure, communication lines, and user offices are shared within the campus hosting the source and target platforms.

> **NOTE**
>
> A DRP includes all elements allowing the rebuilding of an infrastructure in case of a major event at the production site. A BCP offers a lower RTO than a DRP, but at a higher cost.

> **NOTE**
>
> In VMware's terminology, a DRP involves notions of replication with separate ESXi clusters, vCenter, and SRM. This is the technique most often used in VMware. A BCP involves considerations of high availability between sites. It requires an architecture with an extended SAN offering low latency, associated with storage virtualization techniques.

Failover Causes

The most common causes of failovers triggering a DRP are water damage (for example, from air conditioning or piping), electrical problems (such as a malfunction that sends a surge through equipment), natural disasters (such as floods, fires, or earthquakes), or acts of sabotage/terrorism.

DRP Issues in Physical Environments

Business restart or continuity often involves the interweaving of complex needs and processes. In a purely physical environment, this is extremely expensive and complex to manage. First, the source architecture must be re-created on a backup site, which makes management complex because production-platform updates also require the update of target platforms, creating a significant work overload for IT teams.

The procedures that allow the switch to the backup site must then be rigorously tested and validated. For example, documentation can be misinterpreted by the person who must trigger the recovery plan, or the person who initially drafted the plan may no longer be with the company or may be absent on the day the recovery plan must be applied.

Therefore, it is necessary to test switching to the backup site several times each year. This allows teams to train and validate the procedures to guarantee data integrity.

In physical environments, these architectures are usually reserved to very large enterprises with significant financial means, whose application criticality justifies such investments.

vSphere 5 Leverage for the DRP

Because VMs are abstracted from the underlying hardware, the BCP and DRP are simplified. Costs are lowered because creating an identical backup site is not necessary. Thanks to the encapsulation of VMs within files and to replication mechanisms, updating a system on the production site automatically updates the system on the backup site. In a virtualized environment, the DRP can be tested by using VMware *Site Recovery Manager (SRM)*, a scheduler for restart procedures. This reduces errors and improper manipulations. The restart is sequentially orchestrated with priorities based on the criticality or vitality of applications within the company.

STATISTIC

According to a recent market research survey, 63% of companies that have switched to virtualization set up a DRP.

A sophisticated DRP is no longer practical only for large corporations but is available to all types of companies. For many clients, the main reason to switch to a virtualized environment is that it is possible to easily set up a DRP.

Replication

Replication is the act of creating an exact copy (or reproduction) of production data on a backup site (local or remote). Replication can be used to secure a storage array, but it is primarily used for business recovery plans. Replicated data must be recoverable, and business can be restarted when data is consistent at the application level. This allows the restart of operations from the replicated data (called replicas). Ensuring consistency is the first issue that should be considered regarding replication technologies.

The time required to restart applications on the backup site (RTO) depends on this applicative consistency. If it is not guaranteed, it will be necessary to verify the integrity of bases or to use backups, increasing the RTO.

When it comes to replication, key factors are latency and write modification rates.

Replication Solutions

The following techniques allow the replication of data at different levels:

- **Operating system:** This type, called host based, uses replication software such as Double-Take, Neverfail, or Legato. The disadvantage of this technique is the overhead it causes in the OS and the fact that the recovery is crash consistent. Although the mechanism performs well, it is asynchronous. It doubles effort of administrating the operating systems because source and destination machines are active. Replication tool versions must be updated as the OS evolves. The advantage of this type of solution is its relatively low cost.

- **Application recovery:** This technique is based on the manufacturer's replication mechanisms. For example, Microsoft SQL (SQL Mirroring, Log shipping, SQL Server AlwaysOn), Microsoft Exchange [*Local Continuous Replication (LCR)*, *Standby Continuous Replication (SCR)*, and so on], Lotus Domino (Domino Clustering), and Oracle (DataGuard) have replication mechanisms that ensure the consistency of data. There are several types of RPO within the same application (synchronous or asynchronous). The advantage of this type of replication is that it guarantees the consistency of replicated data. Its disadvantage is that expertise is required: Each application uses a different replication mechanism and requires that administrators use several tools.

> **NOTE**
> Some replicated databases occasionally require the application communicating with the database to be coded to understand and support application failover.

- **Low-level (hardware) replication:** This technique, often the best performing and most robust, is generally provided by the storage arrays themselves. Other solutions are based on appliances, hardware cards installed in servers, or physical switches (I/O split). The advantage of hardware replication is having a single tool to manage replications in a heterogeneous environment. There is no OS or application compatibility issue because replication is performed at the data-block level within storage arrays. When using this type of replication, application consistency must be monitored. Here are the main solutions currently available:

  - **EMC:** *Symmetrix Remote Data Facility (SRDF)*, MirrorView, RecoverPoint, VPLEX

  - **HDS**: TrueCopy Synchronous Remote Replication, Universal Storage Platform VM

  - **IBM:** TotalStorage, *Peer to Peer Remote Copy (PPRC)* Global Mirror, and Metro Mirror

- **HP:** StorageWorks Replication Manager, 3PAR Remote Copy

- **NetApp:** SnapMirror and MetroCluster

- **FalconStor:** Continuous data protector

The replication technique typically used in vSphere is storage array replication. In vSphere 5, however, a new feature associated with SRM5 allows replication at the ESXi host level. It is called *host-based replication (HBR)* and brings replication granularity at the VM level rather than for an entire *logical unit number (LUN)*.

Synchronous Versus Asynchronous Replication

As illustrated in Figure 5.12, there are two types of replication: *synchronous* replication (offering an RPO of 0) and *asynchronous* replication (offering an RPO of a few minutes).

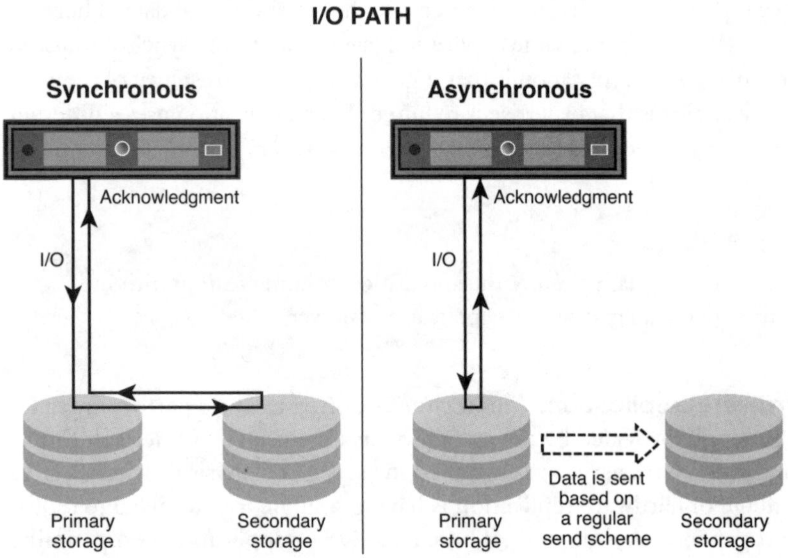

Figure 5.12 Synchronous versus asynchronous replication.

Synchronous replication ensures that each data write from a source array gets written on a target array. When an I/O is sent to the production (primary) array, the I/O is automatically sent to the target array. Host-level acknowledgment is performed only after the I/O is written on the secondary array. Using this mechanism, the data is always identical, and no data loss occurs. If an event occurs on the primary site, the secondary array has data identical to that of the primary array.

The synchronous replication mechanism has a consequence. The time required for the I/O to perform its task (sending the I/O until acknowledgment is received) is called *latency*, or *round-trip time (RTT)*. This latency must be low (usually between 4 ms and 6 ms), or production applications will suffer performance deterioration. This is why the distance between sites to be replicated is limited. (In theory, the maximum is 125 miles [about 200 km], but in practice this distance does not usually go beyond a few dozen miles.)

> **NOTE**
>
> One factor that can cause significant latency is the bandwidth between the sites (pipes). Latency is lower when there are fewer pieces of equipment, so one way to improve this is to use array-to-array connections rather than switches.

Asynchronous replication offers a quicker acknowledgment because it occurs when the I/O is written on the source array. This removes the need to wait for the I/O to return from the secondary site, so there is no latency issue and therefore no distance limitation. Data is stored locally on the source array (in a buffer space that should be planned for) and then sent to the secondary array at regular intervals of a few minutes to a few hours. RPO is not 0, but rather a few minutes to several hours.

To properly define the type of replication that should be used, it is necessary to know the write application load or modification rate, as illustrated in Figure 5.13.

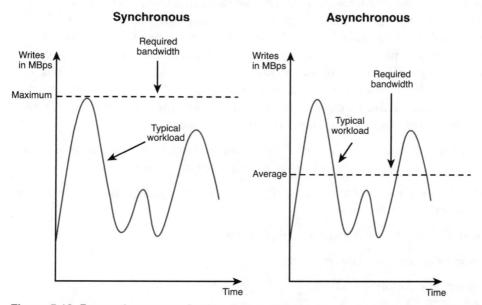

Figure 5.13 For synchronous replication, the bandwidth between the two sites must be at least superior to the peak of the application load to avoid performance problems. If the bandwidth is lower than the peak, asynchronous replication must be used.

Replication can be performed through SAN FC or SAN IP. Some clients use SAN FC for production and iSCSI over a 10-Gigabit network for remote-location replication.

Remember that the object of replication is the reproduction of the primary site's data. It does not protect against deletion errors that corrupt data because the error is propagated to the secondary site. (The replica represents only the last image of the replicated data.) In such a case, it is necessary to resort to snapshots or backups to return to a healthy state.

There are other mechanisms that offer *continuous data protection (CDP)*. This type of solution is very interesting—not only is the data replicated, but a write log is put into place. Through this logging, it is possible to return to any point in the past, which protects the system against bay failure and also protects against data corruption or loss within the bay.

Site Recovery Manager 5

VMware *Site Recovery Manager (SRM)* is a solution that automates business recovery in a vSphere environment and is part of a DRP. This software is sold separately from vSphere 5 licenses but is perfectly integrated into vCenter because it is provided as a plug-in. SRM5 is a task scheduler. It automates business recovery on the remote site (failover) and backtracking (failback). With SRM, the order in which VMs are restarted can be defined, and the IP addresses of VMs can be changed if there is a network switch between the source site and the backup site. It enables administrators to test the DRP without any service interruption, by using isolated networks (testing VLANs or bubble networks). It provides precise reports on run time and also details the performance of each elementary task by indicating its success or failure. In turn, this allows technical teams to analyze these results and validate the switching procedure. SRM is also used for planned maintenance operations (for example, if the production datacenter's power supply is interrupted) to migrate production from one datacenter to another.

SRM also allows the monitoring of datastores that are replicated, and it produces an alert if a VM is placed into a datastore without being scheduled in the recovery plan.

The two available editions, Standard (up to 75 VMs) and Enterprise (unlimited number of VMs), provide the following features:

- vSphere replication or storage array replication
- Testing without service interruption
- Failover automation
- Failback automation (new in SRM5)
- Planned migration

Architecture

Figure 5.14 shows typical SRM5 architecture with storage array level replication.

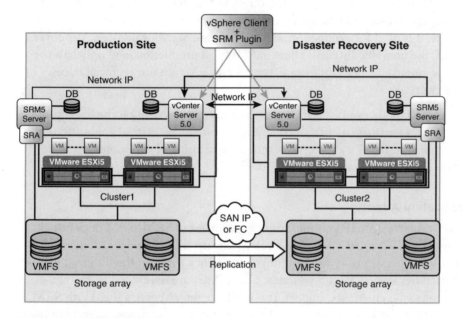

Figure 5.14 SRM5 architecture.

Use of SRM5 requires the following:

- Two vSphere clusters—one vSphere production cluster administered by a vCenter and one backup cluster administered by another vCenter. The two vCenters are interconnected. Peering consists of linking the two vCenters using the SRM plug-in. This allows the vCenters to monitor each other with regard to the availability of resources and the physical availability of datacenters. It also allows SRM instances to communicate with the vCenter that serves as the other's backup and, thus, manipulate objects such as VMs and inventory resources.

- Two SRM5 servers connected to a database on each site.

- Two storage arrays—one primary for production and one backup array on which data is replicated. Storage arrays must be validated in the VMware compatibility matrix with *Storage Replication Adapters (SRAs)*. These arrays must also be compatible to replicate one another. They must both be equipped with additional snapshot licenses (used for testing) and replication licenses when these products are not provided.

- One intersite link with a data replication solution between the two storage arrays.

The Different Modes

SRM5 can work in *active/passive* or in *active/active* mode. The active/active architecture allows half the VMs to run on one site and the other half to run on the other site. Each site is the other's backup. This should be the mode of preference because it reduces the cost of the backup site; it is used for production, not only in case of major disaster. Moreover, if disaster strikes, the unavailability will affect only 50% of production, and only half the VMs will need be restarted—perhaps even fewer if some VMs are not required in cases of deteriorated recovery.

Recovery in degraded mode can be used to limit hardware investment on the backup site. Indeed, for its DRP, IT management can choose to invest only in critical applications vital to its core business. In such a case, VMs should be prioritized and some should be excluded from the recovery plan.

Storage Replication Adapter

Storage Replication Adapter (SRA) is an important component of SRM. SRM does not manage storage array LUNs. SRA serves as a relay between SRM and operations related to storage bay LUN operations. It also monitors consistency between the different datastores if a VM straddles several VMFS volumes. SRA is software developed by storage array manufacturers who ensure its support. It is available on VMware's site. With SRM, SRA controls the array for LUN (failover/failback) snapshot, clone, fracture, and promote operations.

SRAs from various manufacturers can be used in the same SRM server.

> **NOTE**
>
> All arrays from a given manufacturer are not necessarily validated as integrating with SRM5. Check with the manufacturer.

Failover

As shown in Figure 5.15, in the new recovery plan interface, it is possible to choose between Planned Migration and Disaster Recovery.

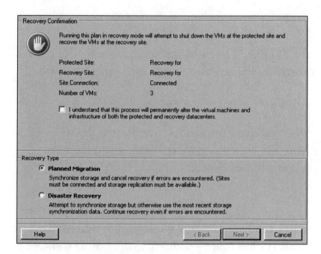

Figure 5.15 Recovery type options.

When a failover (called running the recovery) is initialized, sequencing is as follows:

1. SRM5 stops the first site's VMs (if the primary array can still be reached). Indeed, it is possible for the disaster to have a partial effect, and running VMs require a "clean" stop.

2. Mirror inversion occurs if the primary array exists (if it is not destroyed).

3. SRM contacts SRA to stop replication (called *fracture*) between the primary array's LUNs and the backup array's LUNs.

4. SRM5 makes the secondary site's LUNs available for the secondary site's host servers (performing a promote of the replica on the remote site's server). LUNs from the backup site become primary.

5. The backup site's ESXi servers' HBA cards perform a rescan to discover the LUNs.

6. SRM enters the protected VMs in vCenter's inventory. It remaps vmx with the proper resource at the vCenter level.

7. SRM initializes and automates the restart of VMs stored on replicated LUNs based on configurations. VMs are restarted one after the other. Two factors can trigger the restart of the next VM:

   - When the VM's VMware Tools feature is restarted, it lets SRM know and it starts the next VM.

   - If VMware Tools is not installed, SRM restarts the next VM when the time-out is exceeded (by default, 10 minutes).

> **TIP**
>
> It is worthwhile to validate the functioning of DNS. The SRM servers and vCenters of both sites must be able to resolve themselves correctly and be able to reach each other; otherwise, the SRM solution will not work.

There are two types of service levels: replicated datastores and nonreplicated datastores. Nonreplicated datastores are excluded from the business recovery plan; if production storage is destroyed, a VM restoration phase will be needed.

VM Startup Priority

With earlier versions of SRM, VMs were started based on being assigned to one of three priority groups: High, Medium, or Low. SRM5 has more granularity because, as shown in Figure 5.16, it offers five priority groups (Priority Group 1 to Priority Group 5). VMs part of Priority Group 1 start first, and all VMs from this group must start before those in Priority Group 2 begin to start. The process continues until all VMs from Priority Group 5 have started.

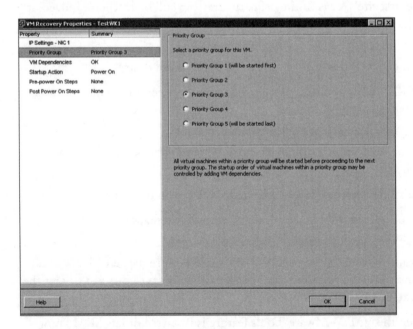

Figure 5.16 SRM5 priority group levels.

It is also possible to define dependencies between VMs within a priority group to ensure that some VMs are started before others. This dependence applies only between VMs of the same priority group.

Planned Migration

Planned migration is very useful when maintenance operations are planned (for example, a power-supply interruption of the datacenter). When this option is selected, all VMs are cleanly stopped (VMware Tools shuts down VM) to ensure application consistency. When stopped, VMs are synchronized one last time before the switch to the backup site.

Testing

The test mode allows a failover test of VMs to the backup site without affecting production. When the test mode is initialized, VMs are placed into an isolated network (test VLAN or bubble network) that does not exit the ESXi host. VMs cannot communicate from one ESXi host to another. If some applications need to communicate with one another, either they must be grouped or a test VLAN must be created that is completely isolated from the rest of the infrastructure.

When the test procedure starts, SRA orders the arrays to show snapshots of the mirrors running on the secondary site. This means production is protected and replication is maintained while tests are performed. At the end of the test, snapshots presented to the ESXi server are destroyed without the need to resynchronize the arrays.

Using these techniques to isolate the network and storage, tests can be triggered during business hours without having an impact on production.

vSphere Replication

SRM5 has a replication mechanism, *vSphere Replication (vSR)*, performed at server level (commonly called *host-based replication*). Replication granularity is performed at the VM level (virtual hardware 7 is the minimum). This allows the choice of which VM can be replicated instead of the entire datastore (as is the case with traditional storage bay replication). Former versions of SRM did not include a replication mechanism. This technique is a form of *Changed Block Tracking (CBT)* requiring an initial complete copy of the VMs. After it is made, only modified blocks (delta blocks) are sent to the target storage space. Up to 500 VMs can be replicated at once, and up to 1000 VMs can be protected in total. vSR authorizes replication between one type of datastore (choices are local disks, SAN FC, NFS, iSCSI, and vSA) and any other type of datastore (for example, a SAN FC datastore to an NFS).

vSR does not work in versions earlier than vSphere 5. This feature is available only with SRM. It is not integrated into vSphere 5 (see Figure 5.17) and cannot be acquired other than with SRM.

vSR's value proposition is to offer a replication solution completely independent from the underlying platform. Replicated VMs can be on datastores from heterogeneous bays (different brands and models) and are independent from the underlying storage protocol (as long as the protocol is in VMware's compatibility matrix). This allows the virtualization of replication, which opens up many possibilities and adds a great deal of administration flexibility.

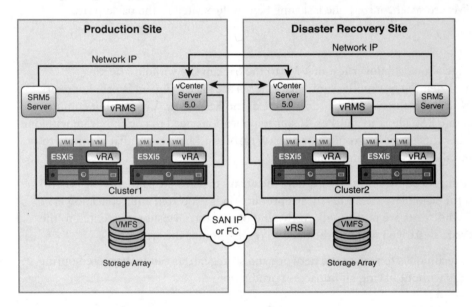

Figure 5.17 SRM architecture with vSphere Replication.

HBR modifies the architecture set up for replication. It requires the following:

- One virtual management appliance *vSphere Replication Management Server (vRMS)* per site (and per vCenter) containing the replication's configuration. A SQL Server, Oracle, or DB2 database is required. vRMS is recorded as a plug-in in vCenter, and it manages the deployment of vRA agents.

- Some *vSphere Replication Agents (vRAs)* in each ESXi host. vRA is responsible for monitoring the write I/O that modifies blocks in the vDisks marked as "protected," and it sends these modifications to the backup site.

- A *vSphere Replication Server (vRS)* on the backup site receiving the modifications from the protected site's vRAs.

NOTE

vRS is autonomous for replication. It continues to run even if vCenter Server, SRM, or vCenter fails.

This replication is limited in the initial version. It is not recommended when there is a need for high SLA demands; only the asynchronous mode is supported, with a minimum RPO of 15 minutes, up to 24 hours. Limitations make this solution suboptimal, and it is a hindrance in situations such as the following:

- There is server-level overhead. Again, the host must be fully dedicated to VMs and applications.

- It is not possible to replicate disks in physical RDM mode, and VM FT, linked clones, and storage DRS are not supported.

- Only running VMs are replicated. VMs that are stopped or suspended, ISO images, and templates cannot be replicated.

- This first version does not offer compression or encryption.

The low-level replication mechanism offered by the arrays offload the host servers from this intensive I/O task. Arrays integrate much more robust features and offer more possibilities, such as synchronous replication, synchronization of modified blocks only during a failback (the array compares the blocks), and compression and de-duplication techniques to reduce the bandwidth necessary between sites.

Array replication offers granularity at the LUN level and allows the creation of coherence groups for application consistency.

TIP

This replication solution can be adapted to small environments but not to enterprise-class environments. For large-scale environments, it is preferable to use storage array replication mechanisms to ensure future scalability.

Failback

Backtracking, called *failback*, is an operation performed after the destroyed primary site is restored. It allows the restoration of all VMs switched over during the DRP to their original locations. Failback is more complex than failover, so more steps are required to properly configure and execute it. Former versions of SRM did not offer failback, so third-party solutions had to be used (notably those offered by array manufacturers). The functionality is standard with this version of SRM.

SRM5 Interface

The interface was modified and improvements were made to simplify the visualization and identification of protected VMs (see Figure 5.18).

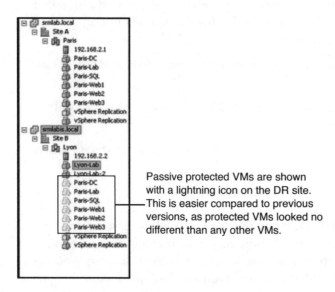

Passive protected VMs are shown with a lightning icon on the DR site. This is easier compared to previous versions, as protected VMs looked no different than any other VMs.

Figure 5.18 Easier visualization of protected VMs in the SRM5 interface.

At storage array level, as shown in Figure 5.19, the direction of replication can be seen.

Figure 5.19 Visualization of replication direction in SRM5.

Stretched Cluster

A *stretched cluster* allows the extension of a cluster onto two physically distinct sites, to provide high availability between two datacenters and to spread the workload between the two datacenters

Adding a distributed storage virtualization solution (for example, EMC VPLEX or NetApp Metro Cluster) is recommended, which offers more flexibility to administrators when compared to traditional replication solutions. Figure 5.20 shows the typical architecture.

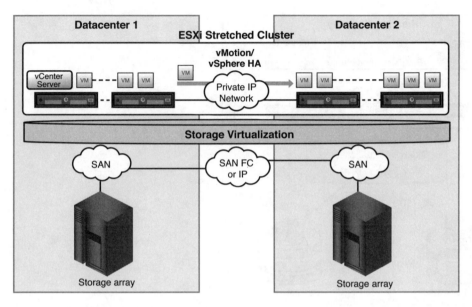

Figure 5.20 Stretched cluster architecture.

In this architecture, VMs can be migrated from one datacenter to another by using vMotion. Storage virtualization leads to a reduction of latency and allows the migration of a VM from one datacenter to another without any service interruption. Therefore, it is possible to be protected from service disruption during planned maintenance operations within a datacenter (called *disaster avoidance*)—for example, the electrical failure of a datacenter. When datacenters are located on several continents, production can also be displaced to be closer to users.

vSphere HA can also be used in the stretched cluster for protection against a complete crash of the production site, forcing VMs to restart on the backup site.

While running in production mode, as shown in Figure 5.21, VMs from Datacenter 1 run on the host servers of Datacenter 1. The storage virtualization solution shows virtual LUNs to the cluster's ESXi host servers. Each write is thus performed on each of the two storage arrays. Reads are performed from the storage array closest to the ESXi host server.

When vMotion is used, as shown in Figure 5.22, the VM is migrated to the secondary site through the private gigabit network. Therefore, components from the first datacenter can be stopped for maintenance operations.

Running Normally
Datacenter 1
Datacenter 2
ESXi stretched cluster
VM
Private IP network
Storage Virtualization
Virtual LUN
vmdk
vmdk
Storage array1
Storage array2

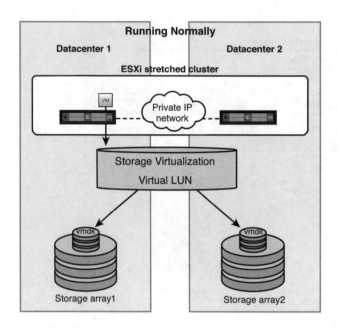

Figure 5.21 Stretched cluster under normal operational conditions.

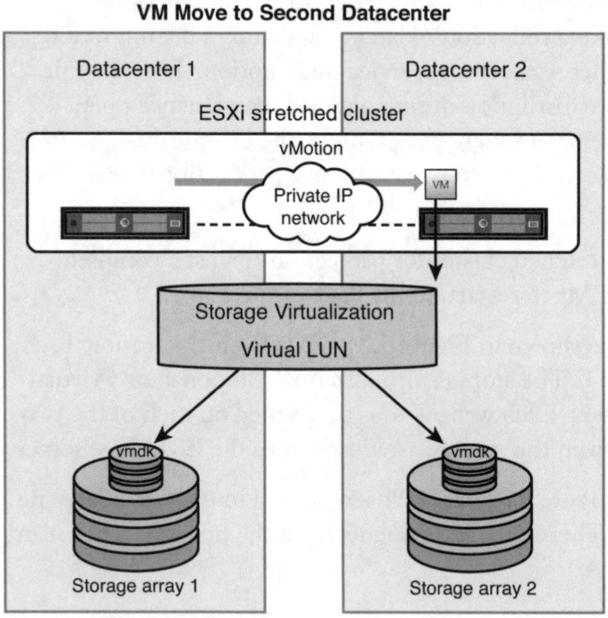

VM Move to Second Datacenter
Datacenter 1
Datacenter 2
ESXi stretched cluster
vMotion
VM
Private IP network
Storage Virtualization
Virtual LUN
vmdk
vmdk
Storage array 1
Storage array 2

Figure 5.22 Using vMotion to enable maintenance operations in a stretched cluster architecture.

NOTE

Without the virtualization layer, it is possible to perform a vMotion in a stretched cluster. In this case, the migrated VMs on the second site access their virtual disk located on the first site. For the VMs to be able to access their vmdk virtual disks on the second array, however, replication must be fractured, and LUNs have to be promoted to the second site's ESXi servers.

Long-Distance vMotion

vMotion is traditionally used within the same datacenter. In the case of a stretched cluster, long-distance vMotion has the following prerequisites:

- An IP network with a minimum bandwidth of 622 Mbps.

- For vMotion, a maximum latency of 5 ms between the vSphere 5 servers and 10 ms for Metro vMotion.

NOTE

vMotion is supported by VMware only if the latency between the source and destination of ESXi is less than 5 ms RTT. In vSphere 5, however, a new feature called Metro vMotion is available with the Enterprise Plus edition and supports a latency of 10 ms RTT.

- The source and destination must be on a private network with the same IP subnetwork and in the same broadcast domain.

- The IP subnetwork on which the VMs run must be accessible for source and destination ESXi servers. This is an important point because, to preserve their communication with external elements, the VMs keep the same IP configuration when they are migrated with vMotion.

NOTE

A stretched cluster is not a prerequisite for long-distance vMotion because vMotion can be performed between two distinct clusters. In this case, however, two separate vCenter Servers are required, causing the loss of the VMs' cluster properties (for example, HA restart priority and DRS settings).

vSphere HA in a Stretched Cluster

It is possible to run vSphere HA in a stretched cluster to enable the restart of VMs on the second datacenter if a major incident affects the first site. In this context, HA restarts the VMs based on the defined priorities. This does not, however, provide as much restart granularity as a classic SRM (such as changing the IP address or restarting according to a workflow).

Expect the Unexpected

For most companies, it is not a matter of if a disaster will strike, but when. vSphere provides many options to minimize the impact of an event, using the portability of the VM as the primary feature. vSphere HA allows for a VM to be restarted on a healthy ESXi host if the host fails. This is a great feature, but if you need to protect the whole datacenter, it's not going to work.

For the whole datacenter, you need to use VMware SRM5. Site Replication Manager provides a comprehensive management and scheduling solution. With SRM5, you can set the protected VMs to go in specific groups, as well as change the IP address to allow compatibility with the destination network. Like backups, the most important thing with high availability is to make sure that the DRP is properly tested. Any DRP that is not tested is not valid, so your organization must make sure that the infrastructure, network, application, and business teams work together to validate the plan. Focusing on both the organizational and technical aspects of your disaster recovery strategy is critical to ensure success.

Chapter 6

Backups in vSphere 5

Moving to a virtualized environment provides the opportunity to perform an in-depth review of backup architectures. Backup technologies and methodologies must be adapted to the virtual environment because of the unique and complex issues involved; a *virtual machine (VM)* is usually not backed up the same way a traditional server is. Successfully implementing backups reveals some of the benefits of virtualization and serves as a lever to reduce costs. The opposite is also true; improper backup implementation can have dire consequences for the entire information system.

Backups: An Overview

Before detailing the key backup issues that can occur in this environment, we define some basic concepts in this section.

What Is a Backup?

A *backup* is the exact (physical) copy of production data, created with the aim of restoring, at will, any data that becomes corrupt or destroyed. This backup copy can be created in different ways:

- By copying the data at given moments
- By replicating the data (The data is always identical to the original, even if the original data is modified.)

Backup Objectives

Backups have three main objectives:

- **Operational:** To restore data in case of accidental data deletion, loss, or corruption (for example, a virus attack)

- **Archival:** To preserve data (for example, e-mails and contracts) for regulatory and legal compliance reasons

- **Business recovery plan:** To restore data in case of major disaster

Business Impact

Always keep in mind that the most important aspect of backup is restoration! We often meet IT managers who have set up backup systems without being concerned about the way in which they will be able to restore the data. The following is a nonexhaustive list of important questions that can have a direct impact on business and should be answered:

- What is the *recovery point objective (RPO)*?

- What is the *recovery time objective (RTO)*?

- What type of data is backed up (for example, applications, OS, databases, messaging, flat files, log files, database logging files, file systems, or video)?

- What backup window is used?

- When and where are restorations performed? What restorations are most frequently requested?

- When an application is backed up, is the backup truly consistent?

- What retention policy should be implemented? How many daily, weekly, monthly, and annual backups should be kept?

- Should backups be sent off-site?

- What is the average daily rate of data modification to be backed up?

- Is the data encrypted or compressed?

Traditional Backup Method

A backup agent is the method traditionally used in a physical environment. It consists of installing an *application agent* whose goal is to make the application consistent before it is backed up so that it has an image that can be restored. At set moments, the agent sends data through the network to the server, which backs it up on the chosen media (such as tapes or hard drives).

> **NOTE**
>
> Historically, backups used magnetic tape, which had the advantage of storing very large volumes at a low cost and which could be stored at an external location at no operating cost. Using hard drives is possible by performing *tape emulation* (called a *virtual tape library* *[VTL]*). It provides more flexibility and quick access times without modifying the existing backup architecture.

In a traditional physical environment, you can use a backup agent because the server on which the application runs usually has available resources. (On average, only 10% of a server's resources are used, so resources are available for a backup agent.)

Although this method is effective, it generates a significant workload for IT teams. It requires deploying agents, updates, and maintenance. Agents consume a great deal of server resources (CPU, memory, network, and storage), and restoration is often laborious (often slower and performed in stages). It also requires managing media, which is subject to handling errors, forgetfulness, and so on.

Backup Issues in Virtual Environments

The following backup issues can occur in virtual environments and should be considered during implementation:

- Risk of contention
- File criticality
- Large volumes
- Increased service levels

The following subsections take a closer look at these issues.

Risk of Contention

One of the goals of virtualization is to attain high levels of consolidation to reduce costs. The available resources of host servers are entirely dedicated to applications. Backup agents make significant use and consumption of these resources. Therefore, the use of agents in a guest OS is not recommended because this can significantly affect performance and generate contentions.

In some cases, however, and for some applications (for example, database and messaging applications), it is necessary to install agents in the guest OS to improve the precision of settings and add granularity for restoration. With messaging agents, for example, it is possible to restore a single email message

File Criticality

The entire content of the virtual disk is represented by a main vmdk file containing the operating system, configuration, application, and data. This file becomes highly critical, and a handling error by an administrator—such as accidental deletion—can lead to disaster. This should be carefully considered, and solutions for rapid restoration should be proposed.

Large Volumes

In a virtual environment, it is possible to back up a VM's entire image. This image leads to very large volumes compared to the data traditionally backed up in a physical environment. Therefore, your deployed technology must be adapted to such volumes, and so should the time frames set for backup windows (usually eight hours at night).

Increased Service Levels

Setting up a virtual infrastructure must considerably improve service levels, and a *service-level agreement (SLA)* should be formally established. Backed-up data must be accessible directly and rapidly, and restoration should take only a few minutes.

In this context, it is understandable that traditional methods of backup (on tapes or VTL) are not optimal. Provisions must be made for high-performance technology to exploit the specific advantages of virtualization.

Backup Methods in Virtual Environments

This section reviews various historical and current backup methods in virtual computing.

Brief History of VMware Consolidated Backup

Because VMs are encapsulated in files, it is possible to back up a VM's entire image. VMware developed *VMware Consolidated Backup (VCB)* for this purpose in *VMware Infrastructure 3 (VI3)*, but that functionality has now been abandoned. VCB was not a piece of software but rather a process (called a framework) that prepared VMs to perform their backup operations. It eliminated network traffic because the backup server accessed the *storage-area network's (SAN) logical unit number (LUN)* directly to take this task off the load of the host server.

Although the solution seemed workable in theory, in practice VCB had several disadvantages. It required a large buffer storage space because vmdk files needed to be copied before being transferred to the backup server. In addition, the framework generated instabilities and required scripts that were cumbersome to develop and had a very limited scope of capabilities (for example, no de-duplication and no possibility of working in incremental mode, difficult file restoration steps, and so on).

To remove these limitations, starting with vSphere 4, VCB was replaced by *vStorage APIs for Data Protection (VADP)*.

Methods in vSphere 5

There are currently two methods of performing backups in vSphere 5, using the following tools:

- VADP
- An agent in the guest OS

Virtualization leverages backups because, using these methods, restoration can be performed at several levels: complete VM, one file in a VM, or backing up data within applications.

We will now examine how these methods work and when they should be used.

VADP

Through these APIs, it is possible to back up an image of the VM's file structure without using the backup agents of the guest OS. Backups are performed "hot" (without any service interruption), which increases the application level of service. Backup application manufacturers can, thus, develop solutions based on the VADP.

> **NOTE**
>
> Available software such as EMC Avamar, VMware Data Recovery, Veeam Backup, Quest vRanger Pro, and Symantec NetBackup natively integrate these APIs.

The advantage of the VStorage APIs is that they create a "mount point" of the VM to be backed up and make it available for a server without requiring buffer space (as VCB did). Backups are simplified, and developing and maintaining scripts is no longer necessary. As shown in Figure 6.1, this task can be migrated to a dedicated server (called a proxy server), leaving all resources available on the host server for VMs and applications.

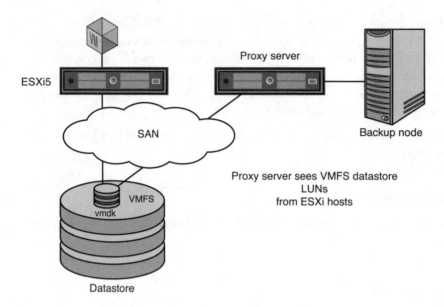

Figure 6.1 The proxy server must be able to access the datastore (LUN VMFS, NFS, and/or RDM) hosting the VMs. Backups are made through a LAN or SAN.

When VADP is used to back up a VM, the snapshot mechanism, discussed later in this chapter, comes into play. Backups made using VADP can guarantee application consistency in certain Windows environments thanks to *Volume Shadow Copy Service (VSS)*. Moreover, with Changed Block Tracking, backups and restorations occur very quickly. (See the section "Changed Block Tracking," later in this chapter.) This reduces the required network bandwidth because only modified blocks are sent to the backup server.

VADP can perform various levels of restoration. Some manufacturers take advantage of the APIs to offer restoration of the VM's complete image (Full VM) or of individual files in the guest OS (File Level Restore):

- **Full VM:** Allows the restoration of the VM as a whole, with all associated files. The advantage of this mode is that it provides a direct backup of the entire VM, including its OS and applications, and allows the restoration of the whole virtual machine. Careful attention must be paid to the volume of space used, which can become extremely large if techniques such as compression or de-duplication are not used.

- **File Level Restore:** Allows the restoration of folders and files within the guest OS without the need to restore the entire VM image. When file level restoration is initiated, the proxy server is shown the VM's volumes as mount points and it is possible to restore only the file needed. No local volume is required on the proxy server because it is a mount point.

NOTE

File level restoration is possible with only some backup software applications, not all. When creating the backup, some software creates the index required to restore the files later because they are incapable of mounting a backup. Consult individual manufacturers about features.

Some manufacturers offer the same possibility by coupling VADP with other APIs, such as the VIX APIs provided by VMware.

Backups with Agents

This traditional method is used mainly for VMs with database-type applications. These VMs are exceptions that need to keep agents within the virtual machine because the management of logs and databases is performed during backups. The agents also allow granular restoration and recordings, whereas with the Full VM mode, the entire virtual machine must be restored to find the missing data. For example, using agents makes good sense for exchange-type messaging servers, where restoring mail might take priority over restoring the entire database. Using agents also have the advantage of not requiring any change to the existing process. Organizations that have a well-developed, agent-based backup solution often continue to use them in VMs initially. Over time, they may gradually transition to a more optimal VADP-based solution.

Snapshots

This section provides an overview of snapshots and how they can be used in a virtualized environment.

Array Snapshots Versus vSphere Snapshots

First and foremost, it is important to distinguish between the snapshots provided by storage arrays (for example, SnapView from EMC and SnapVault from NetApp) and the snapshots used by vSphere. Their granularity is different: A snapshot from a storage array is done at the level of the entire LUN (VMFS volume containing several VMs), whereas a vSphere snapshot is done at the VM level.

A storage array snapshot uses pointers to determine which blocks have been modified since the last snapshot and when modifications are written and committed; a VM snapshot freezes the vmdk file and creates another file in which the modifications will be written.

> **NOTE**
>
> A snapshot is not a backup in a strict sense because the source data is not physically copied to another location. If the data is destroyed, it is impossible to restore it using only a snapshot.

Advantages of VM Snapshots

The snapshot is one of virtualization's main advantages, one that is very useful for administrators. A snapshot is taken when a VM is in a healthy state and before a significant modification. It allows the setup of a simple backtracking solution in case of a malfunction occurring after an application migration, installation of a new service pack or patch, and so on.

Snapshots are also initiated by vSphere 5 (GUI or script) when a backup software application uses them through the VADP.

How a Snapshot Works

A snapshot captures critical VM state information, such as the following, at a given moment:

- Disk state
- VM settings
- Memory state (can be deactivated)

When a snapshot is triggered, all activities on this VM are suspended. (Ideally, snapshots are taken when the VM is less active.) It is important to ensure that the application state is consistent before taking the snapshot. (See the section "Application Consistency," later in this chapter.)

As shown in Figure 6.2, at the moment the snapshot is created, the web.vmdk file is frozen and put into read-only mode. No more data will be written in this original file. All modifications will be written in the newly created file, named web0001-delta.vmdk. This file represents only the differences since the moment the snapshot was taken. It is important to ensure the application state is consistent before taking the snapshot.

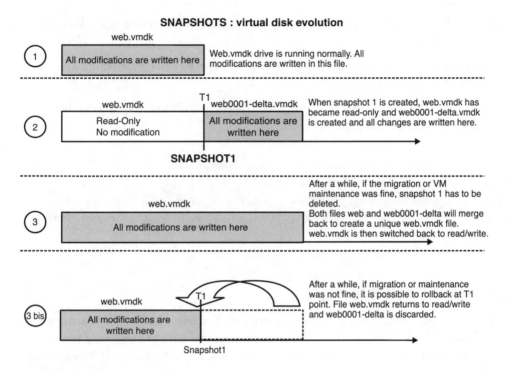

Figure 6.2 VM snapshot process.

Precautions with Snapshots

In a production environment, snapshots must be used for a defined period of time so that observations can be made and the system can be backtracked if something is not working. The advised snapshot duration should not exceed one or two days.

Keeping a vSphere snapshot over a long period is not recommended; the more data is modified, the larger the snapshot becomes. A snapshot that can grow without limit can occupy the entire datastore space and put all VMs in jeopardy (for example, because of crashes or corruption).

Current rules of thumb expect the average modification rate of a snapshot to be 20% of the VM's total volume in a 24-hour period.

REMINDER

vSphere snapshots do not work with Raw Device Mapping in physical compatibility mode (RDMp) disks.

Improper handling of snapshots can render the VM unusable. Therefore, the following points must be considered:

- A snapshot revert is destructive; all modifications, as well as *xxx*delta.vmdk files, are permanently destroyed.

- Never manually delete *xxx*delta.vmdk files in the VM's directory. Use Snapshot Manager in vCenter for these operations.

> **NOTE**
>
> It is important to understand the mechanics and use of snapshots, and it is strongly advised that a procedure be designed and adhered to. If in doubt, make backups before any handling.

Application Consistency

Ensuring application consistency is one of the main challenges to backup performance when applications with elevated I/O rates (for example, database and messaging applications) are running. In a shared storage environment, most I/O activity is performed in the cache memory of array controllers so as to benefit from high performance and reduced latency.

> **NOTE**
>
> The storage array cache component is essential for achieving high performance. Indeed, when a server I/O is written on an array, acknowledgment is sent when the I/O is in the cache, and the I/O is later written on the disk. This allows changing the write order on the disk to reduce the movement of reading heads. This lag in disk writing creates a risk of application integrity loss if data located in the cache is not written (flushed) on the disk.

To follow best practices, the consistency of applications must be guaranteed (as much as possible) before any intervention is made.

When operations such as backups, clones, or snapshots are performed, precautions must be taken to ensure a consistent application state. Sudden hardware crashes can also put applications at risk.

In vSphere, a snapshot (or a backup at the VM's image level) is crash-consistent, meaning it is equivalent to suddenly stopping a production VM before rebooting the server (called a *hard reboot*). Operating systems such as Windows Server (2003 or 2008) or Red Hat Linux easily support this type of occurrence, and the server can be rebooted without the need to reinstall everything. However, for applications, protecting against crash consistency is recommended, as is the use of techniques to ensure a file-system-consistent or application-consistent state.

> **NOTE**
>
> Data inconsistency does not necessarily mean the backup is unusable, but it does mean that during restoration, the use of log files (if present) will be required to put the application back into a coherent state (thereby increasing the RTO). Note that in some cases, corruption is such that restorations are rendered unusable.

> **TIP**
>
> To limit sudden hardware crashes and, thus, the risk of application inconsistency, using a backup battery (in storage arrays or to protect RAID cards) or uninterruptible power supply is strongly recommended to preserve the power to the equipment while the data is flushed (written) on disk.

The following subsections discuss methods that you can use to ensure application consistency.

Volume Shadow Copy Service

Microsoft provides Volume Shadow Copy Service. The goal of this Windows service is to create consistent (coherent) images at precise moments (consistent point-in-time copies, also called *shadow copies*). With this service, the application can be put into an application-consistent state, ensuring the application's integrity upon restoration.

To take advantage of this functionality, the application to be backed up must support VSS (for example, MS SQL Server, MS Exchange, or Active Directory); the guest OS must also support VSS. This service is perfectly adapted to vSphere through VMware Tools (for example, when using snapshots or making backups through the VMware APIs). VSS introduces mechanisms to ensure application consistency. When a request is sent from an application to the VSS receptor, the receptor quiesces the VM. All I/O activity is retained, and all existing data is synchronized. Caches are flushed on disk.

In vSphere 5, Windows 2003 and Windows 2008 Server ensure application consistency with the VSS component.

Earlier versions, such as Windows 2000, do not have VSS; they do not ensure application consistency. With these versions, using pre-freeze and post-thaw scripts, discussed in the next section of this chapter, are necessary.

> **NOTE**
>
> The snapshot *generates* a consistent crash state. With VSS, the VM is *in* an application-consistent state based on the application and the guest OS.

How does VSS work? VSS produces shadow copies by coordinating applications with the backup software and storage. Interaction with VSS is provided by VMware Tools, which run on the guest OS. VMware provides a VSS Requestor and a *VSS Snapshot Provider (VSP)*. When a backup process is launched, the requestor is initiated by VMware Tools. VSP is recorded like a Windows service. It notifies ESXi when the application is quiesced and that a snapshot of the VM can be taken.

There are various levels of consistency:

- Crash-consistent (equivalent to a hard reboot), which theoretically provides consistency at the following levels:

  - At the level of the guest OS (typically no impact for modern OS)

  - At the level of files. (There can be some alteration of files that would not have been written on disk [in cache memory at the time the snapshot is taken].)

  - At the level of applications (possible alteration of the application's integrity, usually a database)

- File-system-consistent, which theoretically provides consistency at the following levels:

  - At the level of the OS (no impact)

  - At the level of files (no impact; all data from the various caches is grouped and backed up onto the disk; no alteration at the file level)

  - At the level of applications (possible alteration of the application's integrity, usually a database)

- Application-consistent, which theoretically provides consistency at the following levels:

  - At the level of the OS (no impact)

- At the level of files (no impact; all data from the various caches are grouped and backed up onto the disk; no alteration at the file level)

- At the level of applications (no impact; all data is backed up and the application is properly shut down, ensuring its integrity)

Generally, it is best to assume that a crash-consistent solution is not consistent at all. With any reliance of the business on a snapshot, it is important to test the ability to recover from it often and comprehensively.

Pre-Freeze and Post-Thaw Scripts

Certain environments that cannot use VSS require scripts to stop services (using the pre-freeze script) and restart them (using the post-thaw script). The hypervisor receives this information through the host agent that transmits it to VMware Tools to trigger the pre-freeze script.

The pre-freeze script for Windows machines must be placed in one of the following folders:

C:\Program Files\VMware\VMware Tools\backupScripts.d

C:\Windows\backupScripts.d

For Linux machines, it must be in this directory:

```
/usr/sbin/pre-freeze-script
```

The pre-freeze script allows the shutdown of some services or the triggering of maintenance the administrator wants to perform in the VM before a VM snapshot is taken.

After this script is executed, a disk quiesce is requested. It allows the flushing of the cache disks' I/O to the VM disks to make files consistent. When the sync driver is done flushing the I/O to the VM's disks, a snapshot of the VM is launched. Disks to be backed up are frozen with consistent data, and modifications occurring within the VM during the backup will be temporarily stored in buffer snapshot files.

After the snapshots are taken, a post-thaw script is triggered (if it was put into place). For example, the script restarts the services stopped by the pre-freeze script. Backups can then start in a manner consistent with operational production.

In Windows, the scripts are located at:

C:\Program Files\VMware\VMware Tools\backupScripts.d

C:\Windows\backupScripts.d

In Linux, the scripts are located at:

```
/usr/sbin/post-thaw-script
```

Troubleshooting Virtual Environments

This section examines some tools and methods you can use to troubleshoot backup issues that can arise in virtual environments.

Changed Block Tracking

Previously, when an incremental or differential backup was made, ESXi would scan the entire VM volume to identify the modified blocks to back up. Starting with vSphere 4.1, the ESXi server was equipped with a map of all the blocks in the VM (see Figure 6.3). Each block bears a time stamp that indicates the location of the blocks modified since the last backup occurred. Scanning the entire snapshot is no longer required for identifying which blocks have been modified since the last backup. This technique makes incremental backup operations much faster (up to 10 times faster; see the graph shown in Figure 6.4), reducing the backup window. This *Changed Block Tracking (CBT)* functionality is deactivated by default because it consumes some resource time at the host server level.

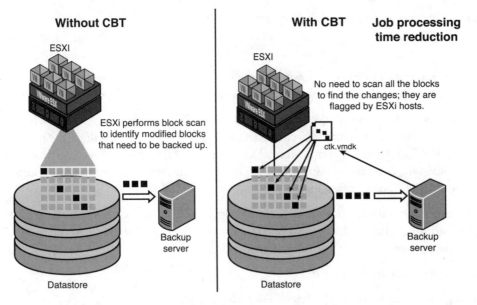

Figure 6.3 Backup process without CBT (left) and with CBT (right).

For VMs with virtual hardware version 7 or 8, this function lists the block changes made (since the last backup) in a -ctk.vmdk file found within each VM's folder for each virtual disk on which CBT is activated (taking up a few tens of MBs). Applications can send a request to the VMkernel to make it send back the blocks of a virtual disk that have been modified since the last backup.

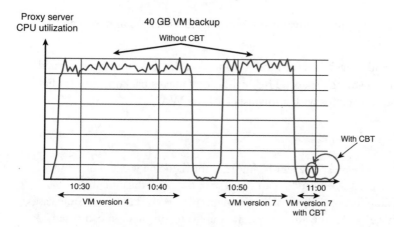

Figure 6.4 Resource utilization with and without CBT.

CBT is available in vmdk and RDMv (not available in RDMp). The following limitations must be noted:

- CBT exists for disks in thin and thick mode on all NFS, VMFS, and iSCSI datastores.
- It does not work if the virtual disk is connected to a shared virtual SCSI bus or VMs with snapshots.
- Activating CBT (ctkEnabled) is done in the VM's advanced settings (version 7 or 8 of virtual hardware only).
- Activation takes effect after the performance of a stun-unstun cycle in the VM. A stun-unstun cycle is triggered by vSphere when one of the following actions is performed:
  - Power on
  - Resume after suspend
  - Migrate
  - Create, delete, or revert a snapshot

> **NOTE**
>
> CBT stems from the vSphere 4 Storage VMotion technology (called *Dirty Block Tracking* or *DBT*) that uses this method to quickly determine which modified blocks must be transferred.

De-Duplication

To reduce the storage space required, advanced technologies such as *compression* and *de-duplication* must be used.

De-duplication copies the identical files (or blocks) found on the disk only once, considerably reducing the required storage space. This technology makes backups more reliable and allows the replication of backups with a low usage of the WAN.

> **NOTE**
>
> De-duplication is definitely the most efficient technology for reducing waste. For example, 300 MB of space might be used when sending an email with a 3-MB attachment to 100 recipients. With de-duplication, only 3 MB of storage space is consumed. In some cases, even less than 3 MB may be used if the attachment has duplicate information contained within it.

Because VMs are often created from a template, it is likely that a significant number of blocks on the disk will be identical. De-duplication makes it possible to significantly reduce the amount of storage space required by only storing redundant data once.

De-duplication at the source is performed at the beginning of the backup process, before the data is sent to the backup solution. Network bandwidth is preserved, which can be worthwhile in some environments, but care must be taken to not consume too many resources from the host server. Many products available on the market offer this technology: EMC Avamar, Symantec PureDisk, Atempo HyperStream, and CommVault are a few.

De-duplication at the target takes place at the level of the backup solution. This frees the source server from an additional workload, but it does not reduce the need for network bandwidth. The choice of technology must be made based on the constraints of the particular situation:

- In a traditional environment, with full incremental backups, the storage capacity growth required is in the order of 150% to 200% per week.

- In a virtual environment, efficiency is impressive; with de-duplication, the storage capacity growth required is only 2% to 7% of data per week.

> **NOTE**
>
> The technologies used by the various solutions available on the market differ. It is important to distinguish the de-duplication performed during backup jobs (during a backup, only nonidentical blocks are sent) from the de-duplication performed only within a VM. Consult manufacturers regarding how their solutions handle these scenarios.

LAN-Free Backups

On physical machines, backups usually go through network cards. But the quantity of data is always increasing, which make the backup windows expand. In most cases, production environments always require more availability, so the backup windows need to shrink.

Virtualization allows backups through SAN links, without going through the network (LAN-free backup), taking advantage of storage and network performance to decrease the duration of backups.

Another advantage of performing backups through the storage network is that, unlike a backup performed with an agent in a physical machine, there is no impact on the machine's processor use. This allows it to provide dedicated CPU power to the hosted application even during backups.

Network Data Management Protocol (NDMP) proxies offload the de-duplication activity to a dedicated server.

Backup Process Through VADP APIs

Figure 6.5 shows the various steps of the backup process used by VMware through the VADP APIs.

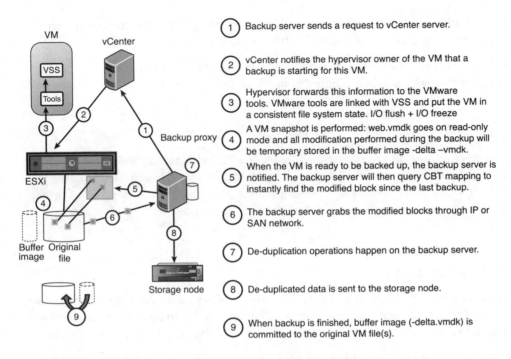

1 Backup server sends a request to vCenter server.

2 vCenter notifies the hypervisor owner of the VM that a backup is starting for this VM.

3 Hypervisor forwards this information to the VMware tools. VMware tools are linked with VSS and put the VM in a consistent file system state. I/O flush + I/O freeze

4 A VM snapshot is performed: web.vmdk goes on read-only mode and all modification performed during the backup will be temporary stored in the buffer image -delta –vmdk.

5 When the VM is ready to be backed up, the backup server is notified. The backup server will then query CBT mapping to instantly find the modified block since the last backup.

6 The backup server grabs the modified blocks through IP or SAN network.

7 De-duplication operations happen on the backup server.

8 De-duplicated data is sent to the storage node.

9 When backup is finished, buffer image (-delta.vmdk) is committed to the original VM file(s).

Figure 6.5 Backup process through VADP APIs.

Data Recovery 2.0

VMware Data Recovery (VDR) is a backup appliance based on CentOS 5.5 64-bit Linux. This tool integrates into vCenter Server as a plug-in. To make it usable, the plug-in must first be installed; then the appliance must be imported. The tool offers a basic backup solution to allow small-scale structures to secure their virtual infrastructure, but it is not suitable for large-scale production environments. VDR allows the use of de-duplication functionalities. It offers mechanisms for integrity control, reinventory (to ensure the de-duplication engine aligns the catalogue on the data actually available), and reclaim (allowing retrieval from the de-duplication store of data that should no longer be placed there because of retention policy rules).

Following are a few constraints to note with VDR:

- VDR can back up a maximum of 100 VMs per appliance, and each vCenter can have a maximum of 10 VDR appliances.

- De-duplication stores are limited to 500 GB on CIFS network shares and to 1 TB for vmdk or RDM format stores.

- NFS is supported as a de-duplication store only if it is introduced by an ESX/ESXi server and the VMDKs are assigned directly to the appliance.

To ensure application consistency in Windows, VDR uses the VSS mechanisms described earlier in this chapter, in the section "Volume Shadow Copy Service."

Backups Are Important, But Restores Are Critical

With so many options for backing up a VM, it's easy to forget that no one cares about backups, only restores matter! Whether using an agent in a VM, or a more modern solution using a VM optimized manner, it is important to test the restores frequently. Different solutions have varying degrees of consistency states, and each one has a place in a recovery strategy. Snapshots, in particular, can allow for quiescence at the OS level, the file level, or the application level.

Backups can use a lot of disk capacity, especially when they are used for archival. Some technologies, such as data de-duplication and compression, can help dramatically, and VMware has incorporated them into the product suite in the form of VADP. In many ways, recovery of a VM can be more complex, but also more comprehensive than recovery of a physical server. When planned well, however, an organization can recover a solution based on vSphere faster, more completely, and with fewer issues.

Chapter 7

Implementing vSphere 5

This chapter walks you through an implementation scenario for vSphere 5. After you size your architecture, you have a number of installation and configuration options to choose from. After reading this chapter, you should be able to determine which configuration works best for you.

Sizing

Before implementing the virtual infrastructure, it is necessary to size the architecture. A question that often arises concerns the sizing of the virtual infrastructure. Sizing requirements will vary depending on factors such as whether you have 50 *virtual machines (VMs)* or 1000 VMs, how heavy the workloads are, and the access type (random or sequential). However, no matter how precise we try to be, some assumptions are usually necessary. For example, you need to consider future (unknown) requirements, and it is important that you don't design something you cannot troubleshoot.

To help you get an idea about the sizing and the target architecture to create, Table 7.1 summarizes the guidance provided in the earlier chapters of this book to lay the foundations for your implementation plan.

Table 7.1 Implementation Size Architectural Options

	Best Practices	Maximum
Cluster		
Number	Between 4 and 8 hosts	32 hosts
DRS	DRS fully automated. Sensitivity: Moderate	
Server		
CPU	Dual processor / Quad processor	160 LCPU / host
	Between 2 and 4 vCPU per core for normal load. 1 vCPU per core for heavy loads	25 vCPU / core
		2048 vCPU / host
Memory	Between 4 and 8 GB per physical core	2 TB RAM / host
Network	Minimum 6 GbE network cards	32 GbE cards
		8 * 10GbE cards
Storage		
LUN VMFS 5	Between 600 GB and 1 TB	VMFS 5: 64 TB
		RDMp 64 TB
		RDMv 2 TB*
	Number of LUNs/hosts: 8	256 LUNs/hosts
		256 NFS mount/host
vmdk	Between 15 and 20 active vmdk concurrent/datastore	2048 vmdk/host
VM		
vCPU	1, 2, or 4 vCPUs/VMs depending on the VM's application	32 vCPU
vRAM	1, 2, 4, or 8 GB vRAMs/VMs depending on the VM's application	1 TB / VM
vmdk	OS: 40 GB	2 TB*
	Application: 100/200 GB. Don't exceed 800 GB. (If more disk is required, use RDM mode.)	

*2 TB minus 512 bytes

The Different Installation Modes

VMware offers several ways of installing ESXi:

- **Interactive installation:** For small-scale deployments with fewer than 10 servers, this installation uses the classic manual method. Insert the DVD, boot from it, and answer the questions when prompted to do so.

- **Scripted installation:** To automate installation, a script containing the ESXi's configuration is created and then placed into a location that the host server can access.

- **Installation through vSphere Auto Deploy ESXi:** This new method allows the loading of ESXi into memory (ESXi takes only 144 MB) without the need to physically install it onto hard drives. When Auto Deploy is activated, the server performs a *preboot execution environment (PXE)* boot by retrieving its configuration using Host Profiles. This mode is used for very large production environments to industrialize the quick commissioning of servers.

- **Customized installation using ESXi Image Builder CLI:** When using this tool for your installation, you can create preconfigured ESXi images (a kind of master related to the company's policy) with the latest updates or patches or with specific drivers.

> **NOTE**
>
> Some manufacturers offer to provide ESXi installed directly (ESXi embedded) onto specific cards (usually SD or USB cards) on some of their servers. In this case, the server boots directly onto the expansion card. This removes the need for local disks and reduces the time required for deployment.

Pre-Installation

The following sections outline the recommended pre-installation steps for deploying vSphere 5.

Checklist

Following is a checklist of the elements required for the installation of a virtual infrastructure:

- Latest update DVD of VMware ESXi 5 or ESXi 5, preconfigured using Image Builder CLI.

- vCenter Server CD (optional).

- License key of 25 characters. (The key can be installed after installation.) The product can be evaluated and used for a period of 60 days following the ESXi's start.

- One server listed in the VMware compatibility matrix with at least one connected network card.

- Network settings (IP address, subnetwork mask, hostname, gateway, DNS).

- One datastore with 5 GB available to install ESXi (except for Auto Deploy mode).

- Root password to be defined.

- Operating system installation CDs or ISO images to install the guest OS, with their associated licenses.

- Windows PC for remote connections.

Prerequisites

This section covers the hardware and software required to install vSphere 5.

For ESXi 5 Server

- **Server:** Before installing ESXi 5, the VMware *hardware compatibility list (HCL)* must be checked to verify the compatibility of the hardware and its internal components. You can find this at www.VMware.com/resources/compatibility/search.php. vSphere 5 allows the management of a very wide selection of hardware components, but confirming compatibility is indispensable to avoid unpleasant surprises during installation. If you are unsure about a component, consult the manufacturer.

- **Processor:** VMware ESXi 5 can be installed only on servers with 64-bit processors supporting LAHF and SAHF instructions.

  - For AMD processors, the revision must be revE or higher.

  - Intel processors must integrate *Virtualization Technology (VT)* instructions and be activated in the BIOS.

- **Memory:** Minimum of 2 GB RAM required, with a maximum of 2 TB per server.

- **Network:** Minimum of 1 connected network card and up to 32 physical GbE network cards (8 cards for 10 GbE) per ESXi server.

- **Storage:** One type of supported storage with 5 GB of space available for ESXi:

  - A maximum of 256 *logical unit numbers (LUNs)* per server and 256 NFS mount points

  - 64 TB for a VMFS5 LUN

- 2 TB in RDMv

- 64 TB in RDMp

- Block size: 1 MB in VMFS 5

Installing VMware ESXi on shared storage array is possible (commonly called boot from SAN [storage-area network]):

- Boot from FC (Fibre Channel) array or iSCSI hardware is supported.

- Boot from NFS (Network File System) and boot from iSCSI software are not supported.

TIP

It is preferable to install ESXi on the server's local disks rather than to use boot from SAN, which is more complex to manage and can be the source of handling errors. The hypervisor is now common and can be reinstalled very quickly. This method will not simplify the *disaster recovery plan (DRP)* (often the goal of boot from SAN). Another method discussed later in this chapter uses Auto Deploy.

For vCenter Server

- **Processor:** Two 64-bit CPUs or one dual-core 64-bit processor greater than 2 GHz

- **Memory:** 4 GB RAM

- **Disk space:** Minimum 4 GB

- **Network:** One network card (gigabit recommended)

- **Software requirements:**

    - Microsoft .NET 3.5 SP1 and Windows Installer 4.5. vCenter Server requires a database: IBM DB2 or Oracle or Microsoft SQL Server is supported.

    - A vCenter Server can manage up to 1000 hosts and 10,000 running VMs.

    - If there is no existing database, a SQL Server 2008 Express database is installed, but it limits the architecture to a maximum of 5 ESXi and 50 VMs. For a complete list of supported database versions, refer to the vSphere compatibility matrix.

    - Update Manager supports SQL and Oracle.

- **Operating system:** vCenter Server can be installed only on 64-bit Microsoft products: Windows 2003 or Windows 2008. (Refer to VMware's site for the list of supported operating systems.)

NOTE

VMware does not support the installation of vCenter Server on an Active Directory domain controller. Choose a static IP address with a valid *Domain Name System (DNS)* rather than *Dynamic Host Configuration Protocol (DHCP)* for vCenter Server. If DHCP is chosen, verify that vCenter Server is recorded in the DNS with the correct values.

TIP

VMware recommends installing vCenter Server in a VM to take advantage of virtualization's service levels. There is one exception in which a physical server is required: when *vCenter Storage Appliance (VSA)* is used, because vCenter ensures the management of the VSA.

vCenter Server Appliance

- **Disk space:** *vCenter Server Appliance (vCSA)* requires a disk of at least 7 GB and at most 80 GB.

- **Memory**:

    - Small-scale deployment fewer than 100 hosts and 1000 VMs: at least 8 GB

    - Medium-scale deployment for 100–400 hosts and 1000–4000 VMs: 12 GB

    - Large-scale deployment for more than 400 hosts and 4000 VMs: 16 GB

vCSA can be deployed on an ESX4.x host or later.

vSphere Client

vSphere Client requires .NET 3.0 SP1 Framework and Microsoft Visual J# 2.0 SE. If they are not found within the system, they will be installed with vSphere Client. vSphere Client can be installed only in Microsoft environments.

Table 7.2 lists the recommended specifications for vSphere Client and vCenter Server.

Table 7.2 Recommended Specifications for vSphere Client and vCenter Server

	Processor (or Core)	Memory	Disk
Up to 50 hosts and 500 VMs			
vCenter Server	2	4 GB	5 GB
vSphere Client	1	200 MB	1.5 GB
Up to 300 hosts and 3,000 VMs			
vCenter Server	4	8 GB	10 GB
vSphere Client	1	500 MB	1.5 GB
Up to 100 hosts and 10,000 VMs			
vCenter Server	8	16 GB	10 GB
vSphere Client	2	500 MB	1.5 GB

Hardware Options

- **Servers:** In our experience, rack and blade servers are used most often for virtualization projects because they allow a considerable reduction in the amount of floorspace used. In some cases, tower formats can be used because they offer more PCI slots to add network or *Fibre Channel (FC)* cards. Each manufacturer offers worthwhile solutions. We recommend choosing well-known brand names such as HP, Dell, IBM, Cisco, Fujitsu Siemens, NEC Computers, or Bull. In all cases, the hardware must explicitly be referenced in VMware's hardware compatibility matrix.

- **Storage:** Storage arrays supporting VMware's *vStorage API for Array Integration (VAAI)* and *network-attached storage (NAS)* VAAI *application programming interfaces (APIs)* are indispensable for optimal use of vSphere 5. If you plan to use *Site Recovery Manager (SRM)*, it is ideal that a *Storage Replication Adapter (SRA)* module is available for the array. Choose arrays with redundancy mechanisms, ALUA mode, and the ability to deal with growth. Some of the best-known manufacturers are EMC, Hitachi Data Systems, NetApp, HP, Dell, IBM, and Oracle Pillar Data System. Confirm compatibility on the VMware HCL.

TIP

Virtualization prolongs the lifespan of architectures. (Lifespan is generally five years.) The solution's evolution must be planned. When choosing the server type, for example, it is important that servers can evolve in a simple manner. They need free expansion slots to add additional components such as network cards, HBA cards, and memory. The same applies to storage. Typically, it must have room for a growth of 20% to 30% of its volume per year.

Preparing the Server

Technology evolves rapidly, so only general advice about preparing servers is provided here.

For BIOS

- Activate all hardware assistance functionalities dedicated to virtualization, such as Intel VTx or AMDv, and options such as Intel EPT and AMD RVI for the *Memory Management Unit (MMU)* between the guest operating systems.

- Deactivate *Automatic Server Restart (ASR)* on certain servers.

- Deactivate all energy management settings.

- Deactivate unused devices such as serial, parallel, and USB ports.

- Activate hyperthreading.

To create RAID clusters

- Activate cache write and use cache backup batteries, or flash backed cache.

- Update the server's various components to the latest firmware (for example, BIOS, ILO-type management and remote-access card, RAID card, network cards, FC HBA cards, hard drives, FC switches, storage, and network components).

- Memory is one of the most critical components, and it will be in constant demand in a virtual environment. VMware recommends testing memory for 72 hours. Tools such as Memtest (www.memtest.org) provide complete and repeated testing.

Consult the manufacturer to find out whether other server elements require configuration.

Installation

This section describes the various vSphere 5 installation options and specifications.

ESXi 5 Server

There are two primary modes of installation for vSphere 5: interactive and Auto Deploy.

Interactive Installation

Installing an ESXi server is easy and quick (10 to 15 minutes). Because ESXi does not have a service console, installation is performed in text mode.

The following information is required:

- VLAN ID

- IP address (can be installed in DHCP)

- Subnetwork mask

- Gateway

- Primary and secondary DNS

- ESXi hostname

- Installation location (minimum disk space required = 5 GB)

- Whether a migration or a new installation (The VMFS version is preserved for migrations.)

- Root password (between 6 and 64 characters)

The screen shown in Figure 7.1 will appear after you boot the server and insert the DVD-ROM.

Figure 7.1 Boot menu.

Follow the instructions and enter the information as required. After ESXi is installed, you will see the interface shown in Figure 7.2.

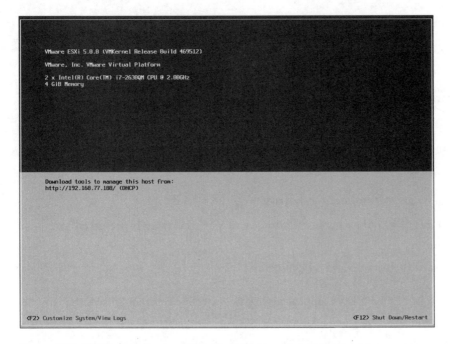

Figure 7.2 ESXi installation completed screen.

Installation with Auto Deploy

Auto Deploy is a new feature in vSphere 5. It is a dedicated solution for large-scale production environments that allows the provisioning of dozens of ESXi host servers from images called *image profiles*. This ESXi image is directly loaded into the host server's RAM when the server boots.

Unlike a traditional installation that requires installing the system onto disks, with Auto Deploy nothing is installed onto the server's local hard drives.

The main advantage of this mode is its very efficient management when upgrades must be made (such as patches or updates) because it is necessary only to update the reference image; when the servers boot, they retrieve the new image. This operation task is much less intensive than reinstalling all servers.

> **NOTE**
>
> The Auto Deploy mode delivers a significant benefit compared with updates made using vSphere Update Manager because backtracking is easier in situations where the physical machines no longer react in a stable manner after corrections are applied.

This solution makes servers completely interchangeable (a server can boot with one image or another, indifferently), which makes it very easy to test new images. Yet although it simplifies deployment, implementing Auto Deploy takes longer to create and configure, and it requires using command prompts through PowerCLI.

NOTE

Do not confuse boot from SAN with Auto Deploy. Although neither method uses local disks to boot ESXi, they are different. In the former case, each server is installed with a dedicated OS (the ESXi hypervisor) and writing is done on disks. In the latter, the OS image is dynamically loaded into the server's memory through the network; it is not, strictly speaking, an installation, but rather an image broadcast (OS streaming).

Boot from SAN is often used to make servers interchangeable and to simplify the DRP. Although this method is proven and works very well, it requires rigorous management of the implementation at the SAN and server levels (for example, zoning, LUN, or masking) to avoid handling errors. Within this framework, Auto Deploy can advantageously replace boot from SAN to minimize risk and make it easier to update the servers' ESXi images.

How Auto Deploy Works

Auto Deploy Server stores and manages images. Through Auto Deploy PowerCLI, administrators create association rules between hosts and image profiles. It is also possible to create a rule to associate a host profile to configure the server.

The host server that uses Auto Deploy makes a remote boot of the ESXi image through the network (called *boot PXE*). To do so, the following are required:

- A DHCP server that will assign an IP address when the server boots.

- A *Trivial File Transfer Protocol (TFTP)* server, which is a light FTP version mainly used for remote boots through the network.

- VMware PowerCLI, because all tasks related to image profiles are made using PowerCLI.

- ESXi Image Builder CLI, which allows the creation of ESXi images packaged with certain specific patch, driver, or software package levels (called *vSphere Installation Bundle [VIB]*) distributed by VMware and partners. A few examples of VIBs include CIM providers, Cisco Nexus, vShield Plugins, Lab Manager, HA agents, Base ESXi patches, drivers, and esxcli extensions.

> **NOTE**
>
> It is possible to add VIBs to an Image Profile if the image is not already assigned to a host server. When adding a VIB, the signature level must be controlled to know who ensures support in case of instability. This level, called acceptance level, can be more or less restrictive: VMware (most restrictive), partners or community (less restrictive, not recommended for production environments).

Host Profiles

As discussed, the role of Auto Deploy is to facilitate ESXi deployments by integrating updates in images. It does not serve to configure the ESXi after the code has been installed in memory. Auto Deploy is complemented by the Host Profiles feature, which allows customization through the predefinition of installation and configuration parameters (see Figure 7.3). This ensures that the infrastructure is homogenous and that all designated servers comply with the defined policy.

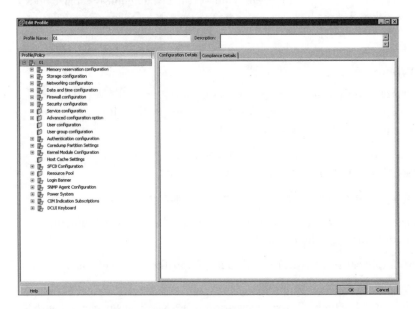

Figure 7.3 Edit Profile dialog for Host Profiles.

Host Profiles provides homogeneity in the configuration and settings of ESXi hosts and allows configuration of the following:

- **Storage:** With VMFS datastores, NFS volumes, iSCSI, multipathing, and so on

- **The network:** Includes using vSwitches, port groups, physical network cards and a related security policy, and NIC teaming

- **License keys**

- **DNS and routing:** DNS server, default gateway

- **The firewall:** Network and service ports (sshd, snmpd, CIM, and so on)

- **The processor:** Using hyperthreading or not

To create a host profile, an ESXi must be configured with parameters allowing the definition of a policy that will serve as a base to create an image called *Gold image*. After this host profile is defined, it can be applied to an isolated host server or to a cluster.

> **NOTE**
>
> A host profile can only be applied when the ESXi server is in maintenance mode.

If Check Compliance is activated, vCenter checks the server's compliance with the defined policy and informs the administrator about the state. Possible states are Compliant, Unknown, and Non-compliant. The Remediation function brings the server back into compliance. It is possible to export the profile configuration in a VPF format file that can then be used elsewhere.

vCenter Server 5 Installation

The screen shown in Figure 7.4 appears after you insert the vCenter DVD.

Figure 7.4 Initial installation screen for vCenter Server.

The following components are available on the vCenter Server installation DVD:

- vCenter Server
- vSphere Client
- VMware vSphere Web Client (Server)
- VMware vSphere Update Manager
- VMware ESXi Dump Collector
- Syslog Collector
- VMware Auto Deploy
- VMware vSphere Authentication Proxy
- vCenter Host Agent Pre-Upgrade Checker

vCenter Server 5 requires a database for the storage and organization of data. You can rely on an existing database. VMware recommends using a separate database for vCenter Server and vCenter Update Manager. vSphere 5 supports Oracle, Microsoft SQL Server, and IBM DB2.

For a complete list of databases compatible with vCenter Server, go to the VMware web site: http://partnerweb.vmware.com/comp_guide2/sim/interop_matrix.php.

The Microsoft SQL Server 2008 Express version can be used if there are fewer than 5 hosts and 50 VMs. Beyond this, it is preferable to use other production versions of Microsoft SQL, Oracle, or DB2.

Upgrading to vSphere 5

Upgrading to vSphere 5 is done in steps. Updates are done in the following order:

1. vCenter Server
2. vSphere Update Manager
3. ESXi servers
4. VMs – VMware Tools and Virtual Hardware

Updates to vCenter Server 5

vCenter Server must be version 5 in order to manage ESXi5. Upgrading vCenter is the first step to upgrading the entire infrastructure. It is possible to migrate the following:

- Virtual Center 2.5 update 6 to vCenter Server 5

- vCenter 4.x to vCenter 5

REMINDER

vCenter Server 5 can be installed only in a 64-bit environment (64-bit OS and servers).

Before upgrading vCenter, remember to back up the database and vCenter Server's certificates, and also ensure that the existing database is compatible by referring to the VMware compatibility matrix. The Pre-Upgrade Check tool, found on the installation DVD, makes it possible to display a report and possibly solve certain problems before installation.

Upgrading vSphere Update Manager

vSphere Update Manager (VUM) 4.x can be upgraded to version 5.0.

Backing up the VUM database is necessary to preserve the previous version's VUM configuration.

NOTE

During installation, VUM uninstalls the obsolete existing patches (for example, corrections for ESX3.x).

After upgrading the Update Manager server, update the Update Manager plug-in in vCenter Server.

Upgrading to ESXi 5

It is possible to perform an update directly from ESXi 4 to ESXi 5 with VUM. The migration of ESX 4 (with Service Console) to ESXi 5 can be done directly, but it must be done with care because numerous configuration files cannot be migrated (such as agents and third-party scripts). It is worthwhile to refer to the upgrade guide to validate the architecture based on the manufacturers' constraints. (See vsphere-esxi-vcenter-server-50-upgrade-guide.pdf.)

It is impossible to perform an update directly from ESXi 3.5 to ESXi 5. In this case, migration requires two steps: a migration from ESX 3.5 to ESX 4, and another to ESXi 5. In the last two cases, however, experience leads us to recommend reinstalling ESXi nodes, one by one, to start from a healthy base, which is preferable and much faster.

Upgrading ESX hosts to ESXi 5.0 from versions that predate 3.5 is impossible without a complete reinstallation of ESXi.

TIP

vSphere 5 includes only the ESXi version. Compatibility with existing solutions must be verified because they may not function without a service console (such as backup and monitoring tools). No rollback is possible after the upgrade is performed (unlike the migration of ESX 3.5 to ESX 4.x, which offered this possibility).

CAUTION

VUM cannot perform the upgrade of hosts already upgraded from the 3.5 version to 4.x.

The easiest way to upgrade ESX/ESXi hosts is through vSphere Update Manager 5.0, shown in Figure 7.5.

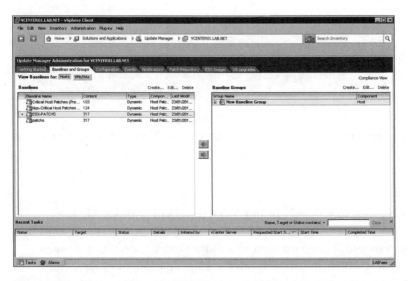

Figure 7.5 vSphere Client Update Manager Administration console.

Other methods can be used for upgrades. Interactive installation (manual) can be done from an ISO image for a limited number of hosts (a dozen). For a large number of ESXi hosts, using scripts is preferable.

Upgrading VMs

It is necessary to begin by upgrading VMware Tools in VMs. This can be done individually for each VM or by using VUM. Note that vSphere 5's VMware Tools feature is compatible with hosts still in version 4.x, so it is not an issue if, during the migration phase, some hosts within a cluster have not yet been upgraded to version 5.

The VM's Virtual Hardware must then be upgraded to version 8 (while VMs are shut down) to take advantage of this hardware version's new functionalities. (See "Virtual Machines" in Chapter 2, "The Evolution of vSphere 5 and Its Architectural Components.") One important consideration when upgrading the virtual hardware is that virtual machines running with virtual hardware version 8 can run only on ESXi 5.0 hosts. The best practice recommends to upgrade a virtual machine's virtual hardware version after all the hosts in the cluster have been upgraded to ESXi 5.0.

> **CAUTION**
>
> Upgrading a version of the virtual machine's virtual hardware is a one-way operation. There is no option to reverse the upgrade after it is done.

The Different Connection Methods

As shown in Figure 7.6, there are several ways to connect to the vSphere 5 environment, including the following:

- Via a local connection on the ESXi server through the *Direct Console User Interface (DCUI)*

- Using vSphere Client for a direct connection to vCenter Server or to an ESXi host server

- Using Web Access on vCenter Server or to an ESXi server

- Using Windows Remote Desktop on vCenter Server

- Using scripting tools (enabling experienced administrators to develop their own scripts and solutions for task automation)

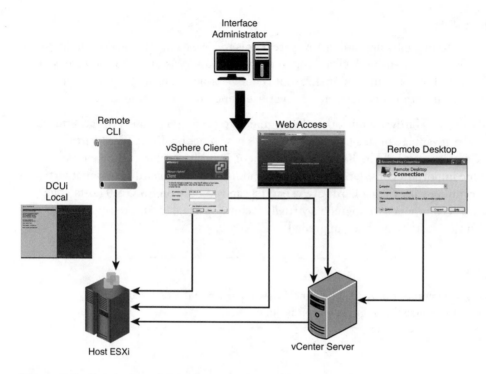

Figure 7.6 vSphere 5 environment connection options.

Direct Console User Interface

The *Direct Console User Interface (DCUI)* allows a local connection to the ESXi server. This enables configuration of the Management IP address (see Figure 7.7). The management network (the only one configurable from DCUI) is automatically created when ESXi is installed. This makes the server reachable and makes configuration possible. It is equivalent to vSphere 4's service console port. DCUI enables you to configure the following:

- Hostname
- Root password
- Diagnostics
- Restart of hostd and vpxa management agents
- Reset, bringing back the initial configuration

> **NOTE**
>
> When the ESXi server is integrated into vCenter Server, a vCenter vpxa agent is installed. The ESXi server's hostd management agent is responsible for retrieving data from the ESXi server and communicating with vSphere Client.

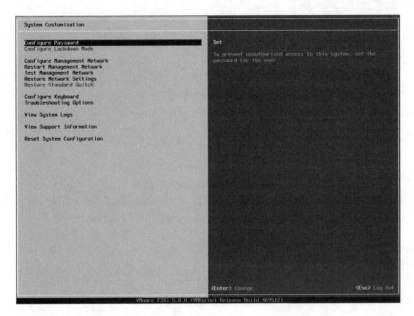

Figure 7.7 System Customization screen.

vSphere Client

vSphere Client can connect directly to an ESXi server or to a vCenter Server. To connect to the ESXi server, the root account (configured at installation) must be used. Connecting with other users is possible. To connect to vCenter Server, a user must have administrator rights or permissions.

To connect to the ESXi server, simply type the server's IP address (or its hostname) with the user name and password defined during installation, as shown in Figure 7.8. vCenter Server uses the Windows user account repository. To connect to it, use either the local accounts of the server on which it is installed or the accounts from the Active Directory the vCenter is joined to.

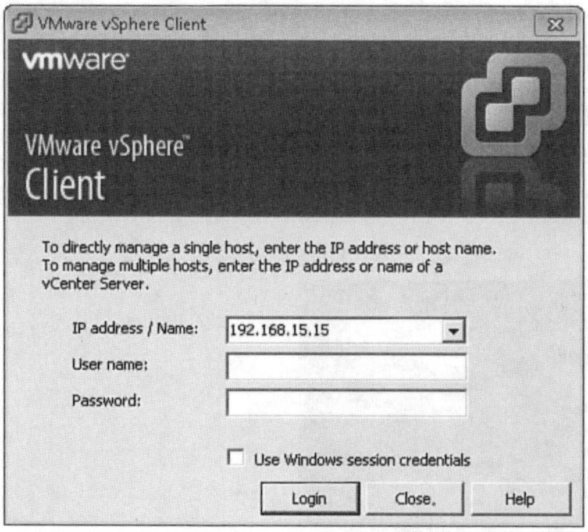

Figure 7.8 vSphere Client login screen.

vSphere Web Client

vSphere Web Access is a web interface, shown in Figure 7.9, developed in Adobe Flex to perform basic administration and configuration actions on virtual and ESXi machines.

NOTE

Web Access is no longer accessible directly on the ESXi, but it can be accessed through vCenter if the vCenter Web Administration module is installed.

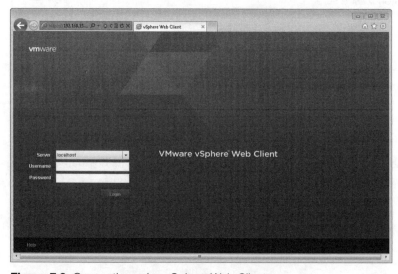

Figure 7.9 Connecting using vSphere Web Client.

Scripting Tools

To automate deployment, VMware developed tools for daily operations. It is possible to create scripts to automate tasks with the same functionality as vSphere Client:

- **vSphere Management Assistant (VMA):** A virtual appliance composed of several management tools. VMA packages include vSphere Command-Line Interface and the vSphere SDK Perl.

- **vSphere PowerCLI:** A command-line tool for the automation of hosts, VMs, guest operating systems, and so on. PowerCLI includes more than 150 cmdlets. (Cmdlets are specific PowerShell commands.)

- **vSphere Command-Line Interface (vCLI):** A utility used to provision, configure, and maintain the host ESXi. vCLI includes numerous commands, including VMkfs-tools, VMware-cmd, and resxtop.

vCenter Configuration

In a VMware environment, vCenter Server is the main management and administration tool. The vSphere Client, connected to a vCenter Server is shown in Figure 7.10.

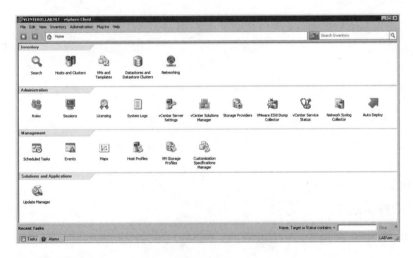

Figure 7.10 A general view of vCenter.

Depending on licenses and the plug-ins installed, you can find the following objects:

- **Inventory group**
    - **Search:** To find objects within vCenter

- **Hosts and Clusters:** To administer and manage host servers and clusters
- **VMs and Templates:** For the creation of VMs and templates
- **Datastores and Datastore Clusters:** To manage the storage space
- **Networking:** To manage the vSwitch and Distributed vSwitch network

- **Administration group**
  - Roles
  - Sessions
  - Licensing
  - Systems logs
  - vCenter settings
  - vCenter Solutions Manager
  - Storage Provider
  - VMware ESXi Dump Collector
  - vCenter Service Status
  - Network Syslog Collector
  - Auto Deploy

- **Management group**
  - Scheduled Tasks
  - Events
  - Maps
  - Host Profiles
  - VM Storage Profiles
  - Customization Specifications Manager

- **Solutions and Applications groups**
  - Update Manager

Licenses

Each ESXi server requires a license key. vCenter Server also requires a license key. (See "vSphere 5 Licenses" in Chapter 2.) If a license key is not entered, a 60-day evaluation period begins.

General Settings

vCenter's other settings are found in vCenter Settings in the Home menu (see Figure 7.11), as described in the list that follows.

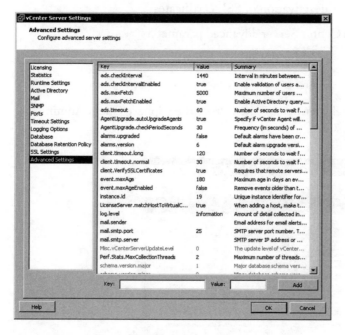

Figure 7.11 vCenter Server Settings, Advanced Settings menu.

- **Licensing:** See the section "vSphere 5 Licenses" in Chapter 2
- **Statistics:** Determines the level of information logged on the components to monitor (the greater the level, the more information generated)
- **Runtime Settings:** For environments with multiple vCenter Server instances
- **Active Directory:** Settings for synchronization with Active Directory
- **Mail:** To send alerts by email

- **SNMP:** To send alerts and *Simple Network Management Protocol (SNMP)* traps to a management console

- **Ports:** To modify ports used by default by vCenter

- **Timeout Settings:** Timeout parameters

- **Logging Options:** Detail level of log files

- **Database:** Maximum number of connections for the database

- **Database Retention Policy:** Settings on the retention of events and tasks

- **SSL Settings:** Activation or deactivation of SSL certificates

- **Advanced Settings:** All vCenter Server advanced parameters

Hosts and Clusters

You can easily perform host and cluster management from the vSphere Client Administration console, shown in Figure 7.12.

Figure 7.12 Client Administration console: vCenter Server objects are shown on the left.

Simply click an object to see tabs corresponding to the various parameters that can be set for that object. For each object modification, status and progression will appear at the bottom under Recent Tasks.

Datacenter Creation

A datacenter must be created before ESXi host servers can be added or VMs created. A datacenter provides a structured organization for all objects in the virtual environment: hosts, clusters, virtual machines and directories, and resource pools. The datacenter must reflect the network architecture following geographic location or functional/departmental organization. This datacenter notion exists only when connected to a vCenter Server. After the datacenter is created, the ESXi server can be added.

> **NOTE**
>
> You can vMotion from one cluster to another within a datacenter, but not to another datacenter.

Managing Permissions

Permissions are very important because they allow the attribution of rights to users who can then perform certain operations. As shown in Figure 7.13, there are three steps to follow:

1. Creating users

2. Creating a role

3. Associating the role to a user to create a permission

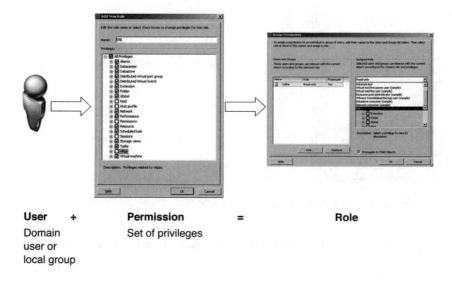

User	+	Permission	=	Role
Domain user or local group		Set of privileges		

Figure 7.13 Permission management steps.

There are two categories of users:

- Users who connect to vCenter Server based on Windows accounts. Users must exist in the *Active Directory (AD)* or locally on the vCenter Server. It is impossible to create or delete users in vCenter; modifications must be made at the AD level. When vCenter Server connects to the ESXi host, it uses the vpxuser account.

- Users who connect to the ESXi server based on a list of accounts internal to ESXi host.

A *role* is defined as a set of privileges that assign certain roles or actions for the objects in the environment. An *object* is anything vCenter Server can manage—for example, datacenter, host, VM, or cluster. When looking at the Hosts and Clusters screen shown in Figure 7.12, objects are listed on the left.

There are predefined standard roles, but others can be created by defining their privileges, as shown in Figure 7.14.

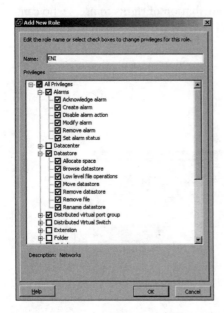

Figure 7.14 Assigning privileges in the Add New Role dialog.

After roles are created, it is possible to associate a role with a user to create permissions.

Storage and Network

Refer to Chapter 3, "Storage in vSphere 5," and Chapter 4, "Servers and Network," which address storage and network configuration in great detail.

P2V Conversion

Physical-to-virtual (P2V) conversion makes it possible to do the following:

- Create a new VM

- Transform a physical server or PC into a virtual instance, using tools such as VMware Converter

> **NOTE**
>
> Other types of conversions are possible—such as between different VMware products (for example, between ESXi and VMware Workstation or Fusion) and *virtual to physical (V2P)*.

VMware offers its VMware Converter as a standalone conversion tool. This tool is well suited to the conversion of a few machines. For large-scale migrations, tools available on the market are better adapted because they can industrialize the process and offer much richer functionalities.

Possible Post-P2V Modifications

Converting a physical server to a virtual one generates changes that must be taken into account:

- The MAC address changes. A new MAC address is attributed to each *virtual network card (vNIC)* in the range 00:50:56:00:00:00 to 00:50:56:3F:FF:FF or 00:0C:29. This can have consequences, notably for licensing, which can be based on the MAC address.

- Virtual hard disks are created. When migrating to a virtual environment, physical disks are converted to virtual disks (vmdk file). This point should be considered in the case of large-capacity disks (several hundred GB) that will take longer to convert. During the P2V, the size of the virtual disk can be modified.

- Licensing mode may change. Software licensing is an important issue to take into account in a migration. It is necessary to verify that manufacturers support their products in virtual mode and that their licensing system is clearly defined. Some manufacturers base licensing on the number of vCPUs, while others base it on the number of physical processors (sockets), or physical cores in the host server.

- Cached credentials are deleted when using Sysprep (a Microsoft tool that creates a new *security identifier [SID]* for the virtualized machine). Some conversion tools use Sysprep for the migration process.

- Before migration, ensure that you can access the server by using a local administrator account. When using Sysprep, all locally stored connection profiles are deleted, along with their associated credentials (called cached credentials). Only the initial installation account is preserved—specifically, the local administrator account. Without this account, it is impossible to establish a connection. Moreover, Sysprep resets the machine's SID. This means that upon its first connection, the machine can longer connect to the domain. It must be reintegrated into the domain manually (but first the previous machine account must be deleted from Active Directory).

Best Practices

Before conversion, the following best practices are recommended:

- Take advantage of conversion to delete useless files (such as temporary files or files unused for months or even years).

- Uninstall applications and deactivate useless services.

- Defragment the hard drive.

- If you do not have access to the machine's local administrator account, create a temporary one to be used only for migration. Remember to delete this account after the migration.

- Stop all services that could hinder the migration process (for example, antivirus, scan disks, and backups).

- When performing a hot migration, it is preferable to stop applications, especially transactional applications such as databases.

- Try to perform migrations while the server is less active. (Migrations can take place at night, for example.)

- Ensure the destination host server has the necessary resources (notably disk space and memory) to run the new VM.

The following best practices are recommended after conversion:

- It is worthwhile to deactivate some VM devices that will not be used (such as the serial port, USB port, parallel port, and disk drive).

- Disconnect the CD-ROM drive in the VM if it is not actively being used.

- Uninstall or stop management and monitoring services and agents related to hardware and no longer required.

- Deactivate software that manages HBA cards or the load distribution of network cards. (VMware manages these.)

- Verify that VMware Tools is installed properly.

- Verify that the virtual hardware was properly installed in the Windows device manager (that is, no question mark or exclamation point icons noting issues).

- Delete devices that generate errors in the event log (for example, the ILO card).

Efficient Management of the Virtual Environment

This section provides information to help you maximize management efficiency in your virtual environment, focusing on the following areas:

- Monitoring the host server
- Alarms and maps
- Resource sharing
- Resource pools
- Consolidation rate
- Server performance
- Clones and templates
- vApps

Monitoring the Host Server

Monitoring the infrastructure requires a combination of proactive actions by the administrator and reactive actions based on defined alerts. With vCenter Server, both methods can be combined. Other tools found on the market can complement vCenter to refine the analysis of information and of object performance.

In a virtual environment, the performance aspect is fundamental because the VMs share the resources of an ESXi host server. Therefore, monitoring the activity of the host and VMs is required to ensure that the VMs have sufficient resources to run their applications. A refined analysis of resources must allow an improved consolidation of the infrastructure, which should lead to significant savings because investing in new servers is not necessary.

An improperly sized server with a significant load can make the server's overall performance collapse. In contrast, a server that is underused, with VMs that exploit only a small part of its resources, causes the company not reap the maximum benefit of the solution.

Alarms and Maps

Alarms are reactive actions based on defined criteria. They can trigger an action such as sending an email to the administrator. Alarms should be used sparingly so that only significant malfunctions are highlighted.

For example, if the VM's CPU usage (%) reaches between 75% and 90%, a warning will be created, and if it goes beyond 90%, an alarm will be sent.

You can associate an action (nonmandatory) such as sending an email or an SNMP trap to a management console. Note that if there is no action associated, an alarm can still be viewed in the alarm section, as shown in Figure 7.15.

Figure 7.15 Alarm definitions viewed in the vSphere Client Administration console.

Resource Sharing

Resource sharing is a fundamental element in a shared environment. VMware provides sharing mechanisms to ensure that VMs have the resources required when contentions occur. These "safeguards" are indispensable and provide peace of mind even when activity is intense. Priority VMs will have the resources they require. Under VMware, different levels of Quality of Service can be set as shown in Figure 7.16.

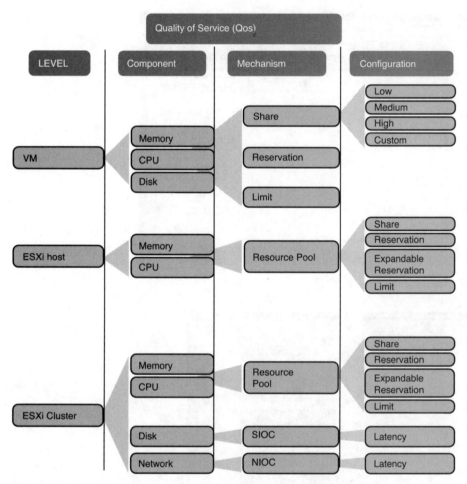

Figure 7.16 It is possible to set quality of Service for memory, processor, disk and network at different levels.

As shown in Figure 7.17, *maps* provide a graphic view of the virtual environment. They make it possible to view the relationship between host servers and VMs, the network, and the datastore.

It is possible to share the memory, processor, and disk within the VM. As shown in Figure 7.18, three settings are available: Reservation, Share, and Limit.

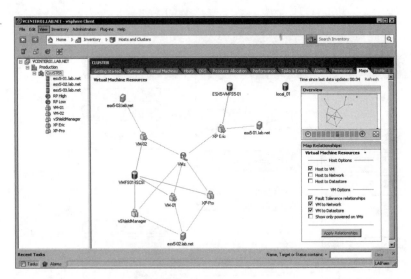

Figure 7.17 Resource mapping example.

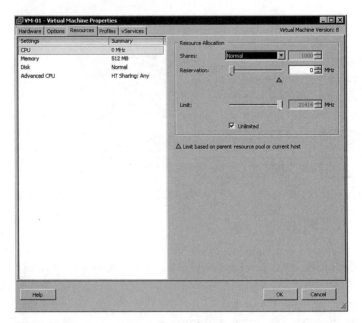

Figure 7.18 VM resource allocation settings.

Reservation

Reservation represents a guaranteed amount of resources for a virtual machine. ESXi authorizes a VM to boot only if the specified amount of resources is available within the

ESXi. This ensures that a VM will have access to a minimum amount of resources at all times, even if other VMs on the same host server experience intense activity. Reservation is divided into the following categories:

- **CPU Reservation:** With normal activity, if a VM does not use the CPU's reserved resources and does not need them, it frees them up for other VMs. However, if the activity of the ESXi host server intensifies, the CPU time is dynamically allocated to VMs based on their configured share and reservation.

- **Memory Reservation:** The amount of memory is reserved on the server's physical RAM regardless of the activity. A VM with a specified amount of reserved memory is guaranteed to have access to this memory regardless of the load level of other VMs. The mechanisms already explained—TPS, swap, ballooning, and memory compression—cannot retrieve that VM's reserved memory. A VM cannot boot if this memory is not available in the RAM. A swap file with the extension vswp is created and equal to the configured memory minus reserved memory, as shown in Figure 7.19.

NOTE

Reservation is a significant element of the slot size calculation when a vSphere HA cluster is used. (See Chapter 5, "High Availability and Disaster Recovery Plan.")

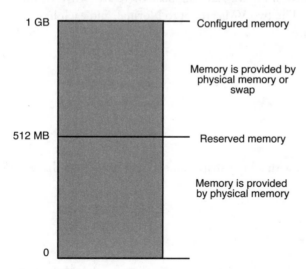

Figure 7.19 Reserved memory is provided by the server's physical RAM. In this example, the swap file takes 512 MB.

> **TIP**
>
> Reservations should not be used too frequently. It should be used for critical VMs (for example, Active Directory, vCenter) or for critical applications (for example, databases, messaging servers). For other, less-critical VMs, it is preferable to work with shares.

Share

Share is a notion of relative importance or priority regarding other VMs. If a virtual machine possesses twice as many resources as another VM, it can consume twice as many resources. There are four levels: Low, Normal, High, and Custom:

- High = 2000 shares per vCPU
- Normal = 1000 shares per vCPU
- Low = 500 shares per vCPU
- Custom = available shares per vCPU defined by administrator

A VM with two vCPUs with a normal share has 2 x 1000 shares = 2000 shares.

Let's look at a specific example, illustrated in Figure 7.20. Suppose there are two VMs on a server with CPU resources of 8 GHz. The two VMs are set to Normal, and each has 4 GHz. Assume the following conditions:

- VM1 = 1000 shares
- VM2 = 1000 shares
- VM1 = 4 GHz
- VM2 = 4 GHz

If a third VM (see Figure 7.21) is booted with a high share value, it will have 2000 shares:

- VM1 = 1000 shares
- VM2 = 1000 shares
- VM3 = 2000 shares

Proportions are calculated as follows:

- VM1 = 1000 / 4000 x 8 GHz = 1 / 4 x 8 GHz = 2 GHz
- VM2 = 1000 / 4000 = 1/4 = 1 / 4 x 8 GHz = 2 GHz
- VM3 = 2 / 4000 = 1/2 = 1 / 2 x 8 GHz = 4 GHz

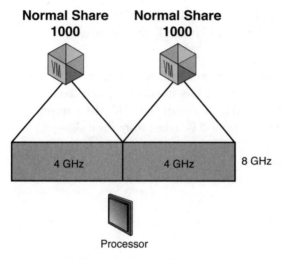

Figure 7.20 Share example with two VMs.

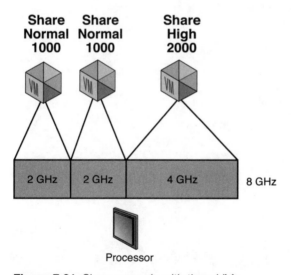

Figure 7.21 Share example with three VMs.

> **NOTE**
>
> It is preferable to set shares and create resource pools rather than use reservations.

Limit

The two limit factors you want to be familiar with are the *memory limit* and the *CPU limit*.

The memory limit is the maximum amount of RAM the VM will be able to take. A RAM-limited VM will have to swap on the disk to have "available memory space," hindering its performance.

In Figure 7.22, the swap file is equal to the configured memory minus the reserved memory: 1.5 GB – 0.512 GB = 1 GB. If the VM needs more than 1 GB, it will not be able to take it from the RAM; the extra memory will be provided by the swap. The 512 MB memory amount (configured memory minus reserved memory) will be taken from the disk swap.

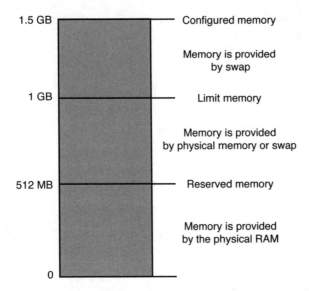

Swap file is 1.5 GB – 512 MB = 1 GB

Figure 7.22 Memory limit example.

NOTE

Because overly large swap files should be avoided, a VM should not be configured with excess of memory.

TIP

Even if the VM is not critical, using limits is of little interest. It is preferable to use shares and not set a limit.

The CPU limit represents the maximum CPU time for a VM. ESXi cannot allocate more CPU time than the specified limit (expressed in *megahertz [MHz]*). CPU limits are used mainly to test performance, to know how a VM behaves with a maximum defined value. For production VMs, it is not wise to use limits; shares should be used.

Resource Pools

With a resource pool, CPU and memory resources can be partitioned in a hierarchical manner, using the dialog shown in Figure 7.23.

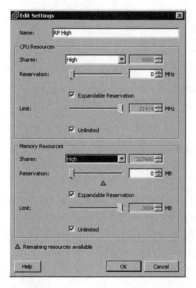

Figure 7.23 Use the Edit Settings dialog set resource pooling hierarchies.

The datacenter's available resources are grouped as several entities, allowing a precise allocation of resources. It is possible to create hierarchical resource pools with children pools that inherit the parent's resources. This management of available resources allows administrators not to allocate resources on each virtual machine, but instead in a global manner.

Figure 7.24 shows a parent and children resource pool.

The creation of resource pools can be done at either the ESXi host or cluster level. As for the CPU and memory, it is possible to set precise values for Reservation, Limit, and Share.

When the Expandable Reservation option is selected (see Figure 7.25), if a child resource pool needs a reservation higher than its own, the resources can be retrieved from the parent resource pool.

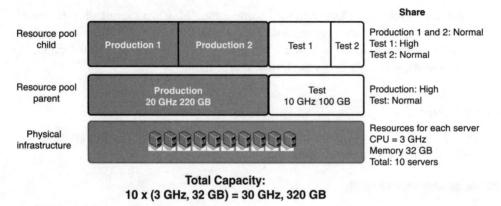

Figure 7.24 Parent and children resource pool.

Resource pools are very useful. Often, three levels are created—low, medium, and high— to define levels of importance. Three groups are also defined for SRM: SRM Low, SRM Medium, and SRM High.

Resource pools are not used to organize VMs; to do so, you must use directories.

Consolidation Rate

The *consolidation rate* is important because it represents the number of VMs that can run simultaneously on an ESXi host server while complying with required performance and service-quality levels. The consolidation rate is directly related to the administrator's mastery of the environment—the more the teams master the technology, the better the consolidation rates.

Of course, establishing the ideal ratio (number of VMs per server) depends on the application load. The best rates are observed in companies using management and automation tools to attain high levels of consolidation.

NOTE

Manufacturers, publishers, and retailers do not necessarily encourage companies to optimize their infrastructure; the company must perform the work itself. Using efficient tools leads to considerable gains. In 2012, hosting more than 30 VMs per server may seem like a lot, but in a few years and with the help of technology, it is likely that consolidation rates will reach hundreds of VMs per server.

Performance in vCenter Server

In a virtual environment, the performance aspect is fundamental because the VMs share the resources of an ESXi host server. Therefore, monitoring the activity of the host and VMs is necessary to ensure the VMs have sufficient resources to run their applications. This is why an administrator must be able to set the best size for all objects in the virtual environment. This can only be done through tools the administrator must master.

In vSphere 5, performance has been improved and, as shown in Figure 7.25, graphs metrics were added to facilitate analysis. These provide a simple view of the status of the ESXi server and associated VMs. Metrics logged relate to the CPU, memory, disks, network, resources, clusters, and system.

Figure 7.25 vSphere 5 performance view using graphs.

The data reported depends on two factors: collection level and collection interval.

Collection Level

There are four collection levels:

- **Level 1 (default):** Collection of general information on the use of ESXi. Metrics logged relate to the CPU, memory, disks, and network, as well as system information: Uptime, Heartbeat, and DRS metrics. This level shows how hardware resources are used.

- **Level 2:** Collection of more detailed information than Level 1, particularly with regard to memory: swap, memory sharing, and active memory. It allows predictions to know whether other VMs can be placed on the same host.

- **Level 3:** Includes the same metrics as Levels 1 and 2 with the addition of device-level information per network card, *host bus adapter (HBA)* card, or core. This includes information on the use of the CPU. It allows the determination of the vSMP's efficiency (by comparing ready time and wait time for each vCPU) and performance.

- **Level 4:** Includes all information supported by vCenter Server. It allows the determination of whether a component is overloaded.

Level 1 consumes very few resources from the host server to collect information. Resources used by Levels 2 to 4 are negligible. Level 4 should be used only to analyze problems over a short period.

Collection Interval

By default, vCenter Server offers several collection intervals: real-time, day, week, month, year, and custom, shown in Figure 7.26. Each interval specifies the duration of the statistics recorded in the vCenter database. Data is collected every 20 seconds.

- Real-time statistics are not stored in the database.

- Day collection takes the real-time collection (every 20 seconds) and consolidates it every 5 minutes: 12 values per hour and 288 values over 24 hours.

- Week collection takes the day collection and consolidates it every 30 minutes: 1 value every 30 minutes, 48 values per day, for 336 values per week.

- Month collection takes the week collection and consolidates it every 2 hours: 12 values per day, for 360 values per month.

- Year collection takes the month collection and consolidates it every day, for 365 values per year.

The longer data is kept, the more space is required to store the database. This is why data should not be kept for too long. Chosen indicators can then be viewed in vCenter, as shown in Figure 7.27.

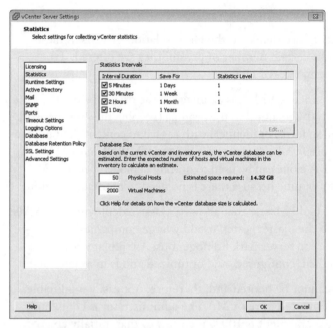

Figure 7.26 Collection statistics.

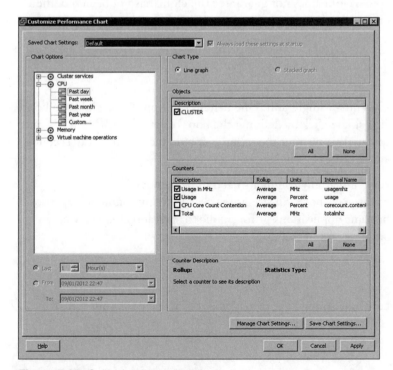

Figure 7.27 Collection interval settings.

Clones and Templates

Virtualization offers great flexibility of use thanks to the encapsulation of VMs in files. VMs can be handled very easily and a certain number of possibilities are offered. To deploy VMs faster, you can create templates or clones.

A *clone* is based on an already deployed active VM. It is an image of the original virtual machine. This new machine can be 100% identical to the original (keeping the same network identifiers: SSID, MAC address, and so forth) or identical with regard to contents, but unique on the network. In this case, the Sysprep tool can generate a unique ID (SID) and a MAC address that differs from the original. A clone can be used to quickly deploy a specific VM from an original VM. This saves a lot of time because there is no need to reinstall everything.

A template is a static image called a Gold Master that allows a massive deployment of VMs from a common base. It is similar to the masters often used by large companies to industrialize server deployment and make the server park homogenous. A template must be created after the VM has been installed, configured, and optimized and is in a stable state.

A template is an inactive VM that cannot be booted and, therefore, not easily modifiable. (To be modified, it needs to be reconverted into a VM.) The administrator is completely certain the template created at a given moment is 100% identical to that initially created.

Because deploying VMs from a clone does not guarantee the clone has not been modified since it was created, using templates is preferable because it reduces the risk of using the wrong image.

vApp

A vApp regroups several VMs into a single unit. One benefit of vApps is the ability to boot (or stop) a group of VMs in a single click by defining the boot order of the VMs. VMs can be booted (or stopped) sequentially one after the other over a defined period (120 seconds by default) or after the boot of VMware Tools.

vApps are valuable when very similar environments need to be deployed in the same manner—for example, for a large corporation's remote sites. Test environments can also use them if they require the same applications or for public (or private) cloud services in order to quickly build a complete architecture.

Best Practices

The following best practices will also improve management efficiency for your virtual environment:

- **Deactivate screensavers:** Screensavers consume CPU time. This consumption is relatively low, but if dozens of VMs run on the same server, this cumulated CPU time becomes significant. This is why deactivating them is preferable.

- **Do not use a desktop background:** Avoid desktop backgrounds. They also use CPU time and memory, often for no reason.

- **Limit antivirus scans and automatic updates:** Avoid scanning disks too often, and plan updates. Antivirus technology that scans disks too often can greatly affect performance. Disk scans should be planned to occur at specific times, avoiding periods of intense activity on the ESXi host server.

- **Check the energy consumption options:** In Windows 2008 Server, the option selected by default is Balanced. Change this to High Performance to fully exploit the VM's performance.

- **Optimize the size of the VM:** Especially memory.

- **Do not allocate additional virtual hardware:** It can consume CPU time.

- **Disconnect all nonessential ports such as the USB, serial, and parallel ports, and the disk or CD-ROM drives:** Guest operating systems regularly access all devices, including CD-ROM drives. If several VMs communicate with the server's physical CD-ROM drive, performance can be affected. It is preferable to use ISO image files.

Well-Planned Architecture Is the Key

In any environment, a well-planned architecture allows for the maximum usage of the technologies. vSphere is no exception, but many of the core designs of it also embrace flexibility. This can make certain decisions seem critical, but you can often also address issues after the fact, too.

It's easy to install vSphere correctly. The ESXi footprint is so small and simplified that it is a snap to install, and vCenter includes a wizard to further help make the install successful. When configuring VMs, it is important to size them correctly. Unlike a physical server, oversizing a VM often negatively impacts performance. vSphere provides ample methods to ensure appropriate performance, such as reservations, limits, and shares. Most production environments make use of these features, but they should always be used sparingly. The VM is a powerful entity, and by implementing the solutions in this chapter, you can maximize its potential for your organization.

Chapter 8

Managing a Virtualization Project

In this chapter, we use the example of a large corporation that has decided to accelerate the penetration rate of virtualization within its information system. This company is already familiar with virtualization technology. Approximately 30% of its server environment has already been virtualized. It wants to move on to the second phase and virtualize on a large scale, including its servers that run critical applications. To ensure the project's success, a project team is set up.

Context

The IT system at this corporation consists of global servers with a high obsolescence rate for both hardware and software. With 362 servers (on x86 systems) spread out between two datacenters, more than 50% are older than four years and will reach the end of the manufacturer's support period at the end of the current year. The cost to replace the servers cannot be covered by IT budget allocations, which shrink every year. Certain archaic applications (10 years and older) are still used but for compatibility reasons cannot be migrated with the current hardware and operating systems. The company doesn't even have the documentation needed to reinstall some of these applications.

The IT department is under pressure. It must answer both to internal clients with new needs (40 new requests per year) and to corporate management, who demand higher service levels coupled with cost reductions. In a tight economic context, internal IT teams bear a significant workload because many agreements with service providers have not been renewed.

The datacenters are another source of great concern—they are reaching their limits in terms of floor space and energy consumption (only a few kilowatt in reserve). No new hardware can be added, which prevents any new project from being undertaken.

A *disaster recovery plan (DRP)* solution is in place, but it is not satisfactory; only 5% of the applications are secured on remote sites, and tests are sporadically performed.

Backups are also problematic; several solutions are in place, but there is no global management, and backup windows are often too narrow. Many restorations from tapes fail due to a lack of backup testing.

The company decides to rely heavily on the virtualization technologies best suited to face these issues. It decides to proceed with a large-scale deployment of virtualization for all applications, even the most critical.

Objectives

The IT department defines its objectives as follows:

- Cost reduction:

    - Reduction in the datacenter's power consumption

    - Infrastructure rationalization

    - Automation of certain tasks performed by administrators

- Securing the production site by implementing a DRP with a *recovery point objective (RPO)* of 0 and an *recovery time objective (RTO)* of less than four hours on the entire IT system.

- The IT system must be the company's growth engine. It must favor innovation, creativity, and new projects.

The IT department also identifies the following future projects that are outside the scope of the immediate objectives:

- Provisioning cloud-type services

- Providing end users and project teams with easy access to IT services

- Implementing chargeback tools

- Implementing a unified backup solution

- Implementing a third replication site

- Standardizing processes

Criteria to Choose a Solution

To evaluate the relevance of existing virtualization solutions in reaching its goals, the company looks at offerings from three top companies: Microsoft, Citrix, and VMware. After an in-depth examination of the different solutions, the company chooses VMware based on the following criteria:

- The product's maturity within large datacenters

- The upgradeable nature of the solution

- The possibility of attaining high levels of service through VMware's advanced features

- A single tool to administer and monitor the virtual platform and DRP; integration of Site Recovery Manager within vCenter

- A robust ecosystem, with numerous options (including migration tools, wide compatibility with backup tools, and reporting)

- The ability to implement a global backup policy

- Preexisting in-house VMware competencies

Project Stages

As shown in Figure 8.1, this virtualization project is planned in four stages: Planning, Design, Implementation, and Management.

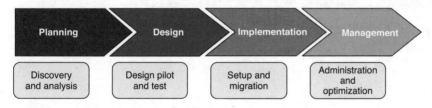

Figure 8.1 Planning stages for virtualization project.

For any virtualization project, including critical production servers, the goal of the planning stage is a preliminary eligibility study. The planning stage includes two steps:

1. *Discovery*, which involves collecting all information on servers, storage, and production equipment to draft a production plan.

2. *Analysis*, which involves interpreting results from the discovery step and drafting optimized consolidation scenarios.

The Design stage involves proposing various target scenarios, taking into account the results of the eligibility study, and providing the technical specifications and performance metrics required for the target platform. This guarantees a level of performance at least equivalent to what it was before virtualization. (In fact, it is often much higher.) During this stage, the detailed reference architecture is drafted. This document serves in the drafting of the equipment specifications so that the various providers offer solutions that meet the needs as defined.

The Implementation stage defines the time phasing of migration for priorities defined by the IT department, such as end-of-server warranty contracts, urgency, or capacity. If the project's priority is to decrease energy consumption (kWh), groups of the most energy-intensive applications will be defined and migrated first. The implementation of the target platform will be accomplished by using *physical-to-virtual (P2V)* tools and in compliance with the detailed reference architecture.

The Management stage allows the application of best practices to add operational efficiency to the environment. Strict rules must be followed to maintain control. Tools complementing those offered by VMware can be used to manage day-to-day operations.

Planning

As mentioned in the preceding section, the Planning stage consists of discovery and analysis (see Figure 8.2).

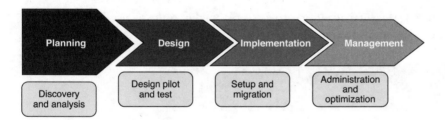

Figure 8.2 At the Planning stage.

Discovery

This stage includes the *production plan*—the exact inventory of the servers and precise information about the use of the various elements over a defined period. Information collected is used to size the target architecture and determine which servers are not eligible for the virtualization project. Information collected is also used for the proper implementation of *Site Recovery Manager (SRM)*.

The project's scope includes x86 processor-based servers. Other types of servers, such as UNIX or mainframe, are excluded.

The study to gather information is realized through a collection server. The infrastructure's physical servers send back all data related to production over a period that is representative of the activity. Usually, a period of 30 days is selected, excluding July and August (months that often are not representative of a typical production plan due to a slowing of business activity). The analysis tool chosen for this particular project is PlateSpin PowerRecon. The analysis stage can begin at the end of the 30-day period, covering the following technical angles listed in Table 8.1.

Table 8.1 Planning Objectives During Discovery Phase

Audit Theme	Goals	Notes
OS type	Verify the compatibility of the OS with VMware vSphere 5's compatibility matrix.	Unsupported operating systems are not eligible, because this means there will usually be no tools allowing P2V or manufacturer support for the OS.
CPU use rate	Allows the determination of the average use rate of the current server park's calculation power. Useful for the sizing of the target architecture.	Servers with intensive CPU use are not usually good candidates for virtualization, but if the goal is to simplify the *DRP*, even a processor-intensive server may be put on vSphere (1 VM for one ESXi host).
CPU usage pattern	Allows figuring whether the CPU activity can be predictable (for specific hours of days of the week) or whether it is random.	Allows the determination of which servers are "at risk." One determining factor to validate a physical machine's virtualization eligibility.
Memory use determination	Allows the determination of the memory's average use rate.	Memory is one of the first elements to take into account when sizing a virtual architecture.
Storage volume sizing	Defines required storage capacities and performance.	The choice of the destination storage architecture is extremely important. Storage is the most critical component of a virtualization environment, because if storage-space and performance (in IOPS) sizing is not defined correctly, the project could fail.
Network connections	Defines prerequisites to ensure network streams in optimum conditions.	The nature of servers (supported applications) and the report scheduling (batch, backups) should be analyzed in detail to determine network activity.
Profiling the application	Allows the determination of the criticality and performance of each application. The switch to virtual should be done only when service levels and performance are at least equivalent.	Special attention should be given to critical applications for their protection and during migration phases.

NOTE

During this period, it is imperative that the data collection operations and the team in charge do not interfere with current production, respecting the company's business reality.

Data collection follows a logical process. The activity of CPU, memory, network, and disk components is collected at all times. Every five minutes, a maximum value is retrieved. After one hour, an average is generated from these maximum values. Each hour is calculated in this manner to establish a profile over 24 hours. In this way, the average value over one month is found for each server. Each server's profile can be calculated, and a graphic representation can be created, as shown in Figure 8.3, showing the activity from all machines. The collection allows the precise determination of the servers' activity and their production plan.

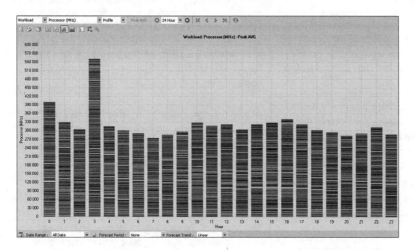

Figure 8.3 Representation of the datacenter's production plan.

In Figure 8.3, each color stacked in the histogram represents the activity of one machine within the datacenter. The collected activity accumulation represents the maximum load observed that the virtualized platform will need to offer when it is in place to ensure, at a minimum, a performance equivalent to pre-virtualization. Note that a large portion of activity occurs at night: backups, batches, database indexing, defragmentation, and so on. On some servers, the busiest time is at night.

As shown in Table 8.2, limit thresholds must be set to determine which servers are eligible for virtualization. These thresholds are based on VMware recommendations as well as our own experience. Every organization may set the limit thresholds differently.

Table 8.2 Limit Thresholds

	Set Thresholds
CPU	6 GHz
Memory	6 GB
Disk	Disk transfer 1700 IOPS
	Bandwidth 20 MBps
Network	20 MBps

Servers above these thresholds will be isolated and not eligible for this virtualization project.

Operating Systems

As shown in Table 8.3, the collection provides a precise description of the servers.

Table 8.3 Distribution of Existing Physical and Virtual Servers

Total Number of x86 Servers	Number of Physical Servers	Number of VMs	Number of Servers Connected to the SAN	Number of VMs Replicated on the SAN
362	242	120	50	35

362 physical and virtual servers are included in the scope of this project. Approximately 30% of the servers have already been virtualized using vSphere 4.1. The majority of servers use internal storage, although some use *storage-area network (SAN) Fibre Channel (FC)* shared storage (50 servers). Only 35 servers are secured on a remote site. The goal for this project is to virtualize the physical servers and to reuse the VMs that already exist. Figure 8.4 shows the operating system environment.

Windows is used in 95% of the environment (four different versions of Windows). The vast majority use Windows 2003, but a trend toward Windows 2008 Server can be observed.

> **NOTE**
>
> All operating systems are found in VMware's hardware compatibility matrix.

CPU Data Collection

Of the physical servers, 50% are uniprocessor servers and 44% are biprocessor servers. Only 6% use quad processors.

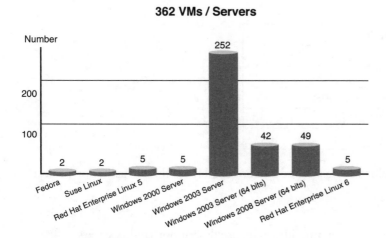

Figure 8.4 Operating systems in use.

NOTE

Experience shows that the more sockets a server has, the more difficult it will be to virtualize because of the presence of an application requiring significant resources.

An in-depth view (see Figure 8.5) of the servers' CPU use shows the activity.

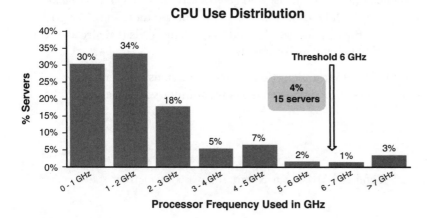

Figure 8.5 Server CPU activity.

As you can see in Figure 8.5, the majority (87%) of servers make reasonable use of the CPU (less than 4 GHz). There are 47 servers (13%) with high CPU activity (more than 4 GHz). 4 percent (15 servers) use the CPU above the threshold set at 6 GHz.

NOTE

These figures are global averages and do not rule out excessive use on a particular server. The average is calculated over periods representative of the activity.

Memory Data Collection

When the memory installed in all servers is added up, you can see that 64% of all memory is used; 36% is free (see Figure 8.6).

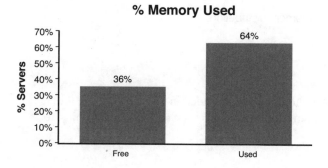

Figure 8.6 Total server memory usage.

An in-depth view, displayed in Figure 8.7, shows how used memory is distributed.

As Figure 8.7 shows, 90% of servers use a capacity equal to or less than 8 GB of RAM; these can be virtualized. Three percent use a significant amount of memory—more than 8 GB. These 10 servers are mainly SQL and Oracle databases. They are above the set threshold and will not be eligible for this project.

Servers with a significant amount of memory used must be analyzed in more detail to confirm whether they can be virtualized. In vSphere 5, licensing is partially linked to the configured memory of the VMs, so this must be taken into account when large memory capacities are necessary.

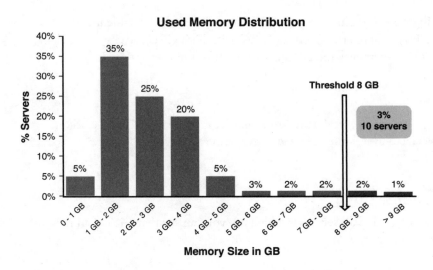

Figure 8.7 Detailed presentation of used memory distribution.

> **NOTE**
>
> A server with significant memory usage should not be excluded in all cases. Indeed, if the main goal is to set up a DRP simply, it can be interesting to keep such a server within the scope of the project.

Disk

There are 312 servers using local storage, and 50 are connected to the SAN. The total storage capacity (local and SAN) of the 362 servers is 25 TB, including 15 TB used, or 55%. This makes an average capacity per server of 40 GB used for 70 GB provisioned. Implementing an architecture with centralized storage will allow consolidation and improve the use rate of the storage.

> **NOTE**
>
> This information serves as a base to size storage. The size needed is one of the indicators used to choose the correct type of disk to use: vmdk, RDMp, or RDMv.

The graph shown in Figure 8.8 illustrates the number of servers per disk capacity used.

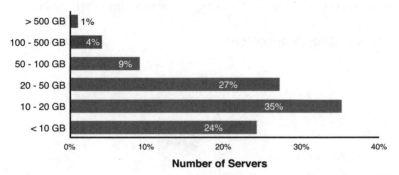

Figure 8.8 Number of servers per disk capacity.

Eighty-six percent of servers use a reasonable capacity, below 100 GB of disk, and these can be virtualized. Fourteen percent have significant volumes, including two above 1 TB. Large-volume servers require an in-depth study.

NOTE

Using *Raw Device Mapping (RDM)* mode disks is appropriate for large volumes.

Bandwidth is an important aspect of eligibility. Generally, a good candidate for virtualization requires an I/O disk bandwidth below 20 MBps. Fortunately, as shown in Figure 8.9, most servers fall below that limit.

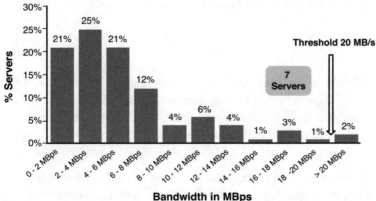

Figure 8.9 Two percent of servers (seven servers) require more bandwidth than 20 MBps.

An in-depth study is needed to identify values and periods. I/O activity, shown in Figure 8.10, is a critical element to monitor when servers hosting virtual machines share disks.

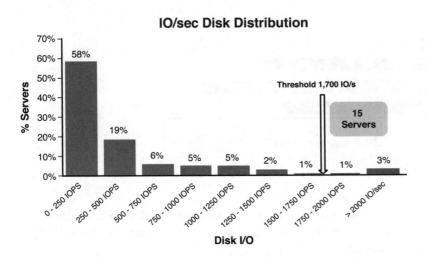

Figure 8.10 IOPS activity.

As you can see in Figure 8.10, the servers' overall IOPS activity is reasonable. Fifteen servers have significant activity, greater than 1700 IOPS, and require in-depth study.

The peaks primarily take place at night. Activity is not necessarily a hindrance in transitioning to the virtual, but it comes at a price. Indeed, for the VM to offer the performance required, it must have its own dedicated RDM disks with a sufficient quantity of disk spindles to absorb the load.

If it is part of the target, dedicating portions of SAN for this VM is recommended. What would prevent virtualization would be caused by financial concerns, not technological reasons.

Network

As shown in Figure 8.11, 264 servers are using bandwidth of less than 20 MB/s. 10 servers use bandwidth greater than 20 MBps. Among these are servers for backups, antivirus software, and scanning applications. In a virtualized environment, 20 MBps is the limit for a machine's network traffic. A Gigabit Ethernet adapter usually does not provide more than 70 MBps.

The peaks primarily take place at night and correspond to backup periods. A discussion involving the client must take place regarding backup issues of the target infrastructure. The network activity can be offloaded if a SAN architecture is set up.

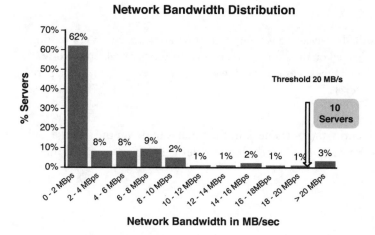

Figure 8.11 Network activity and bandwidth demands.

Applications

The collection provides a precise description of the application environment:

- SQL Server: 124 servers host SQL.

- Oracle Server: 50 servers.

- Approximately 100 existing VMs for tests, development, preproduction, and so on.

- The rest are related to infrastructure servers: *Active Directory (AD)*, *Domain Name System (DNS)*, web, files, printing, BlackBerry, business applications, and so on.

SQL Server: We have found 124 servers/VMs that host SQL. Certain servers have a significant queue length between 5 a.m. and 7 p.m. Performance issues can occur for servers with a queue length beyond 12. If they are retained for virtualization, it will be necessary to increase the number of disk spindles in building these servers' *logical unit number (LUN)*—one disk from the RAID group for every queue length unit above 12. This increase is important, or the contention of target disks could be displaced major concern, which would deteriorate the performance of other VMs.

Oracle Server: 50 servers run Oracle databases. The number of licenses required must be checked directly with Oracle. Some servers are very taxed in terms of CPU and disk I/O. Analyzing these servers will establish whether or not they are candidates for virtualization according to the defined thresholds.

> **NOTE**
>
> The queue length represents the I/O awaiting writing in the operating system. It is a waiting queue for I/O not yet acknowledged on disk. The cause can be an activity peak on the disk or a slowing down between the I/O manager and the file system (for example, an antivirus or a replication driver at the host level).

The queue length audit can identify the bottleneck in the queues between the storage and server. Currently, 14 servers show a queue length that justifies keeping them out of this virtualization project.

Analysis

The average CPU use rate on the company's entire server collection is 19%. This is a good rate compared with what we have seen with many other clients (whose use rate is usually less than 10% to 15%). The large proportion of uniprocessors explains this high CPU use rate. Yet 81% of resources remain unused. The CPU audit identified 24 servers with high activity, including 4 with random behaviors.

The overall server memory use rate is 74%. This is a good average.

In general, ideal candidates for virtualization are servers with predictable activity and relatively low resource requirements compared with what the server can provide.

Collection and analysis provide the average server setup in this company:

> Average CPU activity between 1.5 GHz and 2 GHz, 2 GB of used memory, and storage space of 70 GB (40% of which is used), running Microsoft Windows 2003 Server

This average, provided for information only, serves as a reference.

To determine which physical servers will not be virtualized, *exclusion criteria* are based on the following:

- OS or hardware not found in VMware's hardware compatibility matrix (for example, fax cards, dongles, old operating systems)

- Intensive use of resources as compared with previously mentioned thresholds

- Service or performance levels below those of the physical environment (rare)

- Business reasons (for example, very sensitive applications)

Figure 8.12 shows the result of the eligibility inquiry for the servers in this project.

Eligibility Distribution

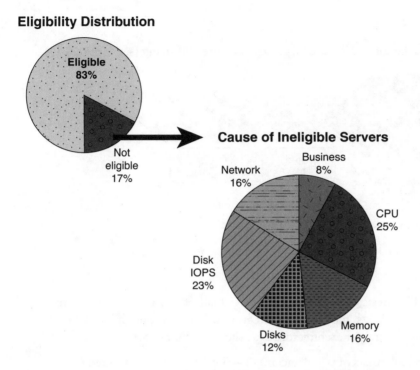

Figure 8.12 Various reasons leading to the ineligibility of servers for virtualization.

Approximately 17% (62 servers) are considered "nonvirtualizable as they are." They will not be considered for this project because decisions must be made quickly and these servers can become hindrances that put the entire project at risk. What matters at this stage is obtaining a good confidence level from users. Subsequently, virtualization possibilities can be explored. These could include the following:

- **Excessive disk and network bandwidth at certain times of night:** Is there a possibility of smoothing out the load?

- **Excessive CPU use rate between 10 a.m. and 7 p.m.:** Can the activity be spread over several VMs?

- **Excessive network bandwidth at 8 a.m.:** Can the charge be spread over a longer period to obtain a use rate below 20 MBps?

- **Significant queue length on several occasions:** To reduce the queue length, use more disk spindles in RAID groups.

- **A great deal of disk I/O over most of the night:** Is there a possibility of decreasing the load? The backup policy must be revised.

Design

In the Design phase, the focus is on the target architecture and sizing (see Figure 8.13).

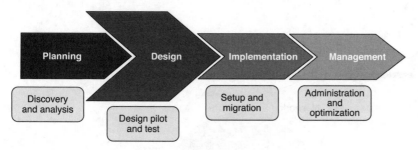

Figure 8.13 Design phase.

Target Architecture

The number of eligible physical servers that will be virtualized is 180 (242 servers minus 62 servers). With existing VMs, the target architecture will have a total of 300 VMs. To meet established goals, the target architecture is as shown in Figure 8.14.

The target architecture consists of two datacenters—Site 1 and Site 2—located 6 miles (10 km) apart. In each location, all ESXi host servers are in a cluster connected to a SAN FC, and the two storage arrays are synchronously replicated. The DRP is taken care of using SRM5.

> **NOTE**
>
> Implementing this type of solution leads to compliance with the Bâle III Agreements published December 16, 2010, requiring (of financial institutions, among others) up to two backup sites.

Sizing

The Discovery stage provides the precise capacities used, which is fundamental information for the best architecture design possible. VMware's SRM5 solution will be implemented to allow the integral recovery of one site on the other in case of a major incident. The architecture is spread over two sites, and all storage is replicated. Servers must be sized to be able to support the load if a site is switched over. The load must be able to handle 300 VMs in DRP. This capacity planning must also take into account upgradeability over three years, on a 30%-per-year basis.

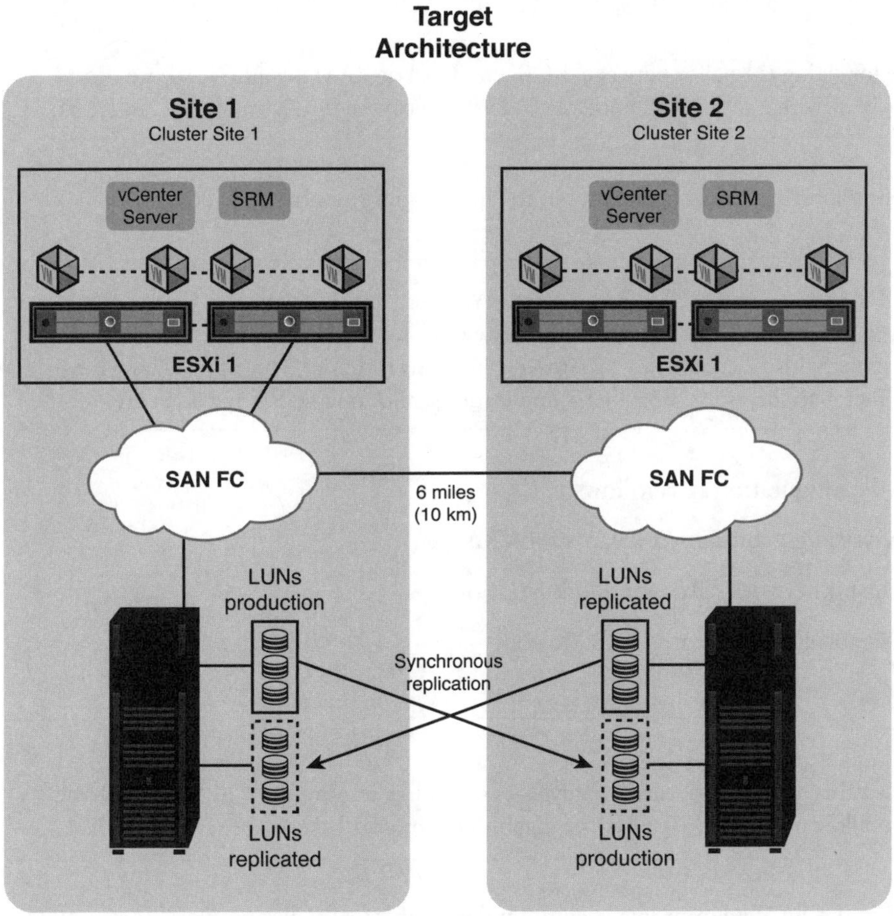

Figure 8.14 The target architecture.

ESXi host server: To provide the power needed in the most demanding scenario, it is necessary to install 16 Intel Westmere E5670 (2 processors, 6 cores, 2.93 GHz) servers (8 servers per site) with 96 GB of RAM per server.

Memory should be one of the first elements considered when sizing the target architecture. The average effective capacity of 2.3 GB per server represents a total memory of approximately 700 GB. Advanced overcommitment memory techniques can guarantee good conditions during activity peaks. They make the amount of memory reliable without the need to oversize the amount of memory.

> **TIP**
>
> A basic rule for sizing is to allot between 4 GB and 8 GB of RAM per physical core. For example, a server with a total of 12 cores should have between 48 GB and 96 GB of RAM.

When choosing a processor, it is preferable to choose a large number of cores.

> **TIP**
>
> Another basic rule for CPU sizing is to allot between 2 and 4 vCPUs per physical core. For example, a server with 12 cores allows 24 to 48 vCPUs to run. This rule applies only for Tier 2 and Tier 3 applications. For Tier 1 applications, allot one vCPU for one core.

Network card configuration is as follows:

- Two physical gigabit network cards for VMs
- Two gigabit network cards for administration
- Two Gigabit Ethernet cards for vMotion

> **TIP**
>
> One Gigabit Ethernet network card usually does not provide more than 70 MBps. A basic rule is to not allow more than 10 VMs per gigabit network card.

With regard to the SAN adapter, we recommend two physically distinct *host bus adapter (HBA)* cards with the addition of redundancy software (for example, EMC PowerPath VE) to take advantage of more advanced features than those offered by VMware (Round Robin). By spreading the I/O load over available paths, this type of software provides administrative comfort and leads to better I/O disk performance without any action from the administrator. If one or several paths are lost, it switches the flux to the remaining paths, automatically detecting HS links.

The required storage sizing is calculated based on the storage capacity actually used for the 300 eligible servers. The following rule is used:

> Capacity to provide = (Effective capacity + 30% for upgradeability) + (Total RAM capacity) + (20% for snapshots) + 10% for safety

Therefore, the total volume is 12 TB + 3.6 TB + 1.3 TB + 3.3 TB + 2 TB = 22.2 TB.

The same volume must be reserved for the DRP, so double the preceding result (Total = 44.4) to arrive at the anticipated capacity (see Table 8.4).

Table 8.4 Anticipated Capacity

Site	Production	Replication	Total
Site A	12.2 TB	10 TB	22.2 TB
Site B	10 TB	12.2 TB	22.2 TB

Expect a 30% increase each year (see Table 8.5).

Table 8.5 Estimated Increase Over the Next Two Years

	2012	2013	2014
Number of ESXi5	12.2 TB	14 TB	16 TB
Number of VMs	300	350	400
Storage TB	22.2	29	38

The DRP involves 270 servers. If a site crashes, all VMs, no matter their environment or rank (there are three levels of criticality), must be active on the remaining site.

TIP

For VMFS datastores, we recommend 800 GB with a maximum of 32 vmdk per volume, with no more than 8 ESXi servers connected.

Figure 8.15 shows the configuration to implement.

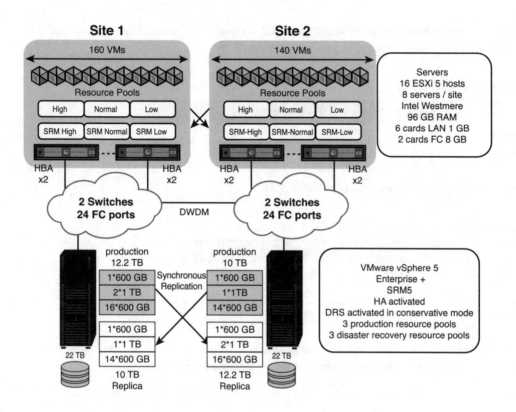

Figure 8.15 Configured target architecture.

Implementation

The previously defined elements are put into service in the Implementation stage, illustrated in Figure 8.16. This stage requires good communication between teams so that the schedule is respected and risk is managed. Prerequisites and deliverables must be rigorously monitored and re-evaluated, if necessary, to limit the zones at risk.

Installing the vSphere 5 Platform

Installation is done in the following order:

1. Physical installation of servers and the storage array in the racks

2. Firmware update of server components and BIOS

3. BIOS configuration

4. Installation of vSphere 5 onto servers

5. Basic configuration of the vSphere server

6. Installation of HBA cards redundancy software

7. Storage preparation, RAID creation, LUN creation, and so on

8. Zoning and masking of the new vSphere server

9. Configuration of local vSwitch and of its administration network

10. Configuration of VMkernel port for vMotion

11. Addition of vSphere server in vCenter

12. Application of host profile

13. Update through the vSphere server's Update Manager

14. Validation of the vSphere server's basic configuration

15. P2V migration

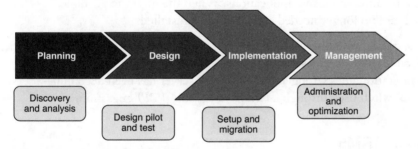

Figure 8.16 The Implementation phase.

P2V Migration

The transformation of physical machines into VMs is organized based on the date at which support ends and on power consumption. The migration will take four weeks. PlateSpin Migrate is selected for the P2V migration because the potential period of time for service interruptions is very narrow. This tool is chosen instead of VMware Converter because it allows the differential synchronization of physical machines to ESXi servers by using planned tasks. Using the same tool, it is also possible to start a target VM and test it in isolation before its final switchover, thus ensuring the VMs indeed boot for critical applications.

Migration scenarios are drafted based on the following priority criteria:

- **Power consumption:** The goal is to rapidly free up energy resources used by the datacenters, using it to deploy all migration waves while ensuring the quality of services if a datacenter is lost. Therefore, the migration of the servers that consume the most power (in kWh) is considered a priority.

- **Hardware obsolescence:** Migrating older servers—some of which are nearing the end of the manufacturer's warranty—lowers the risk of failure.

- **Migration dependencies:** Groups of physical machines must be migrated taking into account their interdependence.

- **New requirements**

Full synchronization is done the weekend before the migration. On the day of the migration, only blocks modified since the last synchronization point are synchronized and sent to the target VM.

Before performing P2V activities, it is necessary to prepare servers by shutting down antivirus software and resource-intensive applications. When the migration is done, hardware-related tools are no longer needed and must be uninstalled.

To decommission the critical physical machines, simply unplug the network cables for two weeks. (This is preferable to physically stopping the server to avoid hard drive problems.) If the virtualization migration goes wrong and the physical server has been decommissioned, it is possible to switch back through a *virtual-to-physical (V2P)* migration.

Implementation of SRM5

To implement SRM5, the following information must be known:

- Which virtual machines are part of the DRP.

- The topology of the VMs (particularly with regard to storage). Certain VMs can have RDM volumes that are invisible from the VM summary.

- What VM dependencies exist, so as to restart them in the proper order.

The boot sequence is based on criteria such as business needs, service-related VMs, infrastructure, and so on.

EXAMPLE

One boot sequence for the VMware environment is Active Directory, followed by DNS, then the vCenter database, followed by vCenter Server, and so on.

SRM requires thorough organization. VMs must find the same hierarchy of resources in the production site and the backup site. Network resources, resource pools, and VM organization files are remapped between both sites. Therefore, it is crucial to organize and name VMs properly so that you can find your way later.

Consistency Groups

Some storage array manufacturer replication solutions enable you to create consistency groups, which are essential.

Some VMs (for example, databases) can be stored in different datastores. Consistency groups for replication (called datastore groups) allow the logical management of the various LUNs as a single LUN, ensuring coherence between all LUNs.

EXAMPLE

If a VM has a vmdk virtual disk on Datastore A and a second vmdk on Datastore B, it is necessary to create a consistency group for storage replication. The consistency group calculates the interdependence of Datastore A and Datastore B. These datastores cannot be separated, and they form a coherent whole.

A VMFS datastore can be a unique LUN or can consist of several LUN extents. If the datastore consists of several extents, consistency groups guarantee that the replication state of the various LUNs used to make up a VMFS is coherent—all LUNs are in the same replication state.

On the two datacenters, a LUN of 2 GB must be introduced to all ESXi hosts within the target cluster; it is called a *placeholder*. It represents the configuration information for each protected VM (the source machine's vmx file) to ensure its business recovery on the target platform.

Mapping Resource Hierarchy

We strongly recommend properly identifying the resource pools between Site 1 and Site 2. For example, on the production site, three resource pools are created: High, Normal, and Low; on Site 2, there are SRM-High, SRM-Normal, and SRM-Low.

The prefix clearly identifies which pool hosts backup VMs and which hosts production VMs. This mapping of dedicated production resources keeps production and backup VMs separate. Indeed, when VM protection is activated, source VMs will be identified in the target environment. If production and backup VMs are not separated, they will be mixed together on the target site, making day-to-day administration more complex.

When the protection group is created, it is possible to add VMs into a datastore. In this case, the "protection group" detects that the VM is not considered as part of the business recovery plan. An email is sent, and a warning appears in the SRM administration console.

Management

After the architecture is set up, it must handle the load. Ensure that the CPU, memory, and I/O disk loads are not saturated, which would lower performance. The management phase, illustrated in Figure 8.17, is where you monitor and optimize the solution.

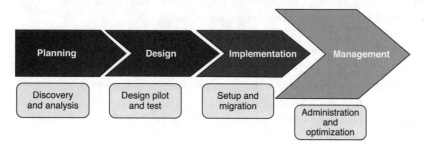

Figure 8.17 The Management phase.

The physical CPU load of ESXi host servers should not exceed 75%. If the CPU load is very intensive, use reservations for critical VMs to guarantee the minimum required. Critical VMs must have high share settings. Monitor the CPU ready time of the VMs' vCPU; it must not exceed 2000 ms.

The DRS cluster is activated in normal mode. FT is activated for four very critical VMs, and HA for 25% of the servers.

Administrators must monitor the ballooning, memory swap in/swap out, and disk R/W latency, which must remain below 20 ms.

A simple action prioritizes resources in case of contentions. It is easy to create three resource pools (High, Normal, Low), which is also efficient for the distribution of CPU and RAM priority based on the VM's criticality. vMotion and Storage vMotion simplify management and planned maintenance operations when acquiring new hardware. This reduces service interruptions during these phases, which would be delicate operations in a traditional physical environment.

Summary and Conclusion

This project is a success. The client is completely satisfied because both the schedule and budget were respected, and all goals set were reached. Cost reduction from energy savings is even above expectations.

Three hundred VMs run on 16 ESXi hosts (8 servers per datacenter). The infrastructure in place provides high service levels with an RPO of 0. Failover tests show the RTO is less than four hours. IT teams are fully trained and perform two annual failover tests.

The system proved itself robust when work being performed by an electrician required a complete electrical interruption of the datacenter. Through an SRM5 planned migration, teams switched all production to Site 2. This operation—usually cumbersome and delicate in a traditional physical environment—was performed without encountering any problem and required a preparation period that had been reduced to a minimum.

New requests (about 50 in the queue) were all addressed quickly as soon as the infrastructure was in place.

The infrastructure rationalization is impressive. At the end of the project, as shown in Figure 8.18, only 78 servers remain instead of the 252 physical servers—a reduction of 69%.

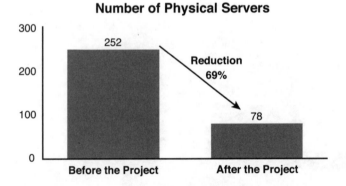

Figure 8.18 Physical server inventory before and after the project.

At completion of the project, a total of 252 existing physical servers 242 physical servers + 10 older-generation ESX servers hosting 120 VMs) were replaced by 78 physical servers (16 ESXi servers + 62 nonvirtualized physical servers).

As shown in Figure 8.19, power consumption after virtualization is 16 kWh; 48 kWh have been freed, resulting in a reduction of 75%.

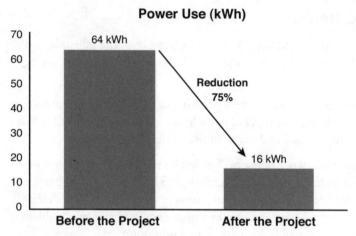

Figure 8.19 Power consumption before and after the project.

As shown in Figure 8.20, floorspace used was significantly decreased, from approximately 740 U (1 U = 1.75 in or 4.445 cm) to 240 U, a 68% reduction. The consolidation ratio is 1:18, a good average. Power use was decreased by 75%.

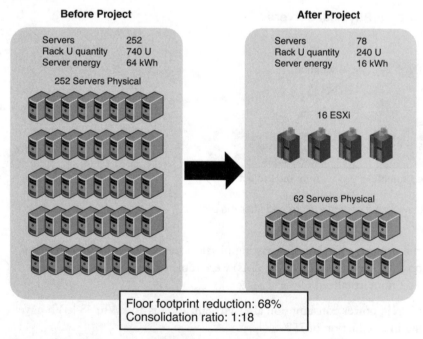

Figure 8.20 Floorspace used before and after the project.

This company now wants to automate a number of procedures and offer service catalogues for internal clients. Backup solutions offering de-duplication are being studied to replace the various existing solutions with a unified solution.

Through this example of a virtualization project, we can see the advantages this technology brings to the datacenter.

A Compelling Story

As you read about the project and challenges that the organization faced, you may have thought that it sounded familiar! In any economy, but especially a bad one, businesses look for any way to reduce costs, and virtualization using vSphere 5 is a great way to do that. In this project, you learned how to size a VM host and a VM correctly, and then converted some physical servers to VMs. To do so, you inventoried the needs of the 242 physical servers, made some decisions about what could best be virtualized, and performed the tasks. The thresholds set in the project were determined by the project team, but every organization may have different thresholds, and vSphere can virtualize most x86 servers. This project also implemented VMware SRM5, so the organization also can benefit from a comprehensive DRP implementation.

The savings were startling, reducing the number of physical servers by 69%, and reducing power by 75%. With green IT initiatives currently underway in so many industries, savings go beyond simply financial concerns. Virtualization saves money, time, the environment, and in some cases, your business!

Common Acronyms

AAM (*Automated Availability Manager*)

ADAM (*Active Directory Application Mode*)

API (*Application Program Interface*)

ASR (*Automatic Server Restart*)

BIA (*Business Impact Analysis*)

BRP (*Business Recovery Plan*)

CBT (*Changed Block Tracking*)

CDP (*Continuous Data Protection*)

CLI (*Command-Line Interface*)

CNA (*Converged Network Adapter*)

DAS (*Direct Attached Storage*)

DCUI (*Direct Console User Interface*)

DMZ (*Demilitarized Zone*)

DNS (*Domain Name Server*)

DPM (*Distributed Power Management*)

DRP (*Disaster Recovery Plan*)

DRS (*Distributed Resource Scheduler*)

ERP (*Enterprise Resource Planning*)

EVC (*Enhanced vMotion Compatibility*)

FCoE (*Fibre Channel over Ethernet*)

FDM (*Fault Domain Manager*)

FT (*Fault Tolerance*)

GPT (*GUID Partition Table*)

HA (*High Availability*)

IA (*Information Availability*)

ICMP (*Internet Control Message Protocol*)

iLO (*Integrated Lights-Out*)

IOPS (*Input/Output Operations Per Second*)

IPMI (*Intelligent Power Management Interface*)

ITIL (*Information Technology Infrastructure Library*)

LUN (*Logical Unit Number*)

MBR (*Master Boot Record*)

MMU (*Memory Management Unit*)

MPIO (*Multi Path I/O*)

MPP (*Multipathing Plugin*)

MRU (*Most Recently Used*)

MSCS (*Microsoft Cluster Service*)

MTBF (*Mean Time Between Failure*)

MTTR (*Mean Time To Repair*)

MTU (*Maximum Transmission Unit*)

NFS (*Network File System*)

NIS (*Network Information Service*)

NL-SAS (*Near Line-SAS*)

NMP (*Native Multipathing*)

P2V (*Physical-to-Virtual*)

POD (*Pool of Datastores*)

PSA (*Pluggable Storage Architecture*)

PSP (*Path Selection Plug-ins*)

PXE (*Preboot Execution Environment*

Index

C

D

O

P

Q-R

S

W-X-Y-Z